EMBRACING
THE BELOVED

Also by Stephen Levine

Grist for the Mill (with Ram Dass)

A Gradual Awakening

Meetings at the Edge

Who Dies?

Healing into Life and Death

Guided Meditations: Explorations and Healings

EMBRACING THE BELOVED

RELATIONSHIP AS A PATH OF AWAKENING

STEPHEN AND ONDREA LEVINE

ANCHOR BOOKS
A DIVISION OF RANDOM HOUSE, INC.
NEW YORK

First Anchor Books Edition, February 1996

Copyright © 1995 by Stephen and Ondrea Levine

All rights reserved under International and Pan-American Copyright
Conventions. Published in the United States by Anchor Books, a division
of Random House, Inc., New York, and simultaneously in Canada by
Random House of Canada Limited, Toronto. Originally published in
hardcover in the United States by Doubleday in 1995.

Grateful acknowledgment is made to the following for permission to
reprint previously published material:

> Quatrain 1246 and "The Question" from *Open Secret: Versions of Rumi,*
> copyright © 1984 by John Moyne and Coleman Banks, reprinted by
> permission of Threshold Books, RD4 Box 600, Putney, Vermont 05346.

> Excerpts from *The Kabir Book* by Robert Bly, copyright © 1971, 1977 by
> Robert Bly. Copyright © 1977 by The Seventies Press. Reprinted by
> permission of Beacon Press.

Anchor Books and colophon are registered trademarks of Random
House, Inc.

Library of Congress Cataloging-in-Publication Data
Levine, Stephen, 1937–
    Embracing the beloved: relationship as a path of awakening / Stephen
and Ondrea Levine.
        p.   cm.
    1. Spiritual life.   2. Interpersonal relations—Religious aspects.
3. Levine, Stephen—1937– 4. Levine, Ondrea.   I. Levine, Ondrea.
II. Title.
BL624.L47   1995   94-19871
158′.2—dc20   CIP

Anchor ISBN 0-385-42527-9

www.anchorbooks.com

Printed in the United States of America
16   15   14   13   12   11   10   9

CONTENTS

CONTENTS

Part II: Deepening the Union

Part III: The Solid Ground of the Path

CONTENTS

CONTENTS

Part VI: Everything That Has a Beginning Has an End

~

INTRODUCTION

F EW RECOGNIZE the enormous power of relationship as a vehicle for mutual healing—physical, emotional and spiritual. Or the power of the "true heart" to awaken us from the emotional trance that relationships sometimes induce. Or the possibilities of seeing our beloved as "the Beloved."

This is not a book about how to "make nice" in relationship. This is about using relationship as a means for profound inner growth. Indeed, much in this book deals with embracing the pained mind that just wants to "make nice"—to maintain safe territory—cowering in the corner, unwilling to engage that which keeps us frightened and absent. This is about cultivating a relationship where the mind turns easy and the heart bursts into flame. This is about the enlightenment of relationship.

This book approaches relationship as spiritual practice. It is a merging of the techniques for clearing the mind and opening the heart. It offers the possibility of a healing relationship. A conjoining on the path toward the heart where the wounds of the past and the confusion of the present are received in mercy and awareness. A relationship that brings one wholly into the present, that allows one to complete their true nature.

This is about how to use relationship as an aid in the exploration of consciousness and the development of a mindfulness and heartfulness that can provide level after level of insight. And perhaps presents a rare possibility of something deeper in each connecting with something greater in both in a mystical union.

We do not mean to imply that relationship is the only way or even a better way than the deeply committed solitary journey of a seeking heart. Indeed, what is being shared here is applicable to a much wider circle of relationship than just our "pair bonding." Each walks a solitary path even with another beside them.

What is offered here is "survival practice at the edge of the flat world." It challenges us to take one more step. To go beyond safe territory, to go into the vastness. To exceed our fear of falling. To watch the mind's fear that if it takes one more step nothing will be there to stay its fall. And to realize that in taking that amazing step into space, we have wholly entered our life—the exploration of our original nature—that floats in the enormity just beyond our edge. And rather than fall, gently we rise, letting go of our suffering, recognizing that only our fear creates gravity and the heaviness around the heart.

Thus, when we hear the statistics that fifty percent of marriages end in divorce, we are not frightened or depressed. Instead, something deep within is reaffirmed that perhaps half of those who get married today may be there for their beloved on their deathbed. Half of the people who marry may be together the rest of their lives! The glass is half full, and there's enough there for all of us. To small mind, fifty percent of life doesn't work. To big mind, even the half available is grace.

And when we discover that relationship can be a spiritual practice as powerful as any, combining the explorations of the body, mind and heart into a single practice, there may develop, at first for moments and then days or even years, an implacable connectedness and psychic interbeing. This mystical union is the fruit of a conscious, committed relationship.

Such relationships are rare and worth all we can give. They arrive on their own schedule. In the beginning they require all you have. As they ripen, they necessitate all you are.

Although this book is written in the first person, it is only the first person singularity of the record keeper. Most of this book, based on years of experimentation and exploration, is derived from notes taken during investigative exchanges between Ondrea and I as our commitment to the manuscript forced us to put into language the intuitive, sometimes prelinguistic, deep inner workings of our process together. We learned a great deal from formalizing our process for the use and possible benefit of others.

The way Ondrea and I work is to brainstorm on a topic and allow our minds to explore its warp and woof. Then we encourage the heart to echo it on paper. Then we eat and digest it. And see what comes up!

The pronoun "I" is so often employed because Stephen transcribes, like Ganesha from Vishnu, the mutual experience of their tandem exploration. The "I" who writes this (on a good day) is only a messenger from the heart of that collaboration.

When we were first searching for a term to describe our collaborative process we explored the term "tandem," but rejected it when the dictionary defined it as one individual leading another. But like two climbers on a single rope, one often precedes the other and supports their progress. And since one can never tell on any given morning who will be a bit lighter or clearer that day, "tandem" has become more acceptable to us.

In truth, on any given day's climb, I need only look to the side to see Ondrea navigating the same rough outcropping. Most often the rope hangs slack between us.

I

~

A HEALING
CONVERGENCE

CHAPTER 1

~

APPROACHING
THE PATH

*This book is not meant to be read in only a linear manner. It
often offers an experiential process. It is as much poetry as
prose. Absorbed phrase by phrase, image by image, it allows
healing to enter the heart, the mind, the body.*

W E SHARE the process from which we are learning daily for
the benefit of all who wish to use relationship as a path
of self-discovery. This work is not to be taken lightly.
This is a book about co-commitment, not co-dependency. These
techniques are not applicable to anything that resembles the old-
style dominant/submissive relationships which have for so long
perpetuated our all-too-human suffering.

When true hearts truly join there is a mystical union. An interconnecting of whole human beings which is the foundation for
great insight and growth. It is a collaboration in healing.

Although we often speak in terms of merging, or becoming one,
or dissolving into oneness—this is not a giving up of one person to
another. It is not as the great German poet Rilke fears of such
commitments, "a hemming-in, a mutual consent that robs one
party or both of their fullest freedom and development."

Indeed, if two people attempt only to become one, they certainly
may get lost. But if the oneness just beyond such concepts is their
ultimate concern—if each heart is committed to the universal heart,

3

our birthright, our original nature—neither stops. And the ongoing aerial act is spectacular.

Indeed, when Rilke says that the most that can be expected is that "two solitudes protect and border and greet each other," he is speaking of the best of the ordinary way. They do not burn for the Beloved. They do not love the truth even more than each other. They refuse to give it all away. To be blessed surveying new frontiers.

The distance from your pain, your grief, your unattended wounds, is the distance from your partner. And the distance from your partner is your distance from the living truth, your own great nature. Whatever maintains that distance, that separation from ourselves and our beloveds, must be investigated with mercy and awareness. This distance is not overcome by one "giving up their space" to another, but by both partners entering together the unknown between them. The mind creates the abyss but the heart crosses it.

A conscious relationship teaches us to treat ourselves and others as our only child. And to do it mindfully. It does not break the heart. A conscious relationship is as healing and life-affirming as an unconscious, old-style relationship is at times harmful and life-denying. The harmful effect of an unconscious relationship is that it keeps us so small, dependent on external circumstances for our happiness. More needs than gifts are brought to such an entanglement. But a conscious relationship offers the possibility of relating across the gulf of I and other all the way into the heart of our beloved. A conscious relationship allows us to remain conscious while in relationship. It's a whole new ball game.

CHAPTER 2

~

ACKNOWLEDGING
THE BELOVED

A FEW YEARS ago Ondrea and I were scheduled to give a talk about healing on what turned out to be Valentine's Day. Coming from the stillness of our mountain retreat to the commotion of the "big city," we were deeply touched by the care and kindness exhibited as the meeting hall filled. So many couples aiding each other. Those alone helped to their seats by the loved ones of the recently departed. The weary, nearly translucent faces of patients, friends and colleagues. So many others drawn with illness or gray with grief. So many returned for healing with their families. Their lovers. Men and women of every description—teenagers and octogenarians, janitors and physicians, car salesmen and poets: black, brown, yellow, and white; gay and straight; sick and well—the loved, the loving, committed to a mutual process. So much buzz and affection. Five hundred gathered for an evening in this beautiful old stone church in an investigation of healing.

These open faces, and the exceptional, nearly initiatory, day we had just had, overwhelmed us with waves of loving kindness.

And we thought what a perfect day to speak about human kindness and maybe even share that term we love so in private but rarely used in groups: the Beloved. A word that incorporates the heart of the sacred into a profound appreciation of our deepest nature. A word that is a "bonding responder" for the way our relationship has become our spiritual practice. And how our practice, our work on ourselves, has become the central core in our connectedness.

And we asked ourselves whether we needed to talk about healing or could just effuse about the Beloved a few times before we realized there was no question. There was no difference. As healing progresses deeper, a more tangible sense of *being* ensues. From that sense of being there constellates the quality of "being present." Being present we come into "the presence": the space in which the process floats: the Beloved.

We find the term "the Beloved" quite functional for many reasons including the obvious parallel between the heart's affinity for such an idea and the draw of the personal toward the universal. And, of course, because it is our practice to meet our beloved as the Beloved.

It is a term used in many spiritual traditions, and is particularly well served in the Sufi tradition, whose mystical, devotional aspect seeks the "hidden mysteries," yearning for the direct experience of the one they call "the Beloved." In perhaps the greatest of all devotional poetry, in the spectacular longings of Rumi, Kabir, Miribai, and Rabia, the Beloved is all that is sought. The Beloved is the context into which the wounded and dismayed may enter, as the ever-injured and uninjurable vastness embraces their pain and transmutes it to mercy. But to all who seek their own true self, whether Sufi or Buddhist, Christian or Jew, Jain, Native American, or agnostic, the Beloved is the ever-experienceable vastness of our true heart, our original nature. And for all it is the possibility of freedom, the divine capacity to transform our pool of tears into the Ocean of Compassion.

The Beloved is neither a person nor a place. It is an experience of deeper and deeper levels of being, and eventually of beingness itself —the boundarylessness of your own great nature expressed in its rapture and absolute vastness by the word "love." It is not for the concept, but for the experience, that we use the term "the Beloved." The experience of this enormity we falteringly label "divine" is unconditioned love. Absolute openness, unbounded mercy and compassion. We use this concept, not to name the unnameable vastness of being—our greatest joy—but to acknowledge and claim as our birthright the wonders and healings within.

As we began to speak on that Valentine's evening, the words "the Beloved" exited our lips with a sigh—a gentle bow to those gathered in the room and to that within each of us, which is only love and boundless being.

And we joined with the group in an investigation of wholeness. The wholeness in which our incompleteness floats, the deep source of being beyond conceptualization, which out of wild exasperation for something to contain its immensity we call the Beloved—whose breath is pure love. The Beloved isn't what you know, it's what you are. It isn't anything you think. It is that in which thought floats. And that which goes beyond thought. It is the heart of being where pure awareness and pure love are indistinguishable. Your beloved is a thought, but the Beloved is the space in which that beloved thought floats.

That sense of presence, of simply being, when investigated brings one toward the experience of the Beloved. At times the heart bursts into flame, the mind kind and clear. But usually it is just a simple spaciousness and ease that lets thoughts float in mercy and awareness and recognizes the evolutionary struggle in everyone they meet.

Kabir, the great God-drunken poet, whispers that the Beloved is "the breath inside the breath." That your heart, like the sun, is always shining. But like the sun, or the heart, any passing shadow can obscure its warmth. All it takes is a slow cloud or an uninvited thought to block its reception. Just as the sun effortlessly shines, so we need do nothing to create the Beloved. The Beloved simply is. In fact, in its exploration—at the center of that indescribable feeling of simply being, of *isness*—the Beloved is discovered spontaneously, self-effulgent, the presence within presence. To meet the Beloved we need gently let go of that which is unloved, judged, concocted from old impressions and old mind clingings. To let it all be

7

healed into the innate vastness which lies just beyond our acquired conditioning.

But we are so befuddled by the mistaken identities of our superficial conditioning that we recognize very little of what we have to share from our depths.

An unfortunate example of the profound unknowing of our true selves is found in the stories of near-death experiences so common nowadays. Many have heard of experiences of people leaving their body, seeing their body perhaps from above, moving through some conduit or tunnel, and then coming out into an enormous sense of presence, a great light. Most who have had such an experience and come back to talk about it speak of meeting Jesus or Buddha, of experiencing Mary or Gaia (the Mother Goddess). Indeed, a few years ago, some of the children who came close and returned mentioned having met Mr. Spock. Nowadays they often return with tales of Donatello of the Teenage Mutant Ninja Turtles. Personifications of omnipotence and great power. But the holder of divine powers, of great wisdom, is once again mispersonified as something, someone, other. It is interesting to note how few return saying they recognized that enormous light, that pervading sense of endless being, of sacred suchness, as their own true nature. "It was me and I am the Beloved." Most, so unused to their own great nature, return saying they met some divinity because they felt such peace and clarity they could not comprehend that it was their own luminous center, the light of their unlimited consciousness gathered into a single-pointed illumination—their own true nature no longer contained, uncontainable as it is.

Normally our consciousness is like the light of an average day. It is random and diffuse, illuminating only the exposed surface it casually falls upon—a tree, a rock, a person, a word, a smell, a taste, a sensation. This thin light casts substantial shadows, but gives little sense of the detail of the objects it passes over. But even on the coldest day of winter, if you take that light and focus it through a magnifying glass, it becomes a blinding point of light capable of igniting whatever it touches. Even the diffuse light of the coldest day, when gathered to one-pointedness, becomes "the flame of awareness," capable of illuminating the dark corners and the bright gateway. Like this thoroughly dispersed unfocused light, consciousness usually slides from object to object without much real experience of its presence. But when that light is focused, when awareness is keen and investigative, it clears the way toward the heart. This is the light we see before us upon death as we approach our true heart. It is the Beloved. It is who we really are when we stop fracturing the light into its prismatic components, attempting to secure "large complementary colors" for the pale mask of our small mind.

Just as few recognize their own nature as the Beloved, so many do not recognize that being across the breakfast table. Few are committed so profoundly to the heart that forgetfulness does not dull their recognition of their true nature, much less their beloved essential being. Most live their lives without much recognition of the enormity available in the shared spaciousness of being—the spacious ease, deeper than thought or thinking, in which we are always interconnected. And can now interact, able to aid healing at levels previously inaccessible.

It is perhaps too much to bear to believe how much we may be missing, that we indeed may be the Beloved. In a way I think there is something in the mind that says it is just too much responsibility. We are so used to our pain, so long trading comfort for known and recognizable suffering.

CHAPTER 3

~

AWAKENING POSSIBILITIES

MANY PEOPLE suffer from relationship senility. The mind has become utterly fatigued from trying. Self-protection and an unwillingness to go further (resistance) have left us confused, insisting we understand.

Many are burned-out and disheartened. The wounds of the past have scarified the heart. The mind has cramped closed. The body atrophied in hard-bellied distrust. But the feeling of loss, and being lost, eventually gets our attention and we see that no one can make us happy but us. And we begin to take responsibility. We begin to build the capacity to respond instead of react. And we focus on our resistance and recognize that relationship is work on ourselves. Taking what a friend calls "the whole catastrophe of relationship" into your merciful heart and investigative mind so the next one will not be a repeat of the last one.

And we commit to "a living dyad," a consecrated relationship, a relationship to consciousness that recognizes the power of a conscious relationship. And work on ourselves, together.

In the boneyard of all our previously unsuccessful relationships

—from which we increasingly learned to successfully relate—we were working *on* that other person. Despising them for not becoming what we hated ourselves for not being. Persecuting them and ourselves in the shadow of our unresolved grief.

But eventually we stop attempting to create, and simply allow, relationship. We begin to sense the possibilities and opportunities missed in the moments we closed our heart to another's pain, moments when it was more important to be "right" than heartful. Moments of unintegrated grief expressed in tones too loud for love. Recognizing that unclear intentions produce unsatisfactory results, we explore the painful recurrence of unforgiveness and resentment. The unfinished business, the passive aggression and aggressive passivity that continually define the separateness between *I* and *other* —the fears of our threatened self-image. The constant displacement of the present by the shadows of the past. The need to be wanted, grinding against the want to be needless. Conflict. Power games. The unwillingness to surrender.

Exploring the charnel ground of relationships we felt did not "work," we awaken as if from a recurrent dream, and relationship becomes what Buddha referred to as "the work to be done."

It means letting go at our edge. Moving out of safe territory into the unexplored and often deeply resisted. It means making a love greater than even our fear of revealing ourselves as unloved and unlovely. A love greater than our fear of pain.

When one commits to practices that clear the mind and expose the heart—such as mindfulness, forgiveness and loving kindness— what once seemed unworkable may well become the very center of the relationship. In those moments when the least movement is possible, the least resolution of our grief, the most minuscule movement is rewarded for its enormous effort. Our intention itself has considerable healing potential. The very willingness not to suffer or cause pain to another becomes the expanse in which healing and peace occur. The open space into which our loved one may let go. Making room in our heart for our own pain, we make room in our heart for theirs.

And our process toward the Beloved becomes a reminder that we are all in this boat together. As Kabir says:

The Beloved is inside you, and also inside me;
you know the sprout is hidden inside the seed.
We are all struggling; none of us has gone far.
Let your arrogance go, and look around inside.

The blue sky opens out farther and farther,
the daily sense of failure goes away,
the damage I have done to myself and others fades,
a million suns come forward with light,
when I sit firmly in that world.

I hear bells ringing that no one has shaken,
inside "love" there is more joy than we know of,
rain pours down, although the sky is clear of clouds
there are whole rivers of light.
The universe is shot through in all parts by a single sort of love.
How hard it is to feel that joy in all our bodies!

Those who hope to be reasonable about it fail.
The arrogance of reason has separated us from that love.
With the word "reason" you already feel miles away.

    Kabir reminds us again that all relationship is with the Beloved. He completes his poem by saying that this work "amounts to one soul meeting another," beyond life and even beyond death. That relationship is simply one being meeting another in beingness. That our unwillingness to explore unflinchingly what limits that meeting leaves us mostly unhappy. And that there is wholeness in a merciful awareness that clings to nothing and condemns nothing, that is simply a presence in which nothing obstructs the natural flow of loving kindness.

~

DYAD BELOVED MEDITATION

S IT TWO OR three feet opposite your partner and close your eyes.

Bring to mind the face of your partner. Try to focus on detail, their eyebrows, the shape of their lips, the form the ear-lobe takes, eye color, skin coloration.

Take a moment to let their image form in your mind.

Be mindful of the process as their image forms in your mind. Do you notice any fear or separation? Are there moments of attraction or repulsion? Investigate the process as the image takes shape in your mind.

Now each open your eyes and look into the eyes of the other.

Let go of any superficial holding to separate aspects of your partner's face and enter wholly the light in that other being's eyes.

Let go of thinking them, and enter their being. Whatever previous images of your partner or yourself are stored in the mind should be acknowledged and relinquished into the deep resonance of the sacred in their eyes.

13

Whatever feelings of unworthiness or doubt arise, observe how they separate you from the Beloved in yourself, in another.

Let yourself be seen.

Let go of whatever prevents your partner from seeing you as sacred suchness.

Let yourself be seen as the Beloved, by the Beloved.

Sense their sacred enormity.

Looking into their eyes, let go of whatever thought or feelings limit your capacity to see them as luminous vastness, their deathless spirit.

Let go. Let go now of what separates.

Even if thought separates, let that go too and rest in being with the Beloved.

Look into the eyes of the Beloved. All that keeps you separate is the mind. Let go of the mind. Let it sink into the heart. There is no separation in the boundaryless spaciousness of shared being.

You are boundaryless space, the vastness of being in which this image of your loved one floats.

Softening the body, softening the mind. Letting the edges, the concepts, the opinions, melt in this enormous inheritance of love and care for your partner's well-being.

You are the Beloved looking into the mirror of beingness reflected in the eyes of your loved one.

You are the Beloved looking for what is looking.

Let go into the eyes of the Beloved.

Meet in sacred emptiness. Meet in the shared heart of being.

Draw healing. Draw mercy from the eyes of the Beloved.

Let yourself soak in the immensity of your partner's care for your well-being.

Let it in. Let the healing in.

Let yourself be the beloved of the Beloved.

Let yourself be love.

You can look the whole world over and never find anyone more deserving of love than yourself.

Let yourself love.

Let yourself be loved.

You are looking into the eyes of the Beloved. And the Beloved is looking into you.

Rest together in the space of beingness in which your individual beings float.

Let go of all that separates and enter the heart of the Beloved.

Enter together the Beloved.

CHAPTER 4

~

COMPLETING
BIRTH

T O BE BORN is to be in relationship. Indeed, our birth pangs are a part of every meeting, and every moment of eye contact. Even before birth a physical, emotional and spiritual interaction is established with our parents. The first tuggings of our personal history this time around. The first momentum of "the long haul."

In the contract of birth, death is not excluded. Either the child at some time will experience the parents' deaths, or the parents will endure the dying of that child. One mother attending her dying son said that these were her "last, and worst, labor pains." Our endings are inherent in our beginnings. This is the nature of relationship to another's heart or to this fleeting moment: only this precious present is " real." The rest, a dream vaguely remembered on the deathbed. A dream birthed in the delivery room.

To make this dream come true we need to awaken. To take birth fully, to become wholly alive. To become responsible to pain and joy, to the world and beyond.

Some theorize that the sense of a separate self arises the first time the infant is denied the breast. Others infer this occurs with the birth experience. Many believe this sense of separation, of *I* as opposed to *other,* comes with the territory: the body. Some believe it occurs when awareness becomes mistaken for consciousness, when the shadowy objects on the screen are mistaken for the light which produced them. The finger pointing confused with the moonlight by which it is seen. But whatever the source of this self-conscious, self-recriminating, self-aggrandizing isolation, when it becomes aware it is aware, it takes birth anew into the possibility of relating *with* another instead of only *to* another. It is, perhaps, from within a recognition of this first sense of separateness that the momentum toward unity begins. And reinforces the longing for this *I* and *other* to become One on the way to oneness.

The deeper the acknowledgment of our separation, the greater the tendency to continue toward birth in the healing heart.

Birth moves outward. But to complete that birth, to be fully born, one then travels inward investigating the nature of the body and mind, the heart and beyond. To the degree we relate to those extraordinary levels of mind we call heart, we will be able to relate a bit more from the spaciousness of being just beneath our seemingly separate trivialities.

When that longing for completion recognizes how incomplete, how partial, our relationships have been, it suggests the possibility of the mind and heart turning fully toward another in a conscious, committed relationship. And we come to recognize that how we relate to the mind and body is how we relate to life itself. To the degree we can touch its pain with mercy—compassion in action—that is the degree we have room to go beyond the old and to enter life wholeheartedly. It is this call to mindfulness and willingness to grow that makes the body and mind a laboratory instead of a prison cell.

And there is another birth that comes after birth. It is a "coming into your own," an individuation of the heart, that opens one to qualities of life and levels of consciousness previously unknown. It is the birth that occurs as the body and mind, born into separation, discover other levels of being. It is the deeper birth that occurs when the born discovers what in Buddhism is called "the unborn," that which precedes birth and exceeds death, the deathless truth of its real nature.

In our experience, much of what we hear on the deathbed is the struggles of life to become fully born. Indeed, it seems that few are wholly born before they die. Most live tentatively, reluctant to put both feet on the ground. Many hop about with one leg still in the womb. And then wonder why death and relationship are so difficult. With so little stability to allow the investigations, explorations and surrenders necessary to move beyond the small old-mind patterns that keep life imbalanced.

But some, acknowledging this great longing for completion, will do anything to become free. Even enter the shadows that the mind casts across the heart. But it takes work to give birth to yourself. It means cultivating the qualities of honesty, patience, watchfulness, forgiveness, kindness, adventure and a willingness to be wholly born, despite the birth pangs and fears which may tempt us to stay in the safe territory of familial pain and rambling confusion. It means developing the capacity to work with a loved one's long-accumulated grief as a part of your work on your own. To be in relationship is to open to the life pain of another on the way into yourself.

Most, attempting the death-defying act of taking birth fully, find a path that leads toward the heart and the possibilities of an unconditioned love. When the heart and mind coincide we complete our birth at last.

Many enjoy what are called "danger sports" because they say it makes them feel "so alive." Forced to be present in order to survive, an increased sense of presence creates an expanded feeling of being alive. But jumping off a precipice with a rubber band tied to your legs or stepping off a cliff with a silk handkerchief held over your head is not the only means of focusing awareness in the moment. The necessity to be present in relationship, too, requires us to be aware in order to survive. Focuses us on the living moment and produces the same "great aliveness" which so many bungee jumpers, hang gliders and rock climbers acknowledge is their near addiction to the sports. Like taking birth in this oddly violent, often struggling world, the uncertainties of relationship catch our attention and cause us to focus on the ground beneath our feet and the space within our mind.

So we see that the ultimate danger sport—the challenge of a lifetime—is intimate, conscious, committed relationship. It uncovers our deepest longings and fears as well as our most essential care for each other. It displays that within us which has so far taken birth as well as that which awaits completion. It allows us to experience, as we step off the precipice, defying gravity, the lightness of being vibrating increasingly within—a greatly increased sense of presence, which when experienced to the core we may tend to call God.

When I was eleven years old, at summer camp, I saw framed on a New England farmhouse wall an aging embroidery which read, "God Is Love." It seemed most bizarre at the time to my tiny, Old Testament mind. But after thirty-five years of spiritual practice, no better definition arises. This is the God we seek: unconditioned love, the Beloved, our inherent vastness. But for many the mind and heart are disunited and each seeks God in its own way. To the mind God is *the* Supreme Being. So mind seeks its "personal best," its highest individual potential, its supreme being. But to the heart, God is not so much *the* Supreme Being as beingness supreme. So it seeks to experience the universal, its common essential nature for which only the word "love" will suffice.

It is said that between incarnations we have the potential to see our "true face." (This may be equally true between relationships.) Whether this is a vision of our root personality uncovered through periods of intense psychological work, or the direct experience of our essential nature due to ongoing spiritual explorations, it is a moment of seeing beyond "the known" and our tiny world. And there is a sense of something being born anew. Such births are often heralded in poetry:

What Was Your Face Before You Were Born

When the heart bursts into flame
history completely disappears
and lightning strikes the ocean
in each cell.

There, before origins
when the double helix
is struck like a tuning fork
there is a hum
on which the universe is strung.

Such is the potential when two humans focus on their humanity, forming a triangle at whose apex is the long-sought truth, the Beloved, and at whose base is the solid foundation of a conscious, committed relationship. Triangulating toward the healing they took birth for. An incarnation of the spirit. An embodiment of the heart.

CHAPTER 5

~

CONSCIOUS RELATIONSHIP

F OR MANY being born onto the spiritual path, it is a quandary how to merge mind-clearing awareness practices with heart-opening devotional practices. How to balance a hard-won increasing sense of presence with an enormous gratitude to the sacred unknown. For those in a conscious, committed relationship, these practices coincide. That is why relationship is the test, as well as the culmination, of much spiritual practice.

To work mindfully with all that arises in the mind that might obstruct the heart is the path of the coincidence of the heart and mind. To use all that arises in relationship as work on oneself, as grist for the mill of deep inner growth, allows yet subtler whispers to become audible, the "unconscious" to become "conscious."

The mind divides the world into a million pieces. The heart makes it whole. To develop a "present heart" is prerequisite to the reception of the enormous gifts—spiritual and psychological—that relationship can bestow. This is one intention of this work: to balance the startling clarity of an inward-focused awareness with the profound urge to join with the mystery, the sacred—as Beloved, as parent, as child, as tree, as sky, as Grandmother Earth.

In conscious relationship these two essential elements merge. Mindfulness, the practice of focusing awareness on the present moment, cultivates a deep willingness to go beyond old mechanical patterns, compulsions and rejections. Brailleing our way toward the underlying reality, feeling our way along moment to moment, noting each nook and cranny, gently spelunking toward the center. This is the quality of investigation which allows conscious relationship to remain conscious, aware of the vicissitudes of the mind, and how their various densities can obstruct the heart of unity and joy.

The devotional quality of a conscious relationship allows us to see the other not as *other* but as self. Then to open to that "other self" as beloved. In the devotional aspect of relationship, one sees one's beloved as the very essence of being, and discovers the divine even in the process of the mind's unfolding, recognizing that what moves thought through the mind is precisely the same energy that moves the stars through the sky. We see in the flow of consciousness the ten thousand manifestations of the sacred. When one sees in this manner, one sees that the other person doesn't have to be perfect in order to be perfect for you. And the nightmare of perfection that warps the pulchritude of another's exquisite heart drops away. One sees the other as a divine gift, a co-conspirator on the path toward the unspeakable enormity. More than just mind, greater than even the heart are lovers who care for each other without reservation, yet care for the Beloved even more.

Then we may experience, as Ondrea did in deep meditation, the divine mother, the Mother of Mercy, approaching us, whispering, "My arms are always around you. All you need do is put your head on my shoulder." And we are overwhelmed with gratitude to our true nature, for our true nature. Tears of joy flow when we recognize that freedom is always just a breath away. Just a breath within the breath away.

Mindfulness teaches us the nature of the shadow. Heartfulness teaches us the nature of the light. Without these qualities in balance, we will evolve either eyeless in the darkness or blinded by the light. Unable in either case to perceive the subtle idiosyncrasies of mind or motion in the shimmering blur of our eagerness for more and our longing not to suffer. But to see straight ahead, one needs to embrace the shadow with the light. To put our world-weary and self-interested head on the shoulder of the divine, our suffering dissolving in tears as we embrace and are embraced by the Beloved. Light is self existent, shadow an interruption of the light by something seemingly solid. Investigating the seeming solidity of things, the shadow too dissolves, melts at the edge and disperses, disappearing into the present heart.

Balancing the practices of heartfulness and mindfulness offers to relationship a quality of workability and open-handedness which brings confidence and joy to the process of our healing. To the process of our merging beyond the mind into the unspeakable loveliness of the heart that is the Beloved.

Conscious relationship can be a path for becoming fully alive by merging the practices of the clarification of mind with an expansive participation in the heart. It is a call to explore the constantly accrued conditioning of the cognitive mechanism we call mind as well as the deep homesickness for God which propels us toward wholeness. Cultivating the devotional quality that sees an *other* as our other, our beloved as the Beloved. These are the history and techniques of surrendering our suffering (the hardest work we will ever do) into the shared heart of our will toward completion; a mixture of moment-to-moment awareness and timeless presence.

Our work is to stay present, available to the universe and vulnerable to the truth. When we are wholeheartedly present, exploring the conditioned mind, who we really are sees who we really aren't. Beyond old ideas of self we find ourselves, as if between incarnations, to be the life spark itself, before it comes into form—before male or female, before rich or poor, before wounded or healed, before the separations of mind—just our true heart, our universal being. Available to love and be loved. Born anew from moment to moment to the incredible journey of the spirit toward the spirit.

As we share these deeper levels of consciousness we call heart, just beyond our conditioned self-image we discover who we may be after all. All that keeps us separate is experienced in the shared heart of our healing. The very act of this release of our suffering into the healing capacity of relationship is an act of bonded commitment to "the healing we took birth for."

Many believe they must select either the path of the contemplative mind, the psychological, mindfulness and the wisdom yogas, or the way of the devotional heart, the mystery, unconditional love, surrender to the Beloved, the celestial song. But relationship is a path that cuts across all other lineages.

In truth, distinctions such as heart and mind are somewhat arbitrary. Heart is just a deeper level of mind, a conduit toward our essential nature. When we go beyond our limited conditioning, our ordinary mind, we enter unconditional love, the heart.

Relationship is one of the highest and most difficult of the yogas. Yoga literally means "union." It suggests the joining of all that is other into the One. One aspect of yoga attempts to join all the disparate parts of the body into the Great Body. Another unites the Great Mind. And at yet a deeper level, it is the union of the "soul" with the Beloved, the personal with the universal. It begins with one being meeting another in love. It deepens and expands until the loved one becomes, in our heart, the Beloved. This approaches the mystical union addressed in so many devotional scriptures. This is the alchemy of hearts merging like halves of the same body, like interdependent hemispheres of the brain. This is where two become one: the Beloved. This is the union of mind and heart, the healing we have sought from incarnation to incarnation. This union is not just with another but with the mystery itself, with our boundaryless essential nature. This union occurs in the realms of surrender where surrender does not mean defeat, but a letting go of resistance to the next moment, the next incarnation. Resistance means an unwillingness to go further. Thus the yoga of relationship entails a willingness to go beyond our resistance, our boundaries, our safe territory. A conscious, committed relationship goes beyond theory, beyond comfortable methods and painful patterns, to the practice of the living truth. To join across that kitchen table the eyes of your beloved.

Conscious relationship is the practice of letting the mind sink into the heart, of healing our frightened and separatist tendencies into the spaciousness of our true heart. It allows a mystical union of such intensity that relationship is no longer differentiated between I and *other,* but united with all that is. It enters the mystery of pure awareness and pure love as being indistinguishable. It goes for broke.

CHAPTER 6

~

RELATIONSHIP
AS HEALING

W HEN ONDREA and I met she had already had two opera-
tions for cancer. In the first operation her cervix and
uterus were removed. In the second, tumors were ex-
cised from the bladder. Clearly if we were to enter together the
remarkable potential for emotional and spiritual healing which
seemed available in our collaboration, we would first have to focus
on the physical body. Having found someone with whom we could
complete relationship, someone who could go all the way and was
committed to do so, our first obligation, while exploring deeper
and deeper levels together, was to focus our attention daily on the
healing of the physical. There was something too precious here not
to direct all our energies into: a healing relationship.

During the first years, physical healing was part of our daily
regimen. Long-held, half-recognized concepts about illness, the
body and even "cure," dissolving one after another as insight into
the depths of what healing might entail opened us to levels of being
that connected the heart with the disheartened. Cure was the
known but distant. Healing was the mystery, the ever-present. Cure

seemed limited to the body alone. Healing seemed ongoing, open-ended, multidimensional. We sensed that if we followed the path with a heart, the body might follow. But the priorities were clear. In a sense, she, we, were no longer healing just for ourselves, but rather for each other and the exploration we had committed to, and ultimately, perhaps, the sentient beings it might serve. As we committed together to the healing we took birth for, the isolation, the fear, went out of the illness. And with each level of deepening awareness came a healing, the mystery becoming more distinct, an increasingly experienced undefined union of hearts.

In those first years there was, of course, the play of bodies and minds introducing themselves to each other (while discovering themselves) as lesser/old ways of relating were auditioned and dismissed. But even in the times when our minds were clouded, beyond such confusion was the ever-present, palpable interconnectedness and commitment that reminded us always to go straight to the heart of healing. At times it was hard to tell if we were pilgrims on the path or clowns in the circus, but the next step was always the same: to let go into love, to deepen mercy and awareness, to put down the load as we were able. A moment at a time. Lightening the burden. Healing.

The potential of a healing relationship is in its ability to triangulate on the mystery with great "don't know"—an openness of mind which no longer clings to the "known" and insufficient, a mind vulnerable to the truth.

About two years into the process, a much-trusted friend, proficient in Oriental medicine, told Ondrea there was a distinct possibility that she might die within the next six months. He is an expert acupuncturist, someone we certainly would have gone to for treatment had we not lived a thousand miles away. But because of his great concern for Ondrea's well-being, he showed me with a pen on her body the acupuncture points he felt must be regularly stimulated for her body to reorient and heal itself. Although I had never applied acupuncture before, he offered me a set of needles and said, "This isn't how I would have chosen to do it, but considering the seriousness of the situation, you really have nothing to lose. Just be sensitive and trust your inner touch."

For the next year, at least three times a week, I inserted needles into extremely sensitive areas of Ondrea's back, knees and abdomen, in hopes this would bring energy to areas of physical imbalance. Sometimes the sessions went very smoothly and she felt instantly revivified. But at other times Ondrea winced in pain due to my ineptitude with the needles, which caused a searing flash to pass through her body. It was one of the most extraordinary situations I have ever found myself in—causing pain to the person I most wanted to be without pain. It was an incredible teaching in helplessness that deepened our trust and commitment.

We trusted on the physical plane what we had discovered on the mental plane: that healing is entering with mercy and awareness into those areas we have so long withdrawn from in fear and judgment. Thus, we followed the path of acknowledging pain, approaching it, exploring its calcified outer ring of thought and resistance, its grief, and entered it with loving kindness. Letting pain float in a moment-to-moment mindfulness and timeless mercy. As this process had consistently aided in the relief and healing of mental pain, so it seemed to aid in the softening and release of physical discomfort. Uncovering layer after layer of wounded holding and antiquated defenses, we experienced the joy of simply being, cured or uncured, healed or unhealed. Quietly listening for what the next skillful step might be.

Sometimes we might both be crying as I turned the needle or placed another deeper. Sometimes the children would come into the bedroom and find Ondrea lying on her stomach, a dozen needles protruding like quills from her back, and as their shoulders crept up about their ears, attempting to hold back the confusion, they often retreated. But even with their aversion to anything that reminded them of pain, they would, at times, just sit in the room and chat—something deep within them trusting the love which permeated.

The need for our absolute surrender and "don't know" trust in the process became a powerful part of the yoga of our healing relationship. It was an extraordinary time.

Now, some years after that period of "heaven/hell," Ondrea's body is devoid of cancer and the toxins which so threatened its existence. Looking back on that time, we are unsure whether it was the acupuncture or the enormity of the love we shared that allowed the healing in. Perhaps it was both, combined with an ever-deepening capacity to give to herself that which she had so long offered to others in her many years of service to those in pain in local hospitals and nursing homes.

If you were to ask either of us, now fifteen years after her last cancer diagnosis, how Ondrea dispelled cancer from her body, we would each have to answer, "Don't know." But it seemed to be a combination of love and our willingness to focus a merciful awareness on the area to be healed—not ostracizing it or sending anger into the illness but inviting it into the preciousness of the moment.

There is a school of thought, now gaining credibility, that is exploring the profound potential of the family and relationship to heal the body. As one might focus mercy and a healing awareness into one's own illness or pain, think how much more powerfully magnified that potential becomes when others, too, are directing their loving attention and mercy into that area. Imagine how healing, on so many levels, it might be when several minds and hearts are focused on a discomforted loved one. Each in collaboration with the source. There is in the family, large or small, as well as in one-on-one relationship, a considerable potential for developing deeper capacities for healing.

As our experiments in healing deepened, we began using our bodies as a kind of laboratory to test these techniques. Living in a large adobe house heated by wood stoves, our arms occasionally came in contact with hot metal when adjusting or adding fuel. Entering directly into the discomfort, watching the initial tightening diminish. Softening to the hard reactions around the pain we noticed that burns healed very rapidly when forgiveness and loving kindness were directed into the multiple tinglings arising there. Often in an hour or two only a red mark remained, rarely a blister. And within a few days the area was completely unaffected. To test this process of embracing that which we so often rejected, we noticed that if we allowed the mind's insistent reaction of withdrawal and fear to remain without the application of these techniques, the effects of the burn might last for a week or more after blistering and generating considerable sensation in that area. Living in the laboratory, it became something of a game to send love to one area of injury but not to another. To see in ourselves, for ourselves, just what this process of healing entailed.

There were also less subtle opportunities to test the effectiveness of this process. Working with my kidney stone, the second in ten years, we sat together on our meditation pillows and focused intensely on the sensations in my urethra where the sharp edges of the stone produced considerable sensation. Within two hours the stone had disintegrated into a fine powder, easily discharged. Had I suspected the potentials of touching so much pain with that much mercy when I had the first kidney stone, I might have saved myself a very painful lesson in how resistance amplifies pain. But I guess that had to be the teaching before this one.

Continuing to apply the healing power of a merciful awareness, we directed this energy at various times over the years into a cracked bone, a strep throat, a pinched nerve and various cuts and contusions, with surprising success. At first we felt that these results were just a bit too good to be true, that perhaps, somehow, we were doing some sort of minor "magic." But as we continued to apply these techniques, we discovered the magic of a deeply focused awareness and the wonderment of mercy and forgiveness to enter that which has become closed off, numbed and perhaps inflamed.

Other opportunities, too, arose. When I was nineteen I learned that I had a "congenital spinal condition." Disks in the fourth and fifth lumbar regions had ruptured when I was in college, causing me to return home for emergency surgery. For some time after the operation, aspirin and limited function were how I dealt with the occasional discomfort in the lower back. Some years later, in my forties, the disks in my neck began to collapse, releasing considerable pain and further decreasing mobility. My initial reaction was to take anti-inflammatory medication and hope it would go no further. But this didn't work. My arm became numb, pain radiating into my right eye.

During the first months of the spinal sensations I bargained with my discomfort. My resistance sought techniques that might relieve me, but as hard-bellied as I was it was like throwing meat to a rabid dog to keep it at bay a moment longer. My discomfort was unaltered. Attempting practices that put my mind elsewhere but hardly investigating that which intensified the disagreeableness of the experience, I went to one of my teachers to ask how I might get rid of the pain. But instead of buying into my escape mechanisms, he said, "Don't look for relief. Look for the truth!" This statement has done much to propel our investigations.

Together we began to explore the sensations, and sent forgiveness instead of fear into the pain. Responding with compassion instead of reacting with anger, a new confidence in our ability to heal arose. Instead of doubt and a sense of failure, we noticed a deeper trust in the process as pain began to diminish. We noticed an increase in the ability to turn my neck. X-rays of the area met with a doctor's frown. His suggestion that surgery would be necessary once again was left behind in a new "don't know" at the possibility of going beyond what others insisted was unhealable. Now, some years later, what was incapacitating is at times only mildly discomforting. The progression of the spinal disintegration seems to have stopped, and I am without symptoms or loss of flexibility for very long periods.

Now any increasing sensation in the shared body/shared heart instructs us once again in mercy and awareness, drawing two hearts into a single focus. It allows us to hum in the laboratory as healing is embraced and the dance continues, slowly turning toward the Beloved.

We are all wounded healers on the way to completion, entering our wholeness just beneath the surface of our superficial holdings. The shared investigation of discomforts leading to a sense of satisfaction and wholeness. Living in the lab, life becomes an experiment in truth.

In the cultivation of a harmonic love, an attunement develops as romance matures into the spirit, that increases the capacity for empathetic synchronistic healing. On the level where we are joined in the mystery—the great unknown vastness beyond our tiny "knowing"—there is the possibility of subtle interactions that affect considerably the body, mind and spirit of our beloved. When hearts touch, other levels seem to open as well, and a subtle interpenetration of awareness, a coincidence of consciousness, sometimes occurs. There is less isolation of that which requires healing. There is a collaboration in healing that focuses on the shared body with the shared heart. Indeed, sometimes one cannot tell whether a thought or feeling or even sensation originated in your mind/body or theirs. And interaction on levels too subtle to have previously been noticed becomes a common experience.

This capacity to directly experience your partner's process creates a bond which enables each to experience the other's mind/body/spirit. And on occasion to even recognize conditions not previously diagnosed but later confirmed by physicians. This mirror effect, pleasant or unpleasant, is just another aspect of what poet David Whyte called "living with the consequences of love."

In some ways, this living with the enormous potentials and difficult healings of the deeper levels of a conscious loving is not unlike what we have come to call "wearing the psychic hat." In workshops we ask the participants, if we had a hat which projected your thoughts to everyone within three hundred feet, who would be the first to volunteer to put on that hat? No one ever raises their hand. But committed relationship is just such an invitation. How long are we going to resist putting on the hat of truth? How long can we stand feeling so unsafe just to maintain the illusion of safety—the smallest of small mind?

And we ask you each, as gently as possible, what keeps *you* from wearing that hat? Are you afraid someone will overhear your insecurities, your sexual fantasies, your angry commentary, your frightened prayers? How much of our life do we feel we need to submerge in order to stay alive? How little mercy has touched this secret pain and longing?

This commitment to the deepest levels of relationship, this openness to wear "the psychic hat," is perhaps personified in the story of a friend traveling in India. During a hiatus between meditation retreats our nearly penniless friend was walking the streets of Benares when he was approached by a beggar who said quite insistently, "Give me money!" To which our friend replied, "I would if I could, but I have none, dear friend." Bowing slightly, he continued on his way. But the beggar would not let him take more than a step before he pulled again on his sleeve demanding once more, "Give me money! Give me money!" To which our friend replied, looking softly into the beggar's eyes, "I would give if I could, but I have no money," and shook an empty pocket to display his sincerity. As he continued slowly on his way, the beggar reappeared in front of him and insisted once more, "Give me money!" To which our friend, soft of belly and open of heart, gently replied that it would give him great pleasure to share what he had, but all he had left after six months of meditating in India was his heart. And that he wished greatly for this man's well-being. The beggar, silent for a moment, looked deeply into his eyes, relaxed his hold on his sleeve, smiled and whispered softly to him, "When you see God in everyone, everyone will see God in you," and disappeared into the crowd. Nothing that came out of this stranger, neither aggression nor anger nor even his obvious need, closed our friend's heart to the moment they were sharing. He was simply present. So, when we see others as the Beloved, that is what they will see in us. When someone reaches out to you, no matter how awkwardly, and you respond with mercy, even when there is nothing you feel you can do—when not even helplessness obstructs your love or your sense of connectedness—you become the beloved of the Beloved. You become love itself, the mystery. It is, indeed, as Rilke wrote:

> For one human being to love another human being: that is perhaps the most difficult task that has been entrusted to us, the ultimate task, the final test and proof, the work for which all other work is mere preparation. Loving does not at first mean merging, surrendering, and uniting with another person —it is a high inducement for the individual to ripen, to become something in himself, to become world, to become world in himself for the sake of another; it is a great, demanding claim on him, something that chooses him and calls him to vast distances.

~

DYAD HEALING MEDITATION

T HIS EXERCISE is done with two people who acknowledge momentarily being either a sender or a receiver of the healing
energies of this experiment, sitting across from each other,
looking into each other's eyes.

Sitting comfortably, look into the eyes of your partner.

Sense the presence, the living suchness, in those eyes.

Let yourself see.

Let yourself be seen.

Feel this person across from you. This being, too, who only
wishes to be happy, who only wishes to be free of suffering.

The person you are looking at now is impermanent. Eventually
they'll die.

And so is the person they are looking at.

Sense this shared predicament, this impermanence and recurrent pain of being human.

Let this pain be shared in the possibility of a new healing.

Senders, sense in the body of your partner any place that

may be calling for healing. Notice any sensations in your body that may be mirroring the experience in theirs.

Approach this discomfort in the shared body with mercy. In your body, in theirs, receiving with heart the disheartened in another.

Receivers, allow that which calls for healing to be seen. Open to that healing. Let it in.

In your heart, let your partner know what part of the body, what aspect of the psyche, needs harmonization.

Nothing to verbalize. Just allow yourself to be received.

Uncover the hurt that wishes healing.

This self-protection, this hard-belliedness is too much to hold onto. Too much suffering.

Let it go. Let it be in your partner's heart.

Those sending, begin to approach your partner's pain with mercy.

Acknowledge the physical, mental, and spiritual grief that resides there.

Notice to what degree the sensations in their body and mind resonate in yours.

Meet these feelings, these sensations, with mercy and loving kindness.

Noticing moment to moment the flow of sensation in that area.

Meeting moment-to-moment sensation with moment-to-moment mercy and softness.

Softening around sensations, around thoughts, floating in the mind/body.

Let them float in mercy and awareness.

Know that there may be a place within them that is all too willing to die, to disappear, world-weary and ready to escape this painful life. We are grieved numb here and there in the body.

Slowly fill those areas that long for your embrace with loving kindness.

Begin to focus into the body of your partner a care for their well-being that touches their pain with love rather than fear. That meets them not within little pities, but in vast compassion.

Don't be too rational about all this. Just let your heart's energy flow into their body's need.

A healing osmosis that nurtures both sender and receiver in the heart of healing.

Senders, sensing a place of pain in your partner, through your eyes send that mercy and that healing directly into their need.

Receivers, notice any place that limits your willingness for your partner to know your pain. Anything that limits the accessibility of your pain to their love.

Let the healing in. Let their love in.

It's so isolating, so lonely, to be alone in pain. Share it with the mercy.

Let their loving kindness be received, be absorbed into your openness to healing.

Open your pain to the possibility of healing. To the possibility of a new mercy and softness.

Notice how doubt can block, how expectation can limit, the accessibility of your pain to healing mercy. Let it in.

Sending, deepen the intensity of this intention to heal. Moment to moment focus your awareness on the sensations subtly imagined, if not felt, in their body.

Waves and waves of healing mercy sent into your partner's pain. Waves and waves of healing mercy received by that pain.

Slowly the hard-held pain softens.

Softly the gentle healing expands, cradling the sensation as if in the arms of the Mother of Mercy or the heart of the Beloved.

Receiving, let your body fill with your partner's concern for your well-being, their compassion and loving kindness. Allow your pain into the shared heart of healing.

Receiving, let them participate in your healing.

Let yourself receive this mercy that is so hard to give to ourselves. Let their care in. Allow yourself to be loved that much.

Let it in. Receive.

Sending, notice any resistance or doubt that limits your capacity to join in the healing.

Let the powerful intentions for your partner's well-being penetrate whatever residual grief may arise. Have mercy on you, on them.

Remember the power, the enormous power of your own great nature.

Like the sound of ten thousand lions roaring.

The power you have to send into that pain.

The power to heal, molecule by molecule, the flesh that holds that discomfort, and the mind that clings to its suffering.

Enter with mercy and loving kindness that which has so often been rejected in judgment and fear. Let the healing in.

Focusing moment to moment on the sensations in your body, send moment to moment an intense care for their well-being, an enormous willingness for them to heal into those areas regaining balance.

Receiving, notice whatever blocks the possibilities of healing. Let it go. Not doubt, not fear, not anger. None of them worth holding onto. This is the moment you took birth for.

Notice how even boredom can block something so important, so precious. Let it go.

Focus again and again on opening to this care, this concern for your well-being.

Feel the great roar of their heart echoing in yours.

Let the roar of their enormous care for your well-being displace the pain and weariness.

Let the healing be sent. Let the healing be received.

Notice any fear of being loved that much. Let it in.

Or any fear of loving that much. Let it come through you.

Let the healing we each took birth for float in each other's heart.

Let it float in your partner's great nature.

Let it be received in your great heart.

> Now both let your eyes close. Let them rest.
> Let the heart just beat.
> Let the breath just breathe.
> Just rest in being, in your own great nature.

Now those who were sending, bring your attention to the place in your mind, in your body, in your spirit, where there's an ache, a pain that calls for healing. Let go of this "power place"

of sending and just receive. Soften. Open to the healing emanating from your partner.

Let your attention embrace that in the body, in the mind, in the
heart, that wishes healing.

Letting go, opening.

Letting your pain be vulnerable to healing. Softening to your
pain. Making contact with the sensations in your body to make
them accessible now to your partner's mercy and care.

Those who were receiving, now filling with the great power of
the heart.

Letting the enormous care you have, the enormous concern,
for this other's well-being, fill your heart.

Those who were receiving, beginning to send. Beginning to
gather the power of their loving kindness.

Touching the pain in their partner with a healing mercy.

Sensing the pain of your loved one, begin to touch it with
wave after wave of concern for their well-being.

Directing into the very center of the sensations and feelings in
their body, a softness and expansive awareness that takes them
wholeheartedly within.

Allowing their care for you in, receiving. Allowing your care for
them out, sending.

This connection is so powerful. Don't think it, be it.

Let it in. Let it in.

Let yourself be loved that much. Let it in. Have mercy on you.

Let your pain be touched by mercy and loving kindness. Let it
in.

There's nothing worth holding the mercy away from the pain.
Nothing's worth it. Let it in.

Let the enormous energy of care, the wave after wave of
loving kindness sent from your partner's heart, through their
eyes, directly into your healing.

And those sending, don't be embarrassed by the enormity of
your love. Let it through. Let it through.

Participating in the healing of your loved one. Sending wave
after wave with each heartbeat, with each breath. Soaking your
loved one in mercy and loving kindness. Drenching them in your
care.

Sending and receiving your birthright, your healing.

And let your eyes close. Just being together.

Just feel this being you're sharing your heart with. Feel the gift. Feel the gratitude. Such gratitude to share this moment with this other being. So precious.

Collaborators in healing. Collaborators in the heart.

CHAPTER 7

~

IN THE
BONEYARD
OF THE
BELOVED

I N WRITING a book about the extraordinary potential for healing, and the miraculous moments of insight, psychological and spiritual, that are the legacy of a conscious committed relationship, it is important that we do not idealize the process. Although this all looks good on paper, the actual doing of it is the work of a lifetime. It is a twenty-four-hour process of self-exposure, exploration, insight, release and healing. No one does it perfectly. Each do the best they can with whatever clarity and heart are available in the moment. Being in the moment one is where healing and the Beloved are to be found.

Sometimes it seems as though this practice of exploring together the sacred in relationship is the work we were born to. And there is a sense that it doesn't matter how long it takes, now that one's feet are on the path and one's eyes, softening, turn toward the light. There is a sense of enormous workability and excitement as new possibilities present themselves.

At other times we may wake, filled with uninvited fear, and look about the room dismayed. Where has our practice gone? What has become of our openheartedness and casual self-confidence? We lie there feeling helpless and hopeless wondering how we ever could have imagined this might work.

It is in those moments when your practice doesn't quite work that you are tested most profoundly. Doubt, shame, fatigue, anger and judgment wither the entrance to the heart, reducing the possibilities of clarity and mercy. Weakened by fear, we cling to the known, to our fundamental suffering. We fall back on familiar hells. We distill suffering from pain. We hide in our wounds.

These moments when the heart is closed, obscured by grief, is for many the bane of relationship. But for some, for those willing to go beyond their pain to discover life itself, the difficulty in relationship is not a curse but a blessing. It is an opportunity to see *other* as *self* and that neither is quite as real or definable as the mind insists. We discover that exploring what closes the heart opens it, and experience, in Thomas Merton's words, "that true love and prayer are learned in the moment when prayer has become impossible and the heart has turned to stone."

Some exclaim that it is the misunderstandings, the emotional ups and downs, the ever-changing boundaries on our personal maps, the balance of care for another with self-interest, the painful remnants of previous unsuccessful interactions, that are "the killers of relationship." And they cultivate distrust and a depressed sense of helplessness. But for the committed heart that wishes to go beyond the mind of suffering, this is the perfect opportunity to let go mindfully of the unheartful and personally painful. It is a ripe field of investigation, a possibility of life anew.

A fellow raised his hand in a workshop recently and said he wanted to speak about what he called "the boneyard" of his previous unsuccessful relationships. He said, with some embarrassment, that he had been married five times and just now was coming to see that "perhaps these divorces were my fault too." He said he had been looking back at "the skeletons left on the battlefield" of his previous relationships, and had to shudder at the depth of the unconsciousness with which he entered each human interaction. At last the pain was too great to ignore. He no longer felt the closed heart was an adequate navigator toward the healing and happiness he had always so frantically sought. His next relationship may well be his first.

We have met many remarkable women and men in our years of spiritual journeying but we have never encountered any who said they were wholly without some "relationship difficulty." In order to be unconditionally loving, we must go beyond conditions and conditioning. To be so alive with love, each moment anew, in what could be called an *unconditioned* love—a love unscathed by previous disheartenments. An effortless expression of the "present heart."

Using the difficulties of relationship as a means of deepening the connection between the heart and the mind, between *I* and *other,* between your beloved and the Beloved is the corpuscle-by-corpuscle, molecule-by-molecule, instant-to-instant effort to explore the present moment as it is. To see beyond denial or fear what closes us, as well as what allows us to remain open. To develop an honesty so profound that it occasionally insults us. It is a commitment to one's self as deep as any relationship known. It is a willingness to die into love, to surrender the mind completely into the heart.

Such a "dying" of the mind into the heart, beyond the imagined separations of self, is wonderfully illustrated in William Buck's extraordinary translation of the Hindu classical holy book the *Ramayana,* in which he tells of the Demon King Ravana, stealing Rama's (the prince of the spirit) bride Sita. The Shadow King has usurped the Beloved. The story details Rama's feats of heroism and his single-pointed drive to regain the light—Sita, the bride of the heart—no matter what the consequences. After extended battles and numerous casualties, Rama the sacred finally faces Ravana the unholy in mortal battle. After enormous effort, the light penetrates the shadow. Ravana is slain.

The next day what is called "the stone letter" is delivered to Rama by one of the slain demon's vassals. Breaking open the letter, Rama reads what Ravana wrote on the evening before his death. In it Ravana praises Rama's extraordinary commitment to the sacred worlds of light and healing. And goes on to say that though he had reveled in the shadow realms, even finding the power to direct the beasts of the mind, he was still unable to experience the immensity of the heart. Feeling he had done all that he could in the essentially unsatisfying realms of control and power, he said that his work was done and that all that remained was for him "to be killed by God." He tells Rama that his original intention in stealing his beloved, and the fierce battles that followed, were all so that he might be slain, freed of his angry desires, by the Beloved, this enormous light. Ravana personifies the hindrances to the heart. It is that part of us calling out for healing, wanting only to be absorbed in the embrace of the sacred.

It might be added here that although this idea of "being killed by God"—an image favored in much spiritual literature—resonates in some poetic chamber of the heart/mind, it can be misleading. The image used here is not to maintain the conspiracy of suffering which insists we "kill the ego" and often results in a kind of spiritual constipation, but as a reminder of the power of the Beloved to heal the unloved. Perhaps someday we'll stop attempting to kill off parts of ourselves and discover what it might mean to be truly *whole*. To meet with mercy instead of hatred that which is confused and is forever attempting to prove it exists. To consider an alternative to slaying the personal self, a healing, an integration of this painful conceit into a more joyous whole. Not killing the ego, just inviting it to peace, offering it whole to the Beloved. And for this gift the Beloved offers us a rose to dismember the body of our suffering and ancient holding. To remind us of who we really are when we let go of our anger, fear and self-hatred. When we go beyond our grief to the heart that knows no "other," but only itself, everywhere it looks.

This is the song and science of using relationship as a means of liberating the heart.

In ancient Chinese, the ideogram for heart and for mind is the same. Relationship is the practice of not only knowing but directly experiencing this truth.

Understanding is not enough. It is only the beginning. Relationship takes our understanding to the solid ground of being.

CHAPTER 8

~

SMALL MIND, SMALL HEART

BIG MIND, BIG HEART

USUALLY WHEN we speak about "the pain of relationship," the difficulty of relating, we are speaking from a place we refer to as "*my* pain," *my* relationship difficulty. In that pain so identified as/with self, there is little room for "the other," much less the Beloved. It loses any larger context. All that is experienced is a personal sense of separation, little me identified with its separate contents. In practical Zen this is called small mind, the mind with only its idea of itself as context.

Like a child holding its breath in tantrum, we refuse to let go of the suffering we create from our pain. We make the whole world "*my* pain." But then just before we pass out, we recognize that this holding only leads to deeper levels of unconsciousness. And we exhale, the great sigh of letting go passing beyond the tiny world of *my* pain, *my* difficulties, to the universality of *the* pain, *the* difficulties. This is big mind.

Small mind is the personal. Big mind the universal.

Small mind relates *from* its contents. Big mind relates *to* its contents.

Zen master Suzuki Roshi, who introduced us to these concepts, said that "everything" is in big mind.

When the small mind's tendency to contract around its pain is released into a merciful awareness, another context, another frame of reference arises. *My* mind becomes *the* mind—small mind becomes big mind as the space in which even the most difficult experiences float becomes included in an expanded focus on the moment. In that greater space, there is a lessening of resistance, a surrendering of our suffering to something gentler and less judgmental which wishes to go beyond old ways of escape and aggression, posturing and aversion.

Small mind only identifies with its content. Big mind only identifies the process.

When we see relationships in pain, when we see the pain in ourselves, and it begins to be received more and more simply as process unfolding, a space starts to open around even afflictive emotion. And we discover it's not just *our* pain, *our* problem, but *the* problem of the separatist mind itself, confronted with having to get out of its own way (and ways) in order to participate wholeheartedly in relationship. The difficulties of having a mind still so laden with conditioning, still so unhealed and deeply wounded, still so full of grief, so dense that it obscures our true nature. Entering the process of *the* mind by focusing on *my* mind, we get a sense that we are part of a great lineage of beings suffering this same difficulty in this same mind and body in this same moment. And "my" pain, "my" difficulties, become "the" pain, "the" difficulties, of being in relationship. And then there is room for the Beloved even in the midst of difficulty.

When we see that the pain we are each dealing with is an aspect of our personal grief, locked in the small mind, with little alternative but to suffer, we enter big mind and stop taking our pain so personally. Watching moment after moment who we wish we were, colliding with how things are, we find ourselves forced to dream conclusions. But in big-mind awareness of the moment as it is, there is no resistance to our resistance. No longer being negative in the negative, no longer surprised or judging the shadows that old mind casts, we see it is not our partner's, or even *our* work, but simply *the* work to be done. The work of accepting responsibility for incarnation. The ability to respond from big mind instead of the compulsion to react to small mind. Living our life fully unwilling to continue posturing through the inordinate pain we each carry.

When we see *my* selfishness, it's almost too much to bear. *My* cold indifference. *My* fear of intimacy. But when we see *the* fear of intimacy, *the* cold indifference, *the* trembling of *the* mind, we come to see the universality of our personal healing.

Mother Teresa, when asked how she could work in the midst of so much difficulty, said that she saw her ill and dying patients only as "Jesus in his distressing disguise." So looking across the breakfast table at another working on the edge of their pain, working to heal a lifetime's confusion and dismay, we slowly see the problem of relationship, the pain we all carry, and begin to recognize our partner in times of such confusion and dismay simply as "the Beloved in its distressing disguise."

When the heart opens to the mind's pain, small mind melts at the edge as our very human condition and conditioning, our ordinary grief, starts to be met, and eventually float, in big mind. When little mind opens from separate suffering to universal participation, it becomes big mind, the path to the Beloved.

Jesus said that when two or more were gathered in his name, he would be there. When two face together the sacred, grace is in constant potential. When we are participating with a merciful awareness in all that arises, not clinging to or condemning anything, we may see directly into the nature of consciousness itself. The process in which *our* process floats. And we come to *experience,* rather than just "know" each other. We no longer trade off the "living truth" for some decrepit model, some old idea that obscures the sentience of that being across the breakfast table.

When two gather toward the Beloved, the ground is consecrated and the priorities become absolutely clear.

And we enter the possibilities of that extraordinary image in Christianity which says we are each cells in the body of Jesus. As delightful an image as that is, it is that much more superb an experience. We are all bubbles in Buddha mind. Buddha bubbles in the body of space, corpuscles of vastness.

Ananda Ma, a remarkable Indian saint, the embodiment of pure devotion, once said, "People come to me and ask, 'Ma, what do you want?' They know what I want, but it's just ego asking. Really, the only thing they can give me is to take that which is separate from the Beloved out of their question and know who they really are." When we wish to give our spiritual partner something to let them know "how much we *really* love them," the most appropriate gift is always to dissolve the separation across which gifts are offered.

Is this so different from what Saint Francis suggested when he chided us to "seek to love not to be loved"? To not seek only to be *a* beloved, but rather to be *the* Beloved. Not to seek, but to *be* love.

Nisargadatta, whose name interestingly enough translates as Mister Natural, a masterful teacher of sacred emptiness and essential nonduality, was once asked what one might do about the qualities of separation that small minds so often manifest in relationship. He said, "Just let go of every thought except 'I am God, you are God.'" He offered them an express ticket. He made the Beloved the conductor. But of course even on this train, after the last stop, you must walk the rest of the way yourself.

This letting go into the great love is the precious gift of relationship available when priorities turn toward the vast healing of our birthright. Embracing and releasing the small triumphs and despairs of our ever-changing past. This is small mind dissolved in big mind, delighted to discover the Beloved to share on the way to being the Beloved.

CHAPTER 9

~

PROPER GRAMMAR

T HE BELOVED is not a noun. It is a verb, it is beingness constantly unfolding. It is *amness* itself. In this same way, at this same level, you too are not a noun but a process unfolding. You too are the Beloved, the energetic suchness to which so much devotional literature, poetry, and scripture refer when attempting to express personal experiences of the sacred.

When we see our partner as a noun, they are somehow not quite as alive as we. They have become an object frozen in our mind, a model, rather than the subject of our heart. We have substituted an idea for the living truth, the mind too small for the Beloved.

Small mind, like a closed fist, has lost touch with its essential openness. Has become cramped closed and finds it painful to let go. Difficult to peel back those fingers palsied for so long around some imagined threat to the imagined self. Small mind is constantly ambushed by its fearful isolation. It lives with one foot on the ground. It refuses to take birth fully. It is drawn to relationship through grief. It measures the world by the degree of its own suffering. But over time this cramping causes muscles to atrophy, and when the possibility of love inspires some joyous pirouette or leap, we discover we do not have the flexibility or the strength. We find small mind too small for our dreams. That the unnameable immensity to which the homesick heart is drawn requires a bigger mind to find its way.

To small mind the Beloved is only an idea. Another confusion. But beyond the separate, big mind means to elude nothing, to push nothing aside. And to stop nowhere. To small mind a "good relationship" is the most that can be hoped for. To big mind it is just the beginning, the base camp from which the ascent originates. The home ground from which the exploration advances into the rarefied levels awaiting.

To small mind the Beloved is at best a goal, something else not "had," another failure, another tightening of perimeters. To big mind the Beloved is an experience, a constant possibility, a constant presence. Small mind thinks the Beloved. Big mind realizes it.

Small mind thinks itself its thoughts. Big mind watches thoughts think themselves.

Big mind tends small mind's longings, as Suzuki Roshi put it, like a large pasture tends a wild horse. He said if you put that wild horse—our ordinary grief, our angry confusion—in a constricting stall (small mind) it will go mad kicking out the slats, a danger to all including itself. But that same wild horse, given the lush green vistas and wildflower expanses of a large pasture (big mind), will buck and snort at first, but eventually settle down, roll in the grass and rest quietly.

Small mind has room only for one. And even then sometimes it's a pretty tight fit. But big mind has room for everything, even the two of you. Small mind hardly has enough space for one thing at a time. Big mind has room for time itself in thing after thing. Small mind floats in big mind quite comfortably.

When you are a verb, you are no longer defined by your limitations, your edges and dualities. And edgeless being, the enormous peace and satisfaction of your true heart, is no longer a threat. Indeed the tragedy is not that someday we must die, but that so often during life we wish to remain numb. No wonder we're in such dull suffering, trying to live so small in such an enormous universe. No wonder relationships can at times be difficult.

CHAPTER 10

~

I AND OTHER

I N ENTERING into relationship, we are treading on one of the most highly charged areas of the mind—the holy/unholy ground of *I and other*. *Other* is our alienation. So, it turns out, is *I*.

The synapse between *I* and *other* is filled with mythical serpents and familiar demons. It is the distance between the heart and mind.

In the process of relationship, this wild terrain must be explored. Noting that on the same level on which resides our sense of a separate self there exists the common grief, the primal terror, that someone will find out we don't really exist.

I creates *other* in the very infrastructure of perception. This cloying self-consciousness doesn't go away by itself. Indeed, it must be examined gently to its root, or the posturing to mask it will reinforce its tendency to view our loved ones, and even ourselves, as *other*. To investigate this sense of separation as a painful, though natural phenomenon of mind (a part of a process unfolding) is a key to a conscious relationship with ourselves and the human heart. When we explore self-consciousness unselfconsciously, when we admit at last how long we have related to ourselves as *other*, *I* and *other* disappear altogether into a mystical union.

Where there is no *other*, the *I* is inseparable from the Beloved. It has the ego of space. It has the body of stellar motion. Although the mind may still produce such separatist images and inclinations, there is little attachment to any reinforcement of their clumsy prod-dings and volitional flickerings. The emotional trance of *I* and *other* is broken and in its place a continuity of heart that goes beyond the mind to discover its whole life.

When you break the conspiracy of *I* and *other*, something of the mystery is revealed. No longer relying on *other* to define our *I*, we approach directly this aspect of mind that we call, depending on our mood, ego or Narcissus or self. Who, you ask yourself, is that crouching in the shadows of small mind, protecting its smallness, defending its pain into suffering? Who is it that wonders who it is, and keeps falling out of love with itself?

Who is it that is offering himself/herself in relationship?

Indeed, before we can fully comprehend what *other* is, we must explore what *I* means. We must inquire within what we are refer-ring to when we say, *I am.*

Settling back and observing this inner dialogue we call *me*, we discover that it seems to be a running commentary on the mind, by the mind. An ever-unfolding flow of consciousness composed of thoughts, feelings and sensations; and of memories and ideas about who is thinking all this. Examining the ever-changing contents of the mind, we see that nothing we call *I* stays for long. That every-thing experienced is in a constant state of change. That what I call *me*, that consciousness, is a process. And how could *other* be any different?! That every thought, every emotion, every experience which has a beginning has an end. That every moment of pleasure, every moment of pain, every sensory experience, every thought and feeling has been impermanent. No wonder the self-image often finds no place to stand, and nothing solid to stand on. When we attempt to make solid the ever-changing unfolding, it leaves us rigid and insecure.

If I ask you, to what does this *I am* refer, the mind will immedi-ately react with a dozen passing identities, I am this, I am that: I am a carpenter, I am a mother, I am a spiritual being, I am a woman, I am a hero, I am a father. But whenever anything is attached to our essential *I am,* we sense we are not telling the whole truth and suffer from a small case of claustrophobia. All the "thises and thats" we cling to are our battered models of correctitude, the dead ends of our spirit. Whenever we attach anything to our essential *amness,* we discard the vast flow of being for something containable and just barely beyond our control. But all that we attach to *I am* is impermanent and our attachment to it is the root of our ongoing suffering. Anything which camouflages our true identity, that attaches to *I am,* reinforces grief and the dread of death and loss, as well as the fear of being in relationship.

Attempting even deeper to answer the question "Who am I?" we find, after tossing a dozen possibilities on the table, nothing independent of conditioning or change, nothing permanent enough to hang your hat on. So, looking yet deeper, we rummage through thought after thought, feeling after feeling, sensation after sensation, seeking something permanent, something solid to identify with, to prove we exist.

But when we explore that to which *I am* refers, we eventually recognize that what we are looking for may not be found in the tiny *I,* but in the vastness of being, in *amness* itself. That *I* belongs to the personal, but *amness* is the universal. Indeed, using "proper grammar" one might say that the *I* refers to the "personal impermanent," and *am* to the "universal immeasurable."

All the experiences of being alive have been impermanent except one. Since the moment you were aware you were aware, whether that occurred in the womb, or at the breast, or the day before yesterday, there has been a single unending experience: the experience of simply being. The experience which, when we settle down and let go of all other experiences, remains. Suspended in the midst of this luminous *presence,* we sense there is more to us than the ever-varying *I.* Letting go of the thoughts that try to define it, and the feelings that attempt to possess it, we enter directly this ongoing experience vibrating at the center of each cell. We explore this sense of presence by which we suspect we exist.

But if I asked you to define it, to answer who indeed you ultimately are, you might have to reply, from the depths of this unnameable suchness, from the midst of the "hum of continuity," simply "*Uh*"—the soft exclamation of the formless essence finding itself in form. This outcasting of the breath in search of a name for that which animates, and is more than, our body and mind ends in exasperation.

Does *Uh* take birth? Does it take death? Or is it the ocean from which these waves are born? And into which each subsides?

This underlying sense of presence, this *Uh* is the only experience of a lifetime which has not changed. It is the space in which change floats. The *Uh* of our universal *amness* is the only constant in the midst of life's inconsistencies.

Everyone's *I* is different, but everyone's *amness* is precisely the same. Indeed, the experience of *amness,* of simply being, never changes. It is the same now as when you were three, or thirty-three, or eighty-three. The experience of *amness* has been the same for all beings from Attila the Hun to Mother Teresa, just *Uh,* just essential being.

And so we see in the ever-deepening investigation of "Who am I?" that nothing impermanent that we attach to the *I* gives relief for long. That only in *amness* are we free. That there at the center of experience, where consciousness originates, is the hum of endless being.

Continuing our investigation into this sense of endless suchness, we come upon life itself vibrating luminous at the center. And enter that which has no beginning and no end, the deathlessness of our underlying nature, our essential *amness.* The *Uh* of boundless being, which for lack of a more expressive term, we call the Beloved.

But even calling it *Uh* we verge on holy war. To name the unnameable is to tempt small mind's tendency to stop at "understanding." Understanding is not enough. It is only the beginning. The idea of the Beloved is like a bubble floating on its vast ocean.

When we come to realize that everything is impermanent but our true nature, that we are *amness* in its distressing disguise, we do not hold so to our suffering, our ever-protected *I,* our defensive smallness. When we surrender into *amness,* when we rest in being, we open to the Beloved, our shared suchness, and notice any sense of separation dissolving in the Inseparable.

We hear of "the battle of the sexes," or of people being "at war with the world," but all skirmishes are fought between *I* and *other.*

Other is the basis of every cruelty, all bigotry and war. In order to harm someone, to lie to someone, to steal from someone, to kill someone, you must see them as *other*—racially *other,* sexually *other,* politically *other,* ethnically *other,* morally *other,* religiously *other,* personally *other.* We see that when the small mind projects its distrust of itself onto another, it is easy to receive that person as *not same:* as nonfamily, nonfriend, nonrelationship, nonhuman, nonfeeling.

And we see that our relationship to *other* is our relationship to self: an other aspect of *amness.* To the degree we judge another, we judge ourselves. Jesus wasn't just moralizing when he said, "Judge not, that ye not be judged." He recognized that the judging mind doesn't know the difference between "I" and "other." It just condemns what does not suit its self-image.

The investigation of *amness* ends the war between *I* and *other.* It stands like Arjuna in the *Bhagavad Gita* between battling clans, examining their fortifications and intentions. It recognizes war as the unfinished business of our unexamined grief. It ends the war by investigating our fear that *I* is essentially different from *other.* It knows that when you say *I* and when I say *I* the flags unfurl, the trumpets blare and the implements of war are unsheathed. It knows, too, that when we reside together in *amness* we are peace. And whatever distances seem to remain between individuals are filled with kindness and wishes for their well-being. No longer attempting to "maintain its space," but to enter directly the unnamed suchness that is the breath of the Beloved.

In Zen, a teacher may hold up two objects such as a bell and a book and ask the student, "Are these the same or different?" If the student says "Same," they are mistaken. If they say "Different," they are equally incorrect. As the old Zen master said, "Such distinctions set heaven and hell infinitely apart." The appropriate reply is often just to ring the bell or read from the book. They are what they are! Each has the same deep essence manifest in a superficially different way. Each is Buddha-nature at a costume ball. Each is susceptible to definition. Each is *other* in precisely the same manner.

So the Zen master might ask, "Is *I* and *other* the same or different?" Don't answer! Don't reply too quickly! If you answer from the *I* and say "Different," you will not be telling the whole truth. If you answer from *amness* and say "Same," you will be equally mistaken. . . . The answer, of course, is not to say it but to be it. To do the psychological (different) work as well as the spiritual (same) explorations to have a whole relationship. Indeed, Rama Krishna says that one of the things that makes God laugh is when bickering lovers say they have nothing in common. Are they same or different? They are the same arguing about differences. The same differences!

And there is nowhere that these *same differences* can be observed more clearly than in disagreements about individual perceptions. Nothing exacerbates the sense of *I* and *other* and creates an emotional trance like two people unable to agree on what occurred during a mutual experience. To disagree about how each sees differently is to be blind. To argue about what is heard is deafening. To contend about what is felt is to be insensate. When it comes to individual perceptions, small mind agreement is, on occasion, nearly impossible. Who's right? Neither if they disagree—both as they shrug into "big don't know."

It is precisely this openhearted, open-minded "don't know" that the Zen master is attempting to stimulate when she asks, "Same or different?" It is the openness beyond conceptualizations, to the truth as it may present itself. In this "don't know" big mind observation, *I* and *other* float in *amness*.

In the mystical wedding, the real joining of real hearts, they do not ask, "Do you take this person . . ."; instead they ask, "Same or different?" And give you the rest of your life to answer—to end the duality that separates mind from heart, and heart from heart, *I* from *other*. *I* and *other* coincide on the common ground of being and the sympathy and harmony it encourages.

When the mind sinks into the heart, is it the same or different?

CHAPTER 11

~

AN EXPERIMENT IN CONSCIOUSNESS

A CLASSICAL ACT OF DEVOTION

TOUCH YOUR forehead to your beloved's feet.

Silently in the heart, send gratitude and blessings.

Sense your forehead touching your beloved's feet as an act of devotion. Sense them as the mother of mercy. Sense them as the feet of Krishna or Buddha or Jesus or Mary, or whoever personifies your heart.

Recognize that you are touching sacred feet.

Wash their feet.

It was good enough for Jesus.

Slowly, perhaps even singing to them, but certainly speaking in the soft tones of loving kindness and interconnectedness, speak of the sacred connection of your hearts. Dry their feet tenderly as though at the foot of the cross, or beneath Buddha's bodhi tree, or in Milarepa's cave. Wash the feet of Gandhi, of Mother Teresa, of your lover, of your children.

Sitting across from the Beloved, bow deeply in gratitude and appreciation. Let go of what blocks bowing. Surrender is not defeat. It is a going beyond resistance. It is the mind sinking into the heart. It is small mind bowing to big mind, entering the heart.

Touching the forehead to the feet. Washing the feet of your beloved, the Beloved.

Acknowledging with a bow their true nature, their sacred essence. Saying in your heart, "I bow to the place within you, and within me, where we share the Beloved, where we are oneness."

And say softly to them, as many in the East do upon meeting and parting, "Treasure yourself."

CHAPTER 12

~

AN EXPERIMENT IN MYSTICAL UNION

SINCE OUR youngest son left home more than seven years ago, we have been committed to a relationship experiment of considerable song and intensity. Having departed the town of Taos, in which we raised our three children, we moved thirty-five miles up into the vast piñon and ponderosa forests of the northern New Mexico mountains. Living in near seclusion, with no phone and few distractions, we committed to an experiment in conscious connectedness. Other than an occasional visitor, there was little to interrupt our process, except perhaps for the "culture shock" a few times a year when we "went out" for a week to do workshops and lectures.

We had always imagined that when our children were grown and out in the world, we would intensify our practice. And when the conditions allowed this to occur, we settled onto a piece of land with not another house to be seen within our sixty-mile vista to the snowcapped mountains. The night sky as amazing as the mind: its perfect mirror: seemingly solid, constantly moving, unknown in origin but appreciated for its luminosity. And by the forest stream, a thousand shimmerings and light plays. A hundred shades of green. The open sky of the southwest as blue as Krishna, as vast as the mind of our deep Buddha. Everywhere we looked was the artful product of Creation. A beauty so effortless and perfect that it made a recent visit to the Museum of Modern Art, a familiar haunt from my distant years in New York City, seem like walking through the corridors of a rag and paint shop. What hung from the walls was more invention than creation. Nothing to compare to a three-hundred-year-old ponderosa or a salamander surfacing to break Narcissus' reflection on the pond. Sitting by the stream, looking toward the mountain just behind the house, we came to realize that the often-quoted statement "Buddha is the blue sky and the green grass" was not a metaphor. That what we call "mountain" or what we label "consciousness" is but a varying density of the same unfolding, that "nature" and what we recognize as "Buddha" are but aspects of a single suchness. And that as we experience the essential nature of the mountain, of the sky, we experience our essential nature as well.

When first contemplating this experiment in silence and seclusion, we projected romantic labels such as "meditation retreat." But we soon discovered, with a sharpening of awareness and an expanding heart, that there was more to the process than even doing "spiritual practice"—that what we really seemed to be about had little to do with what we knew, or even what we did, but was the deepening experience of simply what we were—beingness itself. And all its distressing disguises. As much as it was a meditation intensive, it was that much more a relationship retreat. A daily commitment to remain present. And in the moments we were absent to acknowledge that as well. And to rejoice, in the times we entered together the same level in the same moment, at this "coincidence of heart." A commitment to try to awaken from the long dreams of forgetfulness and self-betraying self-satisfactions. To move beyond the awkward spasms of old mind fear. Connecting first *with* the mystery, and eventually *in* the mystery, we explored beyond fear and the rational, the mind/body/spirit of the moment. Working daily in the laboratory of relationship, quite amazed when the fruits expected from extended periods of meditation began spontaneously to arise in simple silences and passing glances so filled with kind connectedness and the sparkle of the Beloved. Though our meditation practice was interrupted at times over the years due to illness or other factors, there seemed no diminishment of our process. The power, dynamics and profundity of extended periods of clarity and insight was unparalleled in our decades of formal practice. The yoga of relationship defining itself.

As our practice became more a simple resting in being, even the ordinary became quite extraordinary. Mindful of the last breath into sleep, mindful of the first breath on waking, we began to investigate lucid dreaming and other dream-learning experiments. During one period, not moving from the postition in which we awoke, meditating on dream and waking states for between twenty minutes and four hours. The most common of experiences offering up the mystery. Like exploring the desire body's relationship to food, and food's relationship to the process of life. Taking on a "one bowl" practice where for months we ate only one bowl of food a day. During another experiment eating the same meal daily for months. Observing closely the process of eating. Remembering the sacred which is eaten (and which eats). Sleep was at times like going to the Cave of the Sages. Eating like taking birth moment to moment.

During these seven years of experimenting, Ram Dass and Jack Kornfield, two old friends and colleagues, occasionally acted as sounding boards for our process, their perspectives providing some skillful fine-tuning. Indeed when Ram Dass visited our little retreat, he laughed that since we spent all our time together in seclusion, we should by now be celebrating our fiftieth anniversary, adding, that our process together was the most interesting relationship experiment he knew. Some years into the process, sharing with Jack the remarkable healings—physical, mental and spiritual—of our deepening union, he said, "Well of course miracles are happening. You are like a couple of old Tibetans in a cave." Which tickled our lively ego, but in truth we are more like occasionally snow-blind mountain climbers drawn irresistibly by a distant flute.

But it wasn't all heraldic trumpets and angels descending. Much of the grief that lay beneath the noisy ruminations of the mind presented itself. It was an opportunity for healing, an opportunity to meet our lives on many levels with little to interrupt or interfere with the natural unfolding of such healings. It wasn't only the grief of the last fifteen years working as a team with the dying, though in those first months on occasion, the thin, sweet face of a dying patient would present itself in the orange, yellow and black lichen murals on the monolithic outcroppings. But in this stillness could be heard yet subtler griefs, the griefs of a lifetime which now could safely express themselves in an ever-expanding quietude.

At times this grief, this unfinished business with ourselves, presented a confusion of hearts, particularly noticeable when we were changing levels of consciousness and fear was yet holding to the old and fragile security of previously successful strategies.

When we say we undertook an experiment in mystical union, we don't in any way mean to reinforce the painful expectations of "mythical union." We don't mean to make it sound more complicated or easier than it is. Even in a growth-oriented, spiritual relationship, there are times when a couple is out of sync. When we wondered if we shared a common language. Soft-bellied bewilderment and laughter.

Growth experiences, sometimes very subtle, sometimes quite enormous, occur as they will in various ways at various times, each healing at its own rhythm and rate. Different energy movements, healings, openings, closings, can cause two individuals momentarily to communicate at different frequencies. A disattunement may occur as one partner breaks through one aspect while another is preparing its own great leap through hidden mind fields. The work to be done is painfully clear. And nothing but mercy and awareness can do it.

These moments of disattunement were most often received by two hearts willing to go beyond old clingings and fears, which cultivated a gratitude and trust so inexplicably deep that confusion about each other's essential intentions rarely arose. Experiencing love expand naturally and without effort.

In writing about developing a mystical union we do not wish to mythicize relationship, but to demystify the depths available. Mystical unions grow from a shared appreciation of the mystery and a commitment to the co-evolution of consciousness. We have been together since the moment we met more than fifteen years ago, accompanied by an intense commitment and a load-bearing love beyond anything we had previously experienced.

Even in the intensity of our meeting, there was a certain cosmic play that led the heart toward the mystery. The first night we spent together a remarkable thing happened. Having met a few days before in a conscious living/conscious dying workshop, which Ondrea had attended in order to prepare to die from her cancer, we were staying at a friend's home. Just before we retired we noticed that a moth had alighted on a picture of Maharaji—the voice of our heart—placed against a mirror on a dresser across the room. We simultaneously noted how the moth and Maharaji were both phototropic—drawn irresistibly to the light. Some hours later we were awakened by the sound of what seemed like an enormous bird, perhaps an eagle, beating its wings against the terrazzo floor. It sounded like a tethered wildling struggling frantically to be free. As the wings thundered against the ceramic floor in the darkness, we reached out as a reality check to touch each other as we heard in the roar of the wings Maharaji's message to us, "Only fear can destroy this relationship." We listened silently for some minutes before returning to sleep. In the morning we compared notes and found we both received word for word the same message, and had precisely the same experience. In the morning light the moth was nowhere to be found in the closed room. Nor was there any reason to find it. The moth of the moment had told us all we needed to know. The rest was up to us. A thousand times since that experience we have recalled that warning to help clear the mind and open the heart anew.

This was the first teaching in the alchemy of relationship. To transform the frightened, separate and numbed into the confident, unitive and sensate. To convert the ordinary into the extraordinary, transforming our ordinary grief and separation into an inseparability of hearts.

We used to think that Franklin Roosevelt's statement, "There is nothing to fear but fear itself," was a remarkable insight. But then we came to discover there was nothing to fear even in fear. That it, too, was just more "passing show," another boxcar in our train of thought. And fear turned from an instigation to escape to a reminder to be present. That nothing was worth the separation or the guarding of hearts. Reminding us to allow fear its natural impermanence, neither clinging to it nor condemning it, but allowing it to float in something so much greater, the committed heart.

By the time we moved into the woods, our triangulation was well established. We had entered together at the heart level the great joy of a harmonic love. It was the love of two beings sharing beingness, the love that knows the love beyond "knowing."

An example of the difference between the duality which "loves someone" and the experience of being love (the merging beyond distinctions into the heart of the Beloved) was personified for us some years ago on Thanksgiving. Washing the Thanksgiving dishes, I looked up to see Ondrea sitting on the couch with our grandson in her lap and our granddaughter snuggled under her right arm. Beside her was our glowing new-mom daughter. On the other side of her were Ondrea's mother and father. And across the room were our two grown sons, sitting on the floor playing with the dogs. Watching this exquisite familial scene, my mind sighed, "This is as good as it gets!" But a moment later, languishing in the beauty of a healing family reunion, my heart could not deny that even though these personal levels were gratified, our true hearts were not quite acknowledged. The deepest homesickness still unsatisfied. It said, "Yes, this is as good as it gets. But it's only as good as it gets!" All in the room loved each other as much as they could—but there were levels of effortless communion still obscured by the very attachment to this superficial perfection. It was a moment of nearly luminescent beauty, but nonetheless there was a level of joy and connectedness absent that comes from the shared inseparable oneness of being. That offers more than what we usually settle for as "love." As exquisite as the situation, like the state of mind of ecstasy, it was fragile and very much dependent upon the conditions in which it existed. A word or two could have broken it. It was a meeting of minds rather than an unbounded interpenetration of hearts. It was extremely satisfying to the mind, but to the heart, which knew yet deeper levels at which we might connect, it seemed tenuous and temporal. It reminded me that Buddha had said that even the deepest states of concentration and peacefulness acquired in mediation were almost an agitated disquietude next to the unspeakable stillness of our absolute nature.

In these last seven years we have learned that whenever we are anything but the Beloved, our true nature, we suffer. Anything heavier than our original lightness is almost too much to bear.

The commitment to wholeness elevates relationship to mystical heights. When we expand from loving another being to the being-ness of love, alternatives for healing and insight arise. The healing becomes immense. Hope turns to confidence. Fear to fearless mindfulness. And joy, so absent in even some of the most remarkable beings, becomes a common condition. The heart opens beyond the grieving mind. The lotus rises from dark waters.

II

~

DEEPENING
THE
UNION

CHAPTER 13

~

ALONE WITH
THE BELOVED

E XCITED WITH the possibilities of a conscious relationship and
the potentials for triangulating toward the truth, it is easy to
forget that our relationship with that truth is still very much
a one-on-one matter. It is easy to forget that the work to be done
and the fruits of these labors are experienced alone in the solitary
stillness of the heart. That it is our personal practices, our ongoing
investigation of the mind and surrender into the heart that deepens
relationships. As one of our teachers used to say, "Your only friend
is God." In a very real way we are always alone with the Beloved.

Many speak of a gnawing loneliness that blinds the mind so that
the heart cannot see. Some prefer what might be called a "bad
relationship" to being alone with the Beloved. We fear our loneliness, attempting distraction, eating on the run. But if one takes a
few minutes to sit down with this feeling of loneliness that has so
often motivated us, there is something remarkable to be found.
Letting go of resistance to that state, we invite it in, and further
commit to whatever may arise in this exploration. We just sit with
the loneliness and let it eat us alive. Just experiencing moment to

67

moment the varying qualities that comprise this state we call loneliness. Its body pattern. Its tone of voice. Its choice of vocabulary. Its repeated intentions and compulsions. Its desire system. We just sit and let loneliness be, as is.

And the heart, steady as the Buddha under the bo tree, whispers, "If I die of loneliness, so be it. I will continue this investigation until the heart sees clearly." Like the Buddha calling the earth to witness, we touch the ground and persevere, opening to this sense of loneliness we have so seldom related *to*. And so often related *from*. And the loneliness gets deeper. And more insistent. We think we cannot sit a moment longer, so frantically isolated, so abandoned by the world, are we. Lonely, lonely, lonely, and then, in this willingness to just be, the loneliness turns into a state of aloneness. An absolute aloneness which becomes an aloneness with the Absolute. An at-oneness with the universe. Our loneliness transformed into the Great Aloneness where there's nothing left but you and the Beloved. Alone with the Beloved.

When the loneliness becomes an aloneness with the living truth, it makes us patient. We are no longer waiting for the next relationship. We are simply open to it. And in the meantime, we're alone with the Beloved. Then perhaps we can hear into the heart of the gray-haired sixty-five-year-old woman getting married for the first time who said, "It takes a pretty good relationship to be better than no relationship at all." She was not willing to settle, only the Beloved would do.

When we explore and begin to reside in this truth we see that if we cannot be alone with the Beloved, we cannot be present with another. Until we recognize the beloved quality of our true nature, the sacred spaciousness of being, we will be unable to wholly allow ourselves to be the Beloved for another.

We often end our workshops with a Sufi dance. The participants place one hand on their heart, while looking deeply into the eyes of their partner, and with their other hand take their partner's hand and turn slowly in a circle, before reaching out the hand that was on their heart to the next partner and continuing the process. Meeting person after person in deep soft eyes. Because each couple revolves at their own pace, everyone does not reach out for the next partner at the same moment. So, some find themselves having departed from their last partner, but their new partner has n̶ arrived. At this point, we suggest they put both hands over their hearts and give to themselves what they're hoping for from another.

We tell the waiting participants not to grasp at the next partner, but simply to be patient. And add, "There's no life lesson in this or anything!" Most laugh heartily.

Be alone with the Beloved until your beloved comes along. Then share the Beloved in meditation, gardening, working, music, writing, singing, observing, breathing. It is the time that we spend alone with the Beloved that makes us the partner our partner has always been looking for.

> The minute I heard my first love story
> I started looking for you, not knowing
> how blind that was.
>
> Lovers don't finally meet somewhere.
> They're in each other all along.
>
> Rumi

CHAPTER 14

~

LEVELS OF CONSCIOUS CONNECTION

W E EXIST on many levels. There is more to us than meets the "I." There are many strata to our being.

We live on physical, mental, emotional and spiritual planes. These are the levels of *being* that manifest as levels of consciousness: physical consciousness, mental and emotional consciousness, and the multiple experiences and expressions of the deep levels of mind we call heart. And the mystery beyond.

Levels of consciousness coincide with levels of commitment. They are synchronous with the developmental stages called growth: the Survival, Human, Angelic and Mystery stages. As the levels of consciousness deepen, the receptors for relationship broaden.

We connect on many levels. Various qualities interacting. Usually we relate only from the superficial, but there is an enormity to share. There is yet to be offered the unimpeded heart of our true nature.

The first level of connection is physical. It is the biochemical/ neuroelectric level. It is an expression of the earthen body, the born body. It is sensual and very colorful. Most exchanges are on the level of sensation. On this level the travails of *I* and *other* are not much of a problem, as there hardly exists an other.

As a level of consciousness, this is the exploration of sensation: body awareness, mindfulness of sensation, posture and movement. At this dense level, it is not difficult to see how consciousness becomes identified with its sensory objects—and how it tends to relate *from* its pleasure.

As a stage of growth, this is the primal, Survival Stage. It is of prime importance to be familiar with the gross and subtle energies of this level, for it is on this level that a merging joyousness as well as much confusion can be enacted. At this level, softness of belly and openness of heart are interactive.

Although this level can be great "fun," it can be very seductive, drawing consciousness into identification with sensation "as the realest thing happening." Most of its satisfaction comes from the rubbing of small mind against small body. It is often driven as much by loneliness as lust.

On this sensual level, as you discover there is more to you (and other) than the body, you open into deeper levels of mind.

It is important to note that considerable insight is available on each of these levels. Investigated to its root, each of these levels reveals the same truths. That there is more to us than we think or know. It is not that one level is more wisdom-bearing than another, for each offers the teaching of impermanence, process, and grace. As awareness fully occupies each of these levels, it progresses to the next. There is as much mystery in sensation as there are sensations to the mystery.

This is not a linear progression, but a process of expansion that does not so much change levels as include greater depths. Any one of these stages or levels can arise at any time for any number of reasons. One cannot measure one's evolution by the elements of any given level, but by the predominance and re-arising of deeper and deeper stages. In the most balanced relationships, each of these levels displays mysteries which present themselves for investigation and integration into the whole. And more and more evident is the space they're all floating in. The Beloved.

The second level of connection is mental. It is the psychological level; it is an expression of the mental/emotional body. Much of the satisfaction on this level comes from the bargained reinforcement of self-image. It suffers from the mistaken identity of broken dreams and guarded disappointments. If relationship is established solely on this level as refuge from the storm, mistaking water for fire, it can create a prison built for two. It is an interaction of minds very much involved in feelings of being loved and being a lover. It is as much fiction as friction.

Although at this stage the "other" may be considered candidate for beloved, it is still very much filled with isolation and individual agendas. There is mental entanglement. Sometimes it is difficult to dance. Emotional highs and lows are frequent.

It is on this level that "I and other" predominates. Boundaries are drawn and minor border skirmishes occur. On this level if we are not mindful, we get lost in models and expectations. It is as far as most relationships go.

As a level of consciousness this is the investigation of the conditioned mind. Mindfulness of thought and feeling, desires, memory, intention. The content of the body and mind observed in a merciful awareness. Investigated.

On the mental level, where we live most of our lives so small, what we call the subconscious is just subtler and subtler levels of mind—it's only the "subconscious" because we are subattentive.

As a level of growth, this is what might be called the Human Stage, at which psychological beings discover each other. This is the level at which previous injury and grief are healed into deeper stages of consciousness. This is the level of healing on which we integrate our disparate parts into a wholeness, a fullness of being we begin offering wholeheartedly into relationship. This is where small mind closures begin opening into the heart of big mind process.

It is said of this mental level, "If you can make it here you can make it anywhere!" On the mental level, as you discover there is more to you than the mind, you open into the heart. Progressing to the next level of loving individuation.

The third level of connection is the heart. This is the bonding level. It is here that *romantic* love transmutes into *harmonic* love. More than the romantic attachments of the physical and emotional attractions of the first two levels, this love is a state of being, not only a state of mind. This harmonic intermingling is the natural expression of the level of consciousness we call heart. Indeed the phrase "to open your heart" means for consciousness to deepen to this level. In this open space the body and mind are experienced more as process than as content. It is here that the work on the first two levels of reinhabiting the body and clearing the mind opens into the effortless love of a bonded, conscious relationship. The warm attachment of the earlier stages, the growing sense of connectedness, taking a leap of faith into the commitment that bonds hearts while unbinding minds.

The love on this level turns your lover into your beloved—and eventually your beloved into the Beloved. This is the level where the mind and body, like you and your beloved, become spiritual collaborators. On this level where bonding occurs, commitment is wholehearted and without interruption. It is here that the romantic notion of the "magic of love" may actually be experienced. When two minds merge in the heart, thought and feelings commingle. Two minds forming the warp and woof of a whole new fabric. A conjoining of minds and feelings that produces a single tapestry of heart. Boundaries that obstruct the dance floor are relinquished. Boundaries that protect the music are established. We weave and dance, dance and weave. And somewhere near the heart, thought surrenders to intuition as levels of connectedness and interconnectedness present themselves spontaneously. One can almost hear the Melody of the Spheres.

Love turns the chemical to the alchemical. It draws all previous levels up into the heart. At this level bonding occurs quite naturally and spontaneously, as the healing on the lower levels propels our combined energies forward.

It is on this level that triangulation becomes so well established. "I and other" on this level is recognized as a workable quality in the mind, no longer the cause of isolation in the world.

In this alchemy of hearts, minds converge to produce a greater whole than the summation of its parts. It produces a commitment to discovery and liberation so unexpectedly intense that it is capable of turning awareness back onto consciousness, exposing the nature of consciousness itself. Unlocking the mind's secrets and

experiencing directly the simple essence of its seemingly complicated workings. Awareness and mercy bonding like the halves of a
broken heart. Mindfulness and heartfulness keeping the connection
current and alive. The Mystery coming a bit more clearly into view.

It is at this level, if not before, that the partners may well join
into a working team in service to others—in business, in healing, in
teaching, in living.

As we surrender small mind into big mind, our little affections
into our great love, we explore this level of consciousness by entering directly its process. Not grasping at thought after thought but
allowing it all to dissolve naturally into the flow of consciousness.
Discovering realms of loving kindness, mercy and forgiveness, illuminated by the light of our great nature. As a level of growth, this is
the Angelic Stage, a manifestation of the heart body, the body of
compassion marked by a sense of spacious ease and well-exposed
openness.

It brings relationship solidly into the spirit and leads to the next
transformation. When you discover there is more to you than even
the heart, you merge into the mystery.

The fourth level of connection, of consciousness, is the mystery.
It is the level on which a mystical union occurs. "Mystical union" is
a term often used in devotional practices to designate an individual's union with God within. But here we use this term to include
union with the God in each other. The profound connection of
hearts when joined in "depth consciousness." It is an expression of
what we call "the sky body," the space in which the heart's process
and the body and mind's contents float.

On this level, true lovers become wed in the boundaryless vastness which effortlessly expresses itself as wisdom and love. And the
Beloved becomes a constant context in which the process of their
loving unfolds.

It is on this level that remarkable healings, dream interplay, long-
range psychic connection and empathetic communion occur. Many
couples, after some time, can often finish their partner's sentences,
but as the mysteries unite, they may even be able to start the other's
sentence. On occasion, as I am silently trying to recall some teacher
or literary source, Ondrea will turn to me and say, "I can't remember, either!" And neither is certain whether the other spoke aloud

or just thought it. As intuition matures into a mysterious "experiencing" of each other, the process can become so intense that goose pimples accompany its early manifestations.

This mystical union occurs in what is called "the coincidence of opposites," the merging of the seemingly separate into the evidently whole. It is the space in which all opposites and oppositions disappear. It is wholeness without an edge.

As a level of relationship, this is as far as "two" can go. Only *oneness* can take the next step. This is the edge of duality where awareness and compassion are indistinguishable. This is the spaciousness of our own great being.

It might be mentioned here, before we enter what in Zen might be called "the gateless gate" of the last stage, that there really is no way we can rush this process. We can only open to it allowing the possibilities of grace. Indeed, before one can enter each developmental stage, whatever unfinished business remains on the previous level needs to be offered healing before we can go further. This process of integration takes its own time, and only mindfulness and heartfulness will make it smoother. It reminds us that we can't get away with anything, that nothing can be left undone or incomplete.

The fifth realm of consciousness would be abused by any attempt to name or label it. It is that which goes beyond levels. It is the truth that remains when all dualities—all the "I and others," all the "thises and thats," all the gains and losses, all the love and hate —dissolve back into themselves, not relating *from* them or even *to* them, but *as* the space in which they unfold.

In this expansive awareness we are no longer relating to the Beloved, but as the Beloved. The *I* becomes pure *amness*. Not two. Just beings in relationship as a relationship to being.

This is the level of Itself itself. The colorless, formless origin of form and color. Glimpses of this essential reality have been called variously: realization, satori, kensho, pure view, samadhi, or even universal consciousness.

This nonstage stage like every other is, in an ironic sense of the term, an "individual experience." But when both partners are engaged by the same mystical synchronicity into which they ceaselessly surrender, they become a single suchness. Being itself, bowing at the boundary between form and the formless, the known and the unknown. Meeting in the space where there is no *other*. Each being every part of the whole, and the whole it's floating in, and is floating in it. The miracle of our shared existence experienced in the one mind, the one body, of our true nature. It is an expression of the body of suchness or what might falteringly be called the Real Body, the formless body of pure awareness. Our birth body is to the Real Body as a thought is to the mind.

In this spaciousness, in the mystery, nothing seems very mysterious. Just an interplay of energies, nowhere to go until you've gone. Indeed, the mystery only seems that way from without.

And please remember that the last stage, *amness*, is the one that precedes the first.

Each of these levels, like stages of getting born or dying, is a progression from the separate to the universal, from isolation to interconnectedness. Each stage of consciousness or growth or healing can become a level of conscious commitment.

These are the levels of relationship to ourselves as well as another. These are the levels of experience available to our deepening humanness. The enormous possibilities of what we once imagined to be such a small life.

When we open our small lives to the unseen, which we have often subtly felt, our life becomes big. It has room for another and ourselves at last. It reflects the original nature of the heart—spacious, merciful, awake.

CHAPTER 15

~

ROMANTIC LOVE, HARMONIC LOVE

HEN TWO hearts run headlong into each other's arms, there is a collision and interpenetration of consciousness which illuminates the body and sets the mind ablaze. It is the infatuation which begins the journey. Of course, all relationships that ultimately result in a mystical union do not necessarily begin with individuals falling into romantic love. Indeed, some truly remarkable relationships began, as is often the case in Asia, as arranged marriages. Nonetheless, the commitment to growth, focused toward the center of relationship, brought the couples together in a most exquisite and unique manner.

For most, in the initial impact of bodies and minds, there arises an intensity and elation that draws each to the other. We have literally "fallen" in love. We have stepped off the ground and swooned into deep desire and broad emotions. But this chemical euphoria does not last. When the dopamines, norepinephrines and especially the phenylethylamines (PEAs) become chemically neutralized after a year or two of being metabolized, like any drug, the natural high of romantic love falls away.

77

The chemical component of this delightful hysteria gets our attention. But it is what we do with that attention that invites or discourages deeper involvement. Indeed, it is the depth of its focus on what remains "unconscious" that makes a relationship conscious. Romantic love revels on the physical and mental planes, dreaming future paradises in orgies of projection. But exploring together the subtle tug-of-hearts, which trembles at the edge of commitment, we move from the *romantic* to the *harmonic*. This is not the delicate struggle of romance but a harmony of hearts, which includes the sympathetic pains of our ongoing births. And the *sympathetic joy*—one of the Buddha's "great faculties of the heart"—which is the happiness at another's happiness. An attuned compassionate caring.

Romantic love is full of confessions and deceits. Harmonic love is a deep attunement in which self and "other" tend to merge in the Beloved. Romantic love is impulsive and filled with illusions and grief. Harmonic love is present and awake. Romantic love relates to (rather than *with*) another as it imagines them to be. Harmonic love experiences them within, as is.

Love is as close as we get to the Beloved without really trying. It manifests many of the qualities of the sacred. It is characterized by surrender, intoxication, devotion, selfless generosity, joy, uninhibited affection, deep connecting silences and the mercy that goes beyond simple understanding.

Romantic love is as close as we get to harmonic love without really committing. And we wonder why it doesn't last, why the opening heart has frozen in its tracks. But sitting quietly, rolling the question over in the mind, contemplating difficulties and rewards, we begin to see possibilities greater than just the biochemical intensity of deeply desired encounters. Then, instead of lamenting that romantic love is so ephemeral, we begin to deepen its intent. And we come to recognize that romance lasts only as long as it takes for our grief—spiritual, mental and physical—to re-present itself.

Feeling unsafe with nowhere to turn but into the pain once and for all, we explore that which blocks love in a gentle, nonjudgmental manner.

Most romantic attractions originate from well below the threshold of our ordinary awareness. The relationship equation is calculated by a desire system too deep to be recognized by an ordinary unfocused awareness. But as awareness is focused deeper, less arrives C.O.D. from the underdream. And the possibility of conscious love presents itself.

Romantic love believes it owns what it possesses. It abducts the body and the mind. It mimics what it imagines the heart. But a subtler spirit reminds us we cannot own love, only be it. That we cannot possess love, only be possessed by it.

CHAPTER 16

~

BONDING

W HEN ONE speaks of conscious relationship, there may be a tendency to dream. We project ourselves into "golden relationships," imagining the fragrance of jasmine as the orchestra plays the Celestial Melody. But before we can explore the potentials of a conscious relationship, we need to create a common foundation of commitment to growth and the well-being of the other. Flight training occurs on the solid ground of our willingness to heal.

Many people whose relationships are in painful disarray jump at the idea of a conscious relationship. They imagine a "spiritual" interaction; something, anything at all, which might somehow lessen their painful confusion. But before we can enter a conscious relationship (a committed openness and a continuity of the heart), we need to develop the solid ground of commitment and investigation. We need cultivate in our relationship the primary work of settling the mind and opening the heart. We need deepen to the point where bonding is the next natural step. When the time is right, the commitment investigated, there is a powerful bonding exercise which sometimes allows an overlapping of consciousness —an experience of the other person's inner workings that creates an interconnection between hearts not so easily disturbed by the often disconnected mind.

Many, though together, do not experience much togetherness. But when consciousness is retrieved from the ramparts, no longer on guard, it deepens and the path is cleared for further forward movement. In committing to the Dyad Bonding Meditation a few times a week for a few weeks, a considerable power of mutual commitment develops, which allows a glimpse of the possibilities of two entering a boundaryless oneness.

In Asia they speak of two kinds of karma, life momentum. One is the *given* momentum, the momentum we are born into—parents, children, temperament, body type, etc. But most of what comes our way we consider *acquired* momentum—lovers, friends, jobs, education. In this disposable, quick-fix society, most relationships come under the heading of acquired, and somewhat dispensable, momentum, more an option than a given. But when we commit to a conscious relationship, we take our partner as a *given* rather than an *acquired* part of our existence. When we still think of our relationships as acquired, they are disposable and trite. One foot is always kept outside the circle; our bags are never wholly unpacked. Bonding transmutes the acquired into the given. And the level of responsibility—the capacity to respond mindfully instead of reacting mechanically—opens the space wider for yet deeper investigation. When we relate to our lover, our beloved, as an ongoing aspect of our process, considerable forgiveness, noticeable growth and often uncontrollable laughter become its legacy. We recognize that our beloved is not just a temporary houseguest, not just a visitor passing through, but a permanent housemate. Indeed, you "share the rent" on these temporary domiciles we call the body, and these passing states of mind we explore living within. The relationship is no longer caught in, or by, time. What we seek is the timeless quality of their original nature, even before conditioning has distorted the light into the mind's astonishing prismatic effects. Each enters, by whatever door is available, that conditioning and grief which limits further entrance in their beloved as in themselves.

This commitment is not to be taken lightly. Each level of consciousness needs to be integrated. There is no way around "the work to be done." You can't skip a level. Because this is not a linear exploration, but a constantly changing condition in which various qualities predominate—pleasant and unpleasant—only a gentle reception by a merciful awareness will do. It is the willingness to swim in the reservoir of the other's grief. And to share your own. And the futility and joy that accompany growth when we are committed to the long haul. Exploring together the conditioning which usually separates relationships into opposing desire systems, we go, in time, beyond time and conditions to the unconditioned love that spontaneously presents itself when nothing, any longer, obstructs it.

From the viewpoint of the average relationship, bonding practices may seem very appealing, but a forgiveness practice might actually be more appropriate until that which blocks the desired bonding or forgiveness is investigated.

There is no place to go. Don't let this book create a model in your mind of who you are supposed to be and where you are supposed to go. When the heart is open, it knows the way by heart.

Some, fearing "co-dependency"—an imbalance of mutual commitment—question such wholehearted surrender and support as is called for on the solid ground of conscious relationship. And certainly in a relationship that is not co-committed to the living truth such surrender may not be wholly appropriate! Co-dependency is not a bonding, but an entanglement. Indeed, a conscious, committed relationship is like the Great Scale mentioned in the writings of the ancient Egyptians—the scale used by the heavenly deities to weigh the heart against the Feather of Truth. It is that delicate a balance, requiring ongoing attention. Encouraging the mind to enter the heart, to balance perfectly against the "honest truth." Each balancing for the benefit of all.

In co-dependency the scales are always tipped. Often one has to be "down" for the other to feel "up." There is no balance, only dreaded gravity. In a balanced relationship there is no "dominant other," the roles are constantly changing. Whoever has the most stable foothold supports the climb that day.

Ironically, co-dependency is an addiction to our pain while conscious relationship undertakes the healing which dehabitualizes. It is not unlike when a Buddhist monk friend asked his teacher if meditation was a kind of hypnosis, and received the response, "No, it is de-hypnosis!" Conscious relationship can be just such a form of demagnetizing our pain.

Nothing bonds like the truth. Nothing dispels distrust like the revealed heart. Bonding is this willingness to reveal, to simply *be* in the heart of another. To let go of our not-enoughness and self-doubt, making room in our heart for our pain so as to have room in our heart for another's. To see that this woman, this man, is all women, all men. And that this moment is the only moment we have to find the common essence. A conscious committed relationship is a bonding of two "whole" human beings attempting to be mercifully human together.

~

DYAD BONDING
MEDITATION

A N EXERCISE that many have found useful for deepening relationship, and entering the levels of consciousness on which
the bonding that is necessary for conscious interaction occurs spontaneously, is the Ah Breath Bonding Meditation. This
practice, done a few times a week for a few weeks, can open levels
of relationship not previously recognized. It is also a very skillful
practice to share with children, parents, and friends, as it allows, at
times, an overlapping of consciousness in which you feel, sense, the
other in your heart with little or no separation. Indeed, sometimes
one cannot tell whether it is their thought or their partner's thought
arising momentarily in the mind. This practice can act also as a
diagnostic instrument of the separations and separateness we carry
and our unwillingness to surrender, to be bonded mercifully at the
heart.

In a workshop recently, after doing the Ah Breath Bonding Meditation, a woman came to us in tears saying, "I have been married
for nine years, but here in this room with five hundred people
under the most ridiculous circumstances, doing this meditation is

the closest we have ever been and it just shows me how far apart we've been. How could so little cut through so much?"

This is one of the simplest and most powerful exercises to sense the heart we all share, the one mind of being. It allows various levels of connection to be experienced. It can take us through the mind to what lies beyond. It is an exercise in which two people can "see with soft eyes" the levels of intimacy and surrender available to an unobstructed awareness.

Many people use this exercise to deepen the connection within relationships—with lovers, children, parents, the ill, and those one wishes most to serve. It is a guide toward openness capable of giving us a glimpse of our essential spaciousness.

It is a meditation done by two people for twenty to forty-five minutes. Each time this practice is explored, the duration and experience may vary. To make the practice one's own, it is important to become thoroughly familiar with the experiences both of the giver and of the receiver of this technique—though at its deepest point the giver and receiver disappear into the oneness available just beyond the separatist mind.

Do not let the simplicity of this technique cause you to underrate its potential for the two to become one.

Of such a state of boundaryless, nondualistic awareness, Seng-stan, the third Zen patriarch, says:

> For the unified mind in accord with the Way
> all self-centered striving ceases.
> Doubts and irresolutions vanish
> and life in true faith is possible.
> With a single stroke we are freed from bondage;
> nothing clings to us and we hold to nothing.
> All is empty, clear, self-illuminating,
> with no exertion of the mind's power.
> Here thought, feeling, knowledge, and imagination
> are of no value.
> In this world of Suchness
> there is neither self nor other than self.
>
> To come directly into harmony with this reality
> just simply say when doubt arises,

"Not two."
In this "Not two" nothing is separate,
nothing is excluded.
No matter when or where,
enlightenment means entering this truth.
And this truth is beyond extension or
diminution in time or space;
in it a single thought is ten thousand years.

In this exercise, the person with whom you wish to make contact is requested to lie comfortably on a bed or on the floor, as is suitable, with his or her body relaxed. Belts are loosened, glasses removed, arms laid gently by the side, legs uncrossed—open bodies breathing naturally with nothing to do but feel what is happening.

Sitting approximate to their midsection, let your eyes focus on the rise and fall of their abdomen with the inhalation and exhalation of each breath. Encourage your beloved to breathe naturally, not to control the breath or to hold or shape it, but to allow themselves to be naturally comfortable. Without further communication, allow yourself to let go of your normal breath-rhythm and begin to breathe as your partner breathes. As you notice the other's abdomen rising, inhale. As you notice their abdomen falling, exhale. Completely let go of your breath and take on their respiration rate. Breathe their breath in your body.

It is important that once you tune in to your partner's breath, you do not "lock in" but keep the eyes steadily focused on the rising and falling of the abdomen so that you can be attuned to even the subtlest changes within their respiration as different states of mind and different feelings come and go. Even if a state of great peace comes over you, do not close your eyes and disconnect from your partner. Let your attention be very closely attuned to any changes in the rising and falling of your partner's abdomen so that your breath, too, can accommodate these changes.

Taking a few mutual breaths, perhaps eight or ten, begin to breathe their breath in your body. As you both exhale, allow yourself to make the sound AHHHH with each exhalation. AHHHH is the great sound of letting go. With each exhalation, allow this sound to drop deeper and deeper into your body until your belly breathes the AHHHH of their exhalation. It is important that your partner is able to hear your AHHHH, that it is audible and clear. Don't float off into some inaudible whispered AHHHH, which may be pleasant to you but breaks connection with your partner.

Each mutual in-breath is taken silently. As your partner lying before you exhales silently, from your belly, past the heart, out of the mouth, comes this great sound of letting go, the deep AHHHH of release to be heard by them as if it were their own. The person lying down need not make the AHHHH sound.

As with all these meditations, after you make them your own, any type of experimentation is valid. But for the first dozen times you do it allow your partner to maintain silence and find within yourself the deepest natural AHHHH, the deepest letting be of that profound sound within.

Maintain this breath connection for as long as it is comfortable breathing your partner's breath in your body, sounding AHHHH on the exhale. In the course of this practice, any number of states of mind may arise. Some feel a peace beyond understanding. Others moving toward this peace notice unexpected fears of intimacy, sexual energy, or doubt, arising and dissolving momentarily in the breath. Gently stay with it. Let the person lying down know that he or she is in control, and anytime can stop the exercise by simply lifting their hand.

This deceptively simple practice has been found to be exceptionally useful to many. In hospitals, we are familiar with numerous nurses and physicians who use this practice to soften the body and open the mind of those who are in considerable anxiety or tension.

Indeed, many may discover halfway through the meditation that their partner, dropping the tensions of the day, is snoring comfortably. Let it be. Don't force conclusions. Allow the meditation to be the teacher. Any preconceptions are just to be seen as another thought, another bubble floating through the overlapping vastness of a shared reality. Some speak of not being able to tell whose feeling it was that arose at any point during the process. Comparing notes about what was happening during the different stages of the practice refines the connections.

We know of many, working with seriously ill patients, who use this exercise to help them open to healing and release the fear in their body and mind. It even seems to work for patients in a coma. Indeed, a sign of completion noticed with several patients at the moment of their death was deepening of the AHHHH as their breath became thinner and thinner, until at last the soft AHHHH left the body and took life with it. Many have discovered as another dies, the extraordinary possibilities to share that person's death in the deep AHHHH of a profound letting go, which accompanies them to the threshold and allows them to go gently beyond. It is an exercise that has many applications that each will discover as the practice deepens.

Breathing another person's breath in your body, you are paying more intimate attention to that person than perhaps ever before. We hardly listen to every syllable another speaks, much less tune to the microscopic level of each in-breath and the space between, to each out-breath and the resulting stillness. In this deep attention we discover that one does not need to sit twenty years in a cave to get a glimpse of one's shared nature.

The AHHHH Breath is a form of co-meditation, a deep watching of the breath, a profound release of holding that necessitates no dogma or philosophy. The truth is within the truth of it. Whatever is experienced is to be experienced fully.

Wild with the Beloved

I am wild with the Beloved
This speck of dust
the universe, time, and every
act and thought
from mineral to man,
not even a mote in the eye
opened to the terrifying
enormity, the grace that
disturbs our timid understandings
and bursts the waiting heart.

I do not know
what I know
it enters through another door—
even God and the heart
cannot contain it.
Yet here it is
hidden in each breath
revealed beyond reason
and the familiar shape of things.

Do not be betrayed
by philosophies and enlightenments—
the truth destroys all meaning
and the sooner the better.
Let the clear madness come!
Who is there to be separate from
such sacred sanity.

CHAPTER 17

~

TRIANGULATION

TRIANGULATION is a technique for finding out where you are in relationship to the mystery. It is a trigonometric procedure for pinpointing a "distant location" using the perspectives of "two fixed points a known distance apart." In relationship, the distance between these points is "known" through mindfulness and "fixed" by heartfulness. Measuring the separation from each other defines our distance from the truth.

In radio telemetry, triangulation is a method for finding the source of a "mysterious transmission." Two receivers appropriately placed can help solve the quandary. Just as one eye can see, but it takes both to give perspective, "depth of field," so two hearts in combined focus can more readily access the Great Heart, the Beloved.

In our daily affairs, triangulation is not an uncommon means of problem solving. Thus the flourishing trade in marriage counseling. It is the art of two beings approaching a third for wisdom and insight. It is a means of using a third perspective to measure the relationship of the original two.

In "worldly" triangulation we look to the marriage counselor, minister or mentor. In "spiritual" triangulation the two turn toward the One. The context is no longer "How do I get mine?" but rather, "How can we become together all that we might be?"

Once the bond has been established, the base of the triangle secured, and that which separates has been committed to a mutual healing process, the distance and direction to the Beloved, our true nature, can be readily explored.

Relationship clearly is not the easiest method for finding peace, our true heart, but it is one of the most effective for discovering what blocks it.

In the beginning of establishing a relationship triangle the apex is the relationship itself. As this trust and commitment take root in the shared heart, the Beloved takes its proper place and the relationship itself becomes part of the foundation of the triangle.

When a collaboration of hearts connects beings, we experience the pure sweetness of beingness itself. Not being this or being that. Just the simple *whoosh* of being, shared, as two aspects of a single reality.

When compassion becomes a context for relationship, and the pain of another is inseparable from your own healing, your heart becomes a diagnostic instrument perfectly triangulated with the mystery. When the Deathless has become the context for life, only love makes any sense at all.

As a friend said, "Monotheism ruined everything!" Just when we were about to go beyond our dualisms, we stopped short at the One and missed the boundless oneness just beyond. This oneness beyond the One is the mystery unbound by form or meaning. So, in relationship, as the process of triangulation becomes refined, the two do not stop short at simply becoming one or even One. They long for the living truth as much as each other. And relate from the undifferentiated heart to the ever-differentiating mind. There is not even so much "a watcher" as simply the condition of watching. Clear observation. Not watching from some substantial point of view, another monotheism, so much as partaking in the process, floating free in the heart.

Even a relationship that has evolved to a place where two are becoming one still has a way yet to go to heal the deepest sorrows, and allow our sudden wordless understandings to plot the course.

Stopping nowhere, we triangulate upward passing through the heart to experience our sacred suchness. Often sharing an unconditioned love so enormous we are literally *in* love with all that passes through. And that spiritual partner, with whom you began this exploration, is no longer experienced simply as "the person you love" but more profoundly, a process you are *in love with*. When you are in their presence, love spontaneously embraces them. You just float by each other's side in the ocean of compassion.

Conscious relationship is the art of transforming the dystrophy of the mind into the alchemy of the heart. Indeed, when you are "in love" and the open heart closes, it feels as though it has never been so closed before in your whole life. The paradox of this great a love is that the further the heart has opened, the further it has to go to close. This closedness is so painful that the teaching cannot be missed: that any holding in the mind limits access to the heart. That *nothing* is worth keeping the heart closed for even a moment longer. That holding even to the slightest separation, even to a single thought, even to being "right," can create an abyss which our faithfulness fears to leap.

Some speak proudly of how long they are able to maintain their "personal space" and not speak for days in times of conflict. They are proud of how independent they are, how well they have "individuated." And all of this would be true if only they could do it with their hearts open, with self-mercy rather than rage.

Indeed, in the moments Ondrea and I find our hearts closed to each other, it is so painfully evident that we simply can't hold on any longer, and our hearts burst open once again. Thus we are seldom closed to each other for more than a few minutes. And we never go to sleep or part without resolving any "unfinishedness" that might separate us. It is in moments when the heart is closed, when the shadow is most dense, when the light seems farthest away, that our original commitment to this exploration and each other becomes most evident. In love with another, nothing else will do.

Our friend was correct when he said that our monotheisms halt everything. The tendency of the mind, just as it is about to go beyond the duplicity of duality to stop short at the One and miss the enormity of the oneness just beyond, needs to be noted closely. D. H. Lawrence said go deeper than even love for the soul has great depths. Don't settle for safe and recognizable or even "sacred" territory. Don't stop anywhere! When we have passed through the heart of God, relationship enters a state of interrelatedness and only oneness remains. Indeed, to paraphrase a comment by Maharaji: for the average person, their heart is like butter, it melts when near flame. But for the true lover, their heart melts when their beloved's heart is near fire. In such oneness we are "the breath inside the breath," the spaciousness in which we not just merge but emerge.

CHAPTER 18

~

VOWS

I N BUDDHISM there is a major rite of commitment called the Bodhi-sattva Vow. A bodhisattva is one who commits himself/herself to the benefit and liberation of others. The true lover with a steadfast heart, like Suzuki Roshi's bodhisattva, has pledged to the benefit of another and "even if the sun rises in the west he/she has but one way."

Vows taken by committed lovers are like precepts pledged by a monk or nun. They are a support along the high path into the unknown. They are a commitment to ourselves. No matter what circumstances arise, they are the bedrock for the next step.

Vows commit us to the work ahead, psychological and spiritual. They insist we cultivate mercy and awareness. That we do the work it takes to offer all we are. Such vows balance investigations of the personal with doctrines of the universal. They commit to do it all simultaneously. Continuing the broad psychological work to indi-viduate, to come into one's own, so as to be able to integrate the deep spiritual insights. While continuing to deepen spiritual practice to expand the context for their psychological realities. Finding fewer boundaries to their love, true lovers merge for the benefit of the whole—Relationship Bodhisattvas are like that!

Our commitment is in our vows. When Ondrea and I were married, we pledged:

"I offer you my fear, ignorance and old clinging in emptiness and love. I offer you my mind's ever-changing tides—to grow together, uncovering the living truth in each moment we can open to.

"I offer you my heart's love and commitment to help guide us to the other shore.

"My life comes full circle with this vow, to work this lifetime together to go to God, to come to the love that goes beyond form."

Our vow was, and is, a living commitment to the path we share. It is a willingness to live with the consequences of love, to swim in the reservoir of another's grief, to maintain some stillness when agitation approaches. And to bow as it departs. To be completely unreasonable and seldom cautious when the heart intuits a song that will free the mind from itself.

As Stephen Mitchell points out in *Into the Garden: A Wedding Anthology,* in a traditional Zen marriage ceremony there are no wedding vows. Each person simply recites their precepts to maintain mindfulness and heartfulness. They offer no special pledge to one another but only to themselves. Indeed at the beginning of the wedding ceremony the priest says, "You should give up your small selves and take refuge in each other. To truly take refuge in each other means you should take refuge in all things. This is to live together and practice together."

A vow once given cannot be so simply retracted. The same formal energy with which the covenant was created needs be re-created to retract such commitment. It is not a simple matter. (See chapter 29 on sexuality and chapter 50 on conscious divorce.)

The self-image, the imagined boundaries in our unimaginable boundarylessness, may be all too willing to make a vow to bargain with its feelings of unworthiness and incompletion. But vows come more from the heart than from the mind. Before one is certain that a lifetime vow is appropriate to their level of commitment, and is in harmony with their degree of relationship, one might consider a "limited contract" of a few months to test its possibilities.

Find what each expects from the relationship and write it down. Be certain of what you have agreed to before you put your heart's signature on the dotted line. What is expected of you? What do you expect? Contracts for commitment are very powerful examples of our willingness to keep priorities clear.

Indeed some relationships, though sensed not to be for a lifetime, still might be ripe ground for an agreed experiment with the possibilities of commitment. Trial periods of exploration.

Nearly twenty years ago, exploring what this level of commitment might entail, I established a three-month contract with a lover just to see how commitment might play itself out. After the three months two things were perfectly clear: first, that a contract of commitment had enormous power and was certainly appropriate for the next stage of growth; and, second, that the person with whom I had shared this experiment was not. From this experiment in consciousness, it became clear that the high commitment of relationship was as powerful a yoga as any I had ever encountered. One which has allowed me constantly to rediscover my heart in Ondrea.

Because the basis of bonding is trust and commitment, there is one more vow that may be explored to create the kind of safe space in which the required surrender can be accomplished. That is a vow *"never to injure or divulge the secret heart of the other."* This is a sacred pledge, that *under no circumstances* (except spousal violence) will one ever divulge the secrets and feelings that another has confided. That all work done together is sacred and is only between you two and the Beloved. This is the basic ethic, a lifelong commitment to the truth and the mercy which, honored, will set us free. And free the hearts of our loved ones.

This commitment to commitment is very strong. It offers the same power to relationship that a cave offers to a yogi. It is a sanctified space in which to engage the sacred. Here no wobbling will do. This is your commitment to life. This is living, fully alive, with the consequences of love.

We recommit to our vows in a marriage ceremony about every five years. Thus far we have been married by Ram Dass at the Lama Foundation, a Spanish female judge at the Taos Courthouse, a Methodist minister during a five-day relationship workshop in the

Oregon woods, and a shaman tattooist on the day we gave that talk in the church and could not speak of healing without mentioning the Beloved.

In a few months we are planning another ceremony. With each recommitment the vows get simpler. This year we may just bow and kiss.

CHAPTER 19

~

NARCISSUS

MANY BLAME the difficulties in relationship on "ego con-
flicts." What is this ego we are conflicting with? What is
that which insists on only the personal? This is another
aspect of the greatest of all questions, "Who am I?" This is the
exploration of a lifetime.

Perhaps by looking into the archetypal wisdom of ancient mythology, we can investigate this question of what we call ego a bit
less personally.

There is, in Greek mythology, a character called Narcissus, who
for many personifies the ego. Narcissus is the perfect analogy for
the imagined self that each brings painfully to relationship. In that
Greek myth, Narcissus is a beautiful youth who sees his reflection
on the surface of a pond and becomes so entranced by his visage
that he cannot part from it, and remains unto death admiring his
reflection. He is the embodiment of self-concern.

The character Narcissus has long been used to identify a kind of
venal self-interest. We approach Narcissus, as we do ourselves, with
fear and judgment. Its image is as hypnotic to our idea of self as it

was to that youth by the fatal pond. Indeed, it is so magnetic that it has drawn the attention of innumerable writers from Ovid to Robert Graves, Edith Hamilton, Louis Lavelle and Oscar Wilde. In one version, Narcissus suicides. In another, he just pines away. But in most, a new species of flower blooms where he had once kneeled, a white flower with a golden heart, not unlike the huge white blossoms that appeared in Hiroshima soon after the blast had settled.

But in truth, Narcissus drowns in his own reflection. Reaching out to possess himself where once his visage was reflected, now his dead face floats embraced by the still waters.

Narcissus is that part of the mind which thinks about itself. *Though in the old myth Narcissus was male, as a personification of an essential aspect of the conditioned mind, it is neither male nor female.* He is always inventing someone to be. She is seldom patient. It is the overindulged architect of the ever-indulged self-image. Narcissus is a large part of small mind.

Resonating with Freud's nervous tendency to try to legitimize evolving theories by relating them to well-established mythological and classical characters—Oedipus, Electra, etc.—we have employed Narcissus as hod carrier for what early psychoanalysis called "the ego." (Of course, in Latin ego simply means "I am.") But what was being referred to was not the *amness* of being but the "I amness"; the "I am this" and "I am that" identifications with the mind. Freud did not acknowledge there was something beyond the ego, or even a suggested "collective unconscious": that there is a collective consciousness, *being* itself. By shouting ego in a crowded theater, he ignited the audience. And missed the first step, leaving the ego (*I*-ness) dangling groundless without support of its underlying reality (*amness*). He mistook our acquired *I* for our essential *amness*. But it's a common error; one he seems unable to cure. One that must be investigated alone with the Beloved.

When like Freud we stop short at the ego we miss the exquisite truth, choosing the One over oneness once again. Continuing the monotheism of the acquired, rather than the essential self.

Descartes said, "I think therefore I am." To which Zen master Seung Sahn queried, "But when I'm not thinking, then what?"

Thought thinks itself and Narcissus credits himself with all the blame.

Even the old poet Milton threw in his two cents about the myth. He associated it with the origination of Eve, "born into the light in the twinkling of an eye," wondering what her newborn being might be. He suggests that what drew Eve to the apple of self-knowledge attracted Narcissus to the pond. She, however, was more drawn by wonderment than bewilderment.

Not recognizing the process, we attempt to gather the ghostly afterimage of thought into something seemingly solid. This is the essential draw of awareness into consciousness. When awareness is not aware of itself it becomes identified with the passing, impermanent contents of consciousness. We are seldom just *being*. We are constantly *becoming*. Narcissus is the muffled echo of our *becoming*.

Narcissus is the first personification of *amness*. The Beloved is the last.

Narcissus is *amness* in drag. He is that part of us all, self-enamored, self-protective and seemingly isolated in a body and a mind, calling out for recognition. He is our only child, the fragile "I" to which we attribute all our remarkable *amness*. Narcissus is an innate case of mistaken identity. It is a mental construct, a jungle gym of concepts in which we become entangled, imagining we'll benefit from the exercise.

Suzuki Roshi said that ninety-five percent of our ordinary thinking is self-centered. That doesn't leave much room for the truth. Narcissus was the first P.R. man. She was the first to recognize how it can all be done with mirrors.

Narcissus is our smallest I. The Beloved is our biggest.

We are deeply attached to our Narcissus. We are attracted or repulsed by her slightest thought. We are confirmed or denied by his subtlest gesture. We touch Narcissus with fear and anger, withdrawing from, rather than approaching that part of us which so calls out for our embrace. We treat Narcissus as though it were a volitional motif. But Narcissus is part of the basic model, less an option than we would like to imagine. Narcissus is as natural as our will to live.

Narcissus doesn't have to kill himself or be punished. Indeed most imagining they must slay the personal sense of self have seldom considered an alternative: a healing, an integration of this painful ideation into a more joyous whole. Not killing the ego, just inviting it to peace, offering it whole to the Beloved.

This is not an attempt at *killing the ego*—nothing so foolish or egotistical. But to embrace the ego, to embrace our Narcissus. To be kind to it at last. To have mercy on our pain. To know it intimately. To observe keenly its subtlest detail. To not be misled.

Embracing Narcissus is self-acceptance. And as we all know, we can't let go of anything we don't accept. To let go of Narcissus is to free her.

To embrace Narcissus is to relate *to* Narcissus, not just *from* Narcissus. Indeed, Oscar Wilde pointed out that after Narcissus drowned, the pond wept for *its* reflection in Narcissus' eyes.

Narcissus doesn't need to die or be put in chains. Only our painful self-image, our negative attachments, insist on such drastic self-abuse. Narcissus is our bewildered selves, that part of the mind which, like a dandy, lives its life before a mirror. She is in need of mercy, not judgment. He is the ghost of our long-conditioned "someoneness," the persona constantly insulted by the uncontrollable. She is just herself. It is time to stop the war. It's time to make peace. It's time to embrace Narcissus. Our work is not so much to alter Narcissus' possessive nature as to break our addiction to the predominantly "me-thinking" mind. Narcissus is one in a million. One in a million other Narcissuses.

Some say that Narcissus is wholly self-enamored and therefore unworthy of our empathy. But, in truth, Narcissus is like the patient who said she felt like "a piece of crap around which the world revolves."

Ironically, Narcissus' best-known attitude—self-love—was really just a front. Narcissus wears many masks, but beneath them all is the conceit of self-judgment. A feeling of "not enoughness" in the service of which an obsession with appearances ensues. Like most mimics, he would rather look good than feel good. He is the object of so much self-hatred and so little mercy.

Narcissus is just trying to be what she has been told she *should*. Narcissus feels "should on" much of the time, but continues to pretend to exist, insisting her reflection "is as real as she"—neglecting to add, "but no realer!" He only dreams himself. He waits morosely for applause.

Narcissus was not head over heels in love with himself, he just lost his balance. Narcissus is our fear of death, of life, of the next uncontrollable moment. This long-advertised attribute of self-adoration makes it difficult to relate to Narcissus—making him seem a "pretentious other." This lack of a merciful perspective on his pain keeps us from entering the secret teaching armored in shame at the gates of the myth's central chamber. The secret, of course, is to love oneself as Narcissus could not.

When first we acknowledge our Narcissus, we want to turn our back on him. We deride *him* for selfishly seeking his own reflection. But slowly mercy filters in and the mind settles, and sees its own reflection in itself. And priorities change. And we turn toward the pool which long reflected our grief, and dive in. We take the leap of faith. Momentarily frightened as we break our reflection and sink into the waters of our healing, into the Beloved, discovering a peace that goes beyond our angling for control, beyond our desire to be seen as God, in our desire to see as God sees. The peace that comes when we no longer continue to create the world in our image and likeness or insist on acknowledgment as its creator.

When small mind sees itself clearly, acknowledges its illusory reflections held so precious and so fearfully, it becomes big mind. When Narcissus dives beneath his reflection, through the light and shadow just beneath the surface, he takes his first real breath. Beyond the boundaries of his longing he becomes the sacred space in which he floats.

It is time to stop being ashamed of Narcissus. It is the by-product of a mental process which imagines itself separate from the Great Process, but obviously is just an expression of it. Narcissus looks into the reflecting pool to prove he exists. The seeming self-admiration of Narcissus is actually little more than a checking back with reality to make sure the existence we dream is occurring externally as well. When Narcissus looks on his reflection to see if he is dreaming or awake, he can no longer tell. Thought and dream are the skeleton of the imagined self.

But before we can embrace the Beloved, we need to embrace Narcissus. We need to stop taking our self-interest so personally. To observe wholeheartedly the process unfolding. And investigate the insistence by the mind that if there's perception there must be a perceiver, something, someone, separate from the perceived, as it sets heaven and hell infinitely apart, *I* and *other* across the breakfast table.

When Narcissus is accepted as a natural part of mental existence, *I* and *other* no longer empower fear and distrust, but rather become the object of a mutual focus on that in each which is mutually exclusive of the other. Narcissus often would rather play with himself than others.

When we embrace Narcissus, we stop the war. We stop the self-judgment and angry disapproval that follows us like a weeping beast. Narcissus is not at war with the Beloved. He doesn't have the heart for it. Narcissus only wars with the idea of himself. Shadow-boxing. Dream dancing.

There has long been in spiritual and psychological communities the saying "You have to be someone before you can be no one." It is a way of saying that you can't skip over the necessary psychological integrations in order to experience the boundarylessness of your true being. This solid truth points out that without some degree of psychological wholeness, we will not be able to integrate the spiritual insights that arise. That is why some rave about their enlightenment while others just absorb it. Our equivalent of this insight into having to be somebody before you can be nobody is, *you have to embrace Narcissus before you can embrace the Beloved.*

Narcissus requires kind investigation. No force will do. When Narcissus is met, not with judgment or dismay, but with the knowing smile and soft belly of "big surprise!" then one in time becomes not so surprised by the same old thing. Big surprise, the mind has a mind of its own! There is more to Narcissus than we ever imagined. Big surprise. Exploring Narcissus with a nonjudgmental, noninterfering, merciful awareness, we at last allow him simply to be. Just another reflection on the surface of the mind.

But there is more to Narcissus than our superficial reflections may have uncovered. One aspect of Narcissus is self-interest, but yet another is an interest in self. Self-interest is isolation, pride, conceit, posturing and a thousand hasty disguises. Interest in self is quite the opposite. It peels masks. It is an inquiry into the nature of that which calls itself Narcissus. It is the exploratory. Self-interest keeps us well hidden and awkwardly protected in small mind. Interest in self opens small mind separations into big mind healings.

It is time for us to embrace Narcissus. To receive him directly in the heart. To accept her as is. To have a deeper mercy and lighter humor about what Zorba the Greek called "the whole catastrophe," the nature of the conditioned mind. Narcissus is not the enemy. Our attachment, our protection, our unwillingness to explore Narcissus, is what creates discomfort.

Responding to this pain as any other, we embrace it with the mercy and awareness that heals, rather than withdrawing from it in the fear and self-loathing which just creates more of the same. Narcissus is an enemy only to Narcissus. Only our fragile self-image is threatened and takes exception to the term. The small mind judging its small-mindedness.

Narcissus is a ghost seeking incarnation. It is the by-product of a much-misunderstood process: the moment to moment Big Bang of consciousness, and the worlds and wombs it produces for the individual mind to give birth to the universal heart. Although Narcissus imagines himself the viewer of "the movie," in truth she is just another character on the screen. This "me" who seems to watch consciousness pass can be noticed, on closer inspection, to be but another imagistic moment in that passing show. The very idea that there is someone, something, separate from consciousness experiencing consciousness is but another parlor trick of the enormous unfolding. Consciousness experiences itself. Thoughts think themselves in the belly of awareness.

Indeed, as Narcissus attempts again and again to prove that he is the center of the universe, and fails, we find her weeping by a secluded pond. And we approach him with mercy and concern for her well-being. And embrace him knowing, as the mystics might say, that "Narcissus is the mystic bride born to wed the Beloved." They were "promised" at birth.

Narcissus is the betrothed of the Beloved.

CHAPTER 20

~

EMBRACING NARCISSUS

To EMBRACE Narcissus does not mean to indulge its every whim. But to call it out from the shadows and approach it with warmth and clarity. To embrace with mercy and awareness that which we have so long alternately condemned and ordained. To simply observe the self-interested aspect of our ordinary thought. To focus awareness and loving kindness on the process that produces the imagined self.

It is interesting to note that the term "the Beloved" occurs even in spiritual practices that honestly believe one must kill the ego. Because the ego—the self-oriented deeply conditioned mental construct of the "me-thinking" mind—grasps at everything that passes by, we believe we must suppress it. We have forgotten how to simply let it go. To be merciful to the often merciless. To "kill it with kindness."

It is time to bring the caterwauling of the mind into the clear hum of the heart. It is time to stop killing the ego and let it go. Which means let it be. Letting small mind float in big mind without the least need to interfere, judge or condemn. It means making our life *that* big.

Indeed, Buddha and Narcissus are motivated by the same directive: to be real.

Seeking a healing deeper than our conditioning, we stop attacking the ego because it just makes us self-negating and defensive. This "attacking-consciousness" relates to the conditioned mind as if it were the only level of being, and judges every passing thought, attempting to separate the dross from the gold. Forgetting that in Alchemy 101 we were taught that dross was just gold in its distressing disguise.

Those who suppress the ego instead of just letting it recede into the heart make the same merciless error in judgment as those who, attempting to cure serious illness, believe they must "filter out all negative thoughts" in order to be healed. They somehow believe they must be partial to be whole. They do not recognize that what leaves the "negative residue" is not the thought, no matter how dark or fearful, but the negative reaction (holding), as opposed to the healing response (letting go), to that moment. *That a "positive" thought grasped is less healing than a "negative" one met with mercy.* Allowed to dissolve into the golden flow of consciousness. Our thoughts so small, our resistance so enormous.

No longer willing to maintain this heart-crushing self-cruelty, we embrace Narcissus instead of hanging him from the guilt that branches from the Tree of Life. We invite Narcissus off the cross and wash her feet, and soothe his wounds. Welcoming him to join with all the other "creatures of the soul"—the angels and apparitions, the Buddhas and pickpockets, the heartful and the disheartened—on their way to the Beloved like Dorothy passing Oz heading home.

The idea in many schools of spirituality that we must kill Narcissus in order to be free of personal obstructions just results in more constipated yogis and schizophrenic priests. Indeed what is it that wants to kill the ego?! This is an attempt on one level to emulate another, a very unskillful action that hinders deeper spiritual growth and keeps us more mental than heartful.

This mimicking of egoless states, which occur quite naturally at deeper levels of consciousness, can be harmful to the ordinary, unexamined mind. Ego pretense of ego destruction is just someone else to be, another suffering Narcissus. Embracing Narcissus means an end to our guises and disguises, including our ego-filled guise of egolessness. No longer posturing like Saint George at the dragon's throat, we remove our armor and pet the big lizard's belly.

If we wish to end abuse in the world, we must first turn with mercy toward the frightened self and let it just *be,* cultivating a middle way through the mind to the heart of the matter.

Indeed, you can't kill the ego, only lessen your attachment to it. Allowing it to recede into the background and become part of the chorus. Deepening levels of consciousness will produce that same unobstructed openness in which even the ego is just another moment dissolving into the process, floating in the vast spaciousness of being. We don't have to attack the ego. That just keeps us on the battlefield. It will naturally surrender itself as the boundaries of consciousness expand. As one person put it, "You don't have to kill the ego. Enlightenment will do it for you when time and grace allow."

But in truth the ego is not even killed by enlightenment. *Enlightenment does not perfect the personality, only the point of view.* But it shrinks to size when recognized as an infinitesimal bubble floating in the immense ocean of beingness.

Narcissus is captured in his gaze. Our work is to free him of that fixation by focusing that self-interest into an inquiry into self that explores in the mirror of the heart the workings of the mind.

It is neither in the mortification of the physical level nor in the denigration of the mental that access is gained to the heart. Neither penance nor analysis will do what forgiveness can . . . forgive Narcissus. Embrace her. Meet him eye-to-eye, not as an enemy, but simply as a by-product of consciousness. Nothing personal. If you can forgive Narcissus, you can forgive anyone.

We see in the last decade a spirituality growing in which the ego is neither killed nor indulged, but embraced with a mercy and awareness that integrates the whole. Paralleling this expanding spirituality, we recognize a new psychology arising which does not limit the inheritance of being human to just the conditioned and easily recognizable and readily categorized. This is not so much a "spiritual" psychology as one that includes the spirit, the whole of being. A psychology no longer limited to the psyche, a spirituality no longer hampered by addiction to the mind.

On the day the mythic Narcissus got tired of staring at his shoes and went out for a little game of pool we all learned a good deal more about triangulation.

CHAPTER 21

~

THROUGH
THE FIRE
TO THE
BELOVED

T HE REMARKABLE Sufi poet Rumi whispers to us, as if to Narcissus, of the presence of the Beloved "always there before us." He calls us to traverse whatever distances remain. To go through the fire of our deepest griefs and heal the wound of separation from our true nature. To explore with devotion the seemingly separate body, the often isolated mind, the spirit obscured with doubt. He implores us to enter the fires of our holding. To free ourselves for the Beloved.

There is in Rumi's tradition a saying, "This is not a world of my making or even of my choosing, but this is the world into which I am born to find the Beloved." Few would choose this realm of impermanence and holding as a rest stop, but many have discovered its value as a classroom. Birth is our painful initiation into the often awkward realm of relationship and duality. Sliding sideways into whatever niche is available in the family matrix, we attempt to fit our whole ghost into an ever-shifting world of people and things, of liking and disliking, of gain and loss. Born into a realm where most have denied happiness, clinging to momentary enjoyment, we often wander haplessly between pleasure and pain, at times unable to distinguish between the two.

In Zen it is said, "The greater the hindrance the greater the enlightenment." Relationship offers great enlightenment. There, in the midst of the passing show, exploring our pleasure and our pain, examining the light within the fire, we meet ourselves in a brand-new way, and as we look up, there she is, the Beloved, munching toast.

Rumi says that as we approach the Beloved there is:

A fire on the left, a lovely stream on the right.
One group walks toward the fire, *into* the fire, another
toward the sweet flowing water.
No one knows which are blessed and which are not.
Whoever walks into the fire appears suddenly in the stream.
A head goes under on the water's surface, that head pokes out
   of the fire.

Most people guard against going into the fire,
and so end up in it.
Those who love the water of pleasure and make it their devotion
are cheated with this reversal.

He is suggesting from the very heart of a life turned toward the spirit that entering the pain ends the suffering. He recommends we cultivate the profound joy of an unobstructed awareness. Warning that what appears to be the waters of pleasure is indeed a tributary to the reservoir of our grief: denial grasping at pleasure and escape. That the peace and harmony we seek is just beyond the pain and holding we deny.

Rumi, noting that the truth is always available but seldom re-garded, continues:

The trickery goes further.
The voice in the fire tells the truth, saying I am not fire
I am fountainhead. Come into me and don't mind the
   sparks. . . .

Somehow each gives the appearance of the other. To these eyes
   you have now

what looks like water burns. What looks like
fire is a great relief to be inside.

This is the formula for the healing of ancient griefs that the Great Heart offers the small mind. It says that pain is not synonymous with suffering. It offers the mind an alternative. It knows that healing is entering with mercy and awareness areas abandoned in fear and judgment. It embraces pain where it is and experiences it directly, with clarity and compassion. It tells us that the secret to going beyond our resistance is nonresistance: that only our negative holding to pain turns it into suffering and retards its natural dissolution. That it is our resistance to the fire that sets us ablaze.

Fire gets the heart's attention and calls for healing. Water lulls us into the recurring dream of separation that demands satisfaction. Fire consumes what is. Water thirsts for more.

And at last Narcissus stops trying to be someone else. We stop trying to grieve correctly or be a "perfect partner." We stop being model prisoners. We live our life and die our death entering fully the fires of our discomfort. Breaking the conspiracy of suffering in the cool fires of our healing. Again and again reminding ourselves to soften the belly and make room for the Beloved as we work, as we make love, as we sweep the floor, as we take out the garbage.

Sensing the time appropriate to our own process, not dashing into the fire, we take one mindful step closer at a time. Allowing the mind to express its pain to the heart, we sit a moment before taking another step. Gazing into the fire we recognize the flickerings of fear, anger and distrust. And watch our denial panic, seeking refuge in the impermanent and constantly disintegrating. Putting its "best face forward," hiding beneath the mask. The mind looks everywhere for water and is burned. But the heart, knowing better, enters the fire and is cooled. Releasing moment to moment any unwillingness to explore wholly that which separates us from the Beloved, gradually adjusting ourselves to the heat, we enter gently through the molten armoring of the heart. Melting with the pains of our beloved into the spaciousness of the Beloved.

CHAPTER 22

~

SOFTENING
THE ARMORED
HEART

N OWADAYS WE hear poets and psychologists alike speaking of the "armoring of the heart": the long-denied, long-suppressed grief that accumulates layer by layer over the opening to the heart. A shield against further pain tempered over years of disappointment and unexamined grief, amassed at the "grief point" like a stone rolled into the mouth of the cave against our resurrection.

In a workshop some years ago during a grief exploration focused on distrust and fear, a fellow stood in the back of the room and walked hesitantly down the aisle toward the podium. He was growling that this was not a world we could trust. His footsteps were heavy and his tone very frightened and angry. As he approached the front of the room, one could sense a rising fear in some of the participants who viewed this person as "something of a madman and a danger." The group belly had tightened.

Swinging his head from side to side as if expecting an ambush, his frightened heart screamed, "You can't trust this world! It's out to get you! You've got to be ready to fight!" As he approached closely enough for our eyes to meet, I said to him, "I'm glad you came here. This is a good place to work. You know, you're like someone wearing a bulletproof vest." Stopping, he pulled up his sweater, "I'm not *like* someone with a bulletproof vest. I *am* someone with a bulletproof vest." Beneath his shirt was displayed the shiny gray Dacron of his trembling heart's defenses. "But," he asked me, "what am I to do about armor-piercing bullets?" To let down his guard would have been, for him, to step off the edge of a flat world. There was no safety anywhere. He was terrified Narcissus seeking to protect the armoring of the heart from being penetrated.

It was clear that only kindness would do. Anything "rational" I might have said would have just fed into the well-established paranoia of his grief. Calling a "bathroom break" for the workshop, I walked a dozen feet to where this fellow stood, shaking. As I went to put my arms around him he stiffened. But when I whispered, "The arms of the mother are always around you, all you need do is put your head on her shoulder," he began to sob. His armoring broke and his enormous heart exposed itself. He was the personification of our grief, sequestered layer by layer over the heart. He was all the parts of ourselves we have armored ourselves against. His bulletproof vest was a cast for his broken heart. He was the wounded angel of us all.

This armoring of the heart is recognizable as a hardness in the belly. The belly has become rigid with holding. It is a reflection in the body of the imprisonment of the mind. It is the perfect feedback device for our holding. When there is holding, self-protection, fear, distrust, the belly armors. This hardness reminds us to soften, to let go into healing. Soft belly is open belly, is direct access to the heart.

When we begin to soften the belly, we discover we have room for it all. Room to be born at last. Room to heal. Room even to die with an unencumbered heart.

Directing awareness into the belly, one discovers a holding, a tension, that may have been there all through life, but has just been recognized this moment. A rigidity so well established we have somehow gotten used to the pain and imagined it a given in life.

Softening the muscles, softening the tissue, softening the flesh in deep belly—letting each thought breathe itself in the increasing spaciousness—we begin to find ourselves at home even in the midst of the inhospitable. Warring factions are brought to the peace table in soft belly. Levels and levels of letting go into soft belly.

When the belly is soft the passageway between the heart and the mind opens and we begin to see with a soft belly. We begin to listen from soft belly and hear softly the hard world we have so often feared and so seldom embraced. We begin to talk from soft belly, the words soft and for the benefit of all sentient beings. We begin to feel the whole body opening to receive sensation, to let life in at last.

The practice of softening the belly is a key for transforming small mind to big mind. It is the physical act of letting go which accompanies the mental act of release. A physical trigger for a mental phenomenon that re-minds the body of the opportunities for peace.

Because the mind is given to inexplicable moments of fear and closedness, our awareness of the hardness in the belly becomes a perfect biofeedback mechanism for the "letting-go response." Hard belly is a diagnostic device for our holding, our hiding, our posturing. Softening the hardness, we white-flag the war; surrendering our suffering into our pain. As soft belly opens small mind into big mind, it expands awareness of the mind/body—responding *to* thoughts, feelings, and sensations, instead of reacting *from* them.

The way to our heart is through our belly. Letting go of level after level of holding, softening the muscles, the tissue, the flesh, we let the whole breath breathe itself as it will in soft belly. Life entering itself without obstruction, as enormous as our letting go.

In its deeper levels this practice opens the body into the mind, as it dissolves into the heart. Softening level after level to *your* beloved opens level after level of the Beloved.

~

SOFT BELLY
MEDITATION

F IND A COMFORTABLE place to sit and settle in there. And bring
your attention into this body in which you sit.

Feel this body. Let awareness come to the level of sensation in the body.

Feel the breath breathing itself in the body. Sensations of
body breathing. And gradually focus awareness in the abdomen. Sensations of the breath. Feel the breath breathing itself in
the belly.

Sensations of breath coming and going. Each inhalation the
belly fills. Each exhalation the belly empties. The belly rising and
falling with each breath. Sensation arising with each breath.

And begin to soften the belly. Softening the belly to receive
the sensations of the breath. Softening to receive life in the
belly. Breath. Sensation in the belly. Received in a new softness.

Softening. Softening the hardness, the holding in the belly
that resists the breath, that resists sensation, that resists life.
Softening that hardness.

Sensation floating in mercy and awareness. Softening. Let the breath breathe itself in the softness.

Letting go of the resistance, of the fear, of the holding of hard belly. Letting go of the grief and distrust. Meeting them with mercy. With loving kindness in soft belly. Letting go. Letting go of the hardness, breathing it out.

Letting in the mercy, the patience, the kindness, with each inhalation. Soft belly. Merciful belly.

Have mercy on you. Softening to the pain. Softening the holding. Breathing it out. Breathing in mercy. Breathing in healing. In soft belly. In merciful belly.

Softening. Letting go of years of posturing and hiding. So much holding in the belly. So much fear. So much grief. Softening.

Levels and levels of letting go. Levels and levels of softening. Levels and levels of letting go. Levels and levels of healing.

Softening the muscles. Softening the flesh. Softening the holding that resists, that limits life so.

The armoring of the heart is discovered in the hardness of the belly. Meet this pain with mercy, not fear. Meet this grief in softness. In loving kindness.

In soft belly, we have room for it all. Room to be born at last. Room to heal, to be. Room even to die in soft belly.

All the fear, all the anger, all the distrust held so long in the belly. Have mercy on you. Let it go. Let it just be. Gently, in the softness. Met by mercy and awareness moment to moment. Breath to breath.

Softening. Softening.

Even a single thought can tighten the belly, can reestablish separation and fear. Let thoughts come. Let thoughts go in soft belly.

Expectation, doubt, confusion, harden the belly.

Soften.

Thoughts arise uninvited. Let them float like bubbles in the vast spaciousness of soft belly. Moment to moment letting go. Moment to moment being in soft belly. In merciful belly.

Softening. Making room for the heart. For mercy and compassion in the body, in the mind—for soft belly.

Nothing to hold to. Just the vast spaciousness. Just the mercy. Just the letting go of soft belly. In soft belly we have room for our pain and room for our healing. Soften. Letting go of the holding, of the mercilessness.

Letting the universe be our body. Vast spaciousness of soft belly. There's room for it all.

There's room for it all. Let it all float in soft belly.

Breathing in the mercy. Breathing out the holding.

Levels and levels of being in soft belly. Even if some hardness is discovered in the midst of this softness, no resistance. No hardening to the hardness. Soften. Rest in being.

Let the hardness float in the softness. Nothing to change, no urgency in soft belly. Just trusting the process. Just being.

Let the sound of these words pass right through you. No holding anywhere. Even to understanding. No grasping at more. No tightening. Just a gentle letting go of the pain moment to moment. Letting it float in soft belly. Letting the spaciousness of being receive it all in mercy. In loving kindness.

Let the sound of these words pass right through you.

Let all that arises pass through the spaciousness of soft belly, touched by mercy and awareness. Floating in the spaciousness of being.

And gently let your eyes open. Let them open now.

And as your eyes open, notice at what point the belly tightens once again. Even trying to understand can tighten the belly. Being anything but our own great nature tightens us, removes us from the joy of our essential nature. Fills us with mind and confusion tightening the body. Limiting the senses.

Soften with the eyes wide open to the world. Notice at what point that someoneness reasserts itself and you feel a need to protect. Send mercy. Send a blessing to that someoneness so in pain. Soften to it. Let it float in who you really are.

Softening to the pain we all share. And the legacy of healing exposed in this deep softness.

CHAPTER 23

~

OPENING
THE HEART
IN HELL

S ONE WILY teacher put it, "Relationship is good practice, it
can teach you to open your heart in hell."
As a Tibetan lama was dying, his students gathered around
him, praying that he be reborn in heaven realms. His eyes fluttered
open and he said, "Stop, I don't want you to do that! I want you to
pray that I be reborn in hell." His students, in dismay, said, "Oh,
but you have been such a wonderful teacher. You deserve to be
reborn in heavenly realms." To which he replied, "No, I pray that I
be reborn in hell. Where is loving kindness and awareness more
needed?" Where is the Beloved more precious than in hell?

Indeed, how different is this from Meister Eckhard saying, "I
prefer a hell with Jesus to a heaven without." We are all burning at
the edge. To the degree we are working on ourselves, that fire also
illuminates the unknown, the next step. All of our growth is clearly
an expanding beyond our small selves into the spaciousness of the
Beloved. When we are moving gently and without force toward our
edge, toward the fire, hell transforms to heaven—letting go of the
pain into something greater. Letting it all float in the Beloved means

not changing or getting rid of anything—no resistance—simply meeting the old in a brand-new way. Cradling our pain in the arms of the Beloved. Fear arises, joy arises, anger arises, and each dissolves in a mind that does not close. Breathing in and out of the heart together, each the breath of the other, each the breath of the Beloved.

But we are so addicted to our suffering we will fight to the death to protect it. And woe to the person who, even unintentionally, triggered that pain. We hold our ground, even though it is hell. Resistance stops us in our tracks, unwilling to go beyond its fiercely defended edge. Fear (actually a sign of growth at the edge) demands we withdraw to safe territory, old strategies, old pain, a familiar hell. But in relationship, growth insists we let go and expand into the unknown.

Hell is the absence of the Beloved.

Everything in form, including concepts of formlessness, casts a shadow. Even the idea of heaven can produce a hell of resistance to what seems otherwise. The idea of the Beloved can be hell if it creates judgment of self and other. But it is heaven as a direct experience. If we come to imagine that the heart must always be open in order to know heaven, we'll never be able to look the Beloved in the eye. It is quite extraordinary to come to that place where we are able to open our heart even to our heart being closed. Big surprise, big mind has room for it all. Big surprise, mercy and awareness convert hell, our holdings, into heaven, the birthright of our heart.

As the third Zen patriarch pointed out, holding to anything "sets heaven and hell infinitely apart." That holding is hell. That letting go is heaven.

We know some very exceptional beings but we know no one whose heart is open all the time. Even those wise and compassionate enough to take the Bodhisattva Vow—like those who did not recognize their own true light on their deathbed—may not have realized fully that they, too, are one of those sentient beings they have vowed to liberate, "unto the last blade of grass."

To open the heart in hell is to embrace small mind with big mind. To see that what we hold to cramps and atrophies us. That what we hold to leaves rope burns as it is pulled beyond our grasp.

That holding to ourselves as the content of the mind is hell. That opening to ourselves as a process of consciousness is heavenly.

To open the heart in hell is to open even to our resistance with a mercy and awareness, a kindness, a compassion, that reminds us of the Beloved.

Are you looking for me? I am in the next seat.
My shoulder is against yours.
You will not find me in stupas, not in Indian shrine
rooms, nor in synagogues, nor in cathedrals:
not in masses, nor kirtans, not in legs winding
around your own neck, nor in eating nothing but vegetables.
When you really look for me, you will see me instantly—
you will find me in the tiniest house of time.
Student, tell me, what is the Beloved?
It is the breath inside the breath.

Kabir

CHAPTER 24

~

THE
GRIEVING
HEART

THERE IS AN ache at the center of the chest. It is a pain we wish not to see. It's the fire, it's the loss, it's uncontrollable impermanence, our everyday ordinary grief. It's the afflictive emotions that arise in the mind to block the natural openness of the heart.

The heart is always open, it's just that consciousness does not at the moment reside there. It is busy elsewhere. Though we might speak of the heart being closed, it is a misnomer. The heart never closes, it just becomes obscured in the shadows cast by our unexamined grief and ancient holdings.

That ache in the chest, often referred to as the armoring over the heart, is an extraordinary feedback device, like soft belly, for the degree of pain, of holding in that moment.

This ache at the center of the chest is called the grief point. It is a prime area for investigation. In it lies the personal history of our pain, and an unwillingness to expose our anguish.

Many do not acknowledge or even notice this ache. We have become numb from holding. Many recognize it only when a loved one dies or things get "out of control." We only mention this ache when the pain becomes too great to deny or elude. When escape mechanisms are insufficient to suppress our grief, the grief point rumbles like rising magma.

This ache in the chest is like a compass that directs us toward the path of heart. It is a constant reminder of how painful it is to be closed. And what a wonder openness can be. And how much room for the world there is in the big mind of an open heart.

We are all grieving the Beloved. We are all aching our birthright, longing to be free. Our homesickness for God drives us from sensation to sensation, from thought to thought, from emotion to emotion, seeking in the cacophony of consciousness an essential stillness, unobstructed love.

Whether we recognize it or not, we are seeking the sacred in every moment of perception, in every breath . . . No wonder we're so dissatisfied! Big surprise, we get depressed. But depression says the old ways don't work, and that all our attempts to elude it just drive it deeper.

But, when together we enter our grief, there is the combined strength to heal. A profound concern for the well-being of each other creates the safe space necessary for the deeper investigation of our feelings of distrust and insecurity.

When we each enter the grief point, so sensitive when discovered that it is hardly able to be touched, we allow each other the space to let go of whatever is appropriate to release. We do not extract the pain from another, but simply offer that into which it can be expressed and healed. Working together at the grief point, opening to long-disregarded pain, ancient sufferings begin to melt. The buck stops there! Breathing in and out of the ache at the center of the chest with a new mercy and awareness that relates to our halfheartedness wholeheartedly, we free ourselves from the tribulations and hard conditionings of personal history. We begin to forgive our pain, making peace with the past. Breathing in and out of the grief point as it becomes the touch point of the heart. Experiencing joy where once grief was felt, there arises a new confidence and gratitude.

As the grief point transforms into the touch point of the heart, we find ourselves breathing in and out of the heart through this newly opened conduit. And that sweet ache of connection becomes like Krishna's flute calling, offering its pain to the Beloved.

~

THE GRIEVING HEART
MEDITATION

T HE ARMORING around the heart is the accumulation of our
everyday, ordinary grief. All the moments we have put ourselves out of our heart. All the times we have given ourselves
and others so little mercy. On the way to healing the mind and
body into the heart, our daily grief must be explored to go beyond
the holdings of old mind and open to the potentials of this instant.

Some may be drawn to this meditation because of a specific
blockage to the heart—a wound that calls for healing. Others, because the common pain is too much to bear. But most are led to
this practice by the ongoing disappointment of unfulfilled dreams
and losses too numerous and subtle to enumerate: embracing the
common grief that dulls perception and limits the heart.

This meditation connects with the tears unshed, the laughs un-
laughed, the moments unlived. One need not have experienced the
death of a loved one in order to find this exploration a very useful
endeavor. It makes room in our heart for our pain, for our joy, for
our life.

There is a point on the chest, on the sternum, roughly between the nipples about two or three inches above where the rib cage comes together. It is the focal point for this process. Investigate the breastbone to find this point of sensitivity. It is a place where we hold much grief. It may be extremely sensitive. For many when they find it, it will be unmistakable. There may even be a slight indentation there. Take a moment to explore the breastbone to see where it may be evident. Some may find it immediately. For others it may not be as obvious. In this case you "sense" where it may be, mid-sternum, and work with whatever sensations arise there. This point has correlations in many healing technologies. In acupuncture it is "Conception 17." It exists in all traditions which view the body as an energy system. It is the heart center.

After you discover the grief point, place your thumb onto it. As you push into this point with your thumb, you will feel something pushing back. Obviously there is the sternum, the bone plate, but there is also something subtler which is received—a desire to protect yourself, to stay in control, to push away feelings. All the moments of hiding, of protecting ourselves from life, add layer upon layer over the heart of the matter. Thousands of such moments accumulating to become thick as armor. A density of self-protection and an unwillingness to enter directly and emerge from the pain so long suppressed, which pushes back as you push into it. A resistance to life. A resistance to birth. A resistance to healing that asserts itself like a shield against the light. Living in the shadows instead of entering directly the suchness of "just this much." The resistance of a lifetime pushing back against the thumb probing the grief point, opening the way to the heart along the pathway of sensations created.

If you have long fingernails, be careful to use the pad of your finger and not press in with your nail. It doesn't matter whether you use the tip of the finger or the knuckle, just as long as you can exert pressure to bring attention to that area. One of the qualities to be aware of as you start to push into the grief point, to touch the grief, is that the pressure doesn't turn investigation into punishment. You want to push in, to stimulate that point to feel the pushing back, not to cause pain. This is not an exercise in endurance. This is an exercise in opening. We don't have to cause ourselves any more pain to be aware of how much pain already exists.

A simple pressure exerted in that very sensitive area connects the mind/body with the heart center. On the way into the heart, the millions of times we have abandoned ourselves become all too evident. Gently exert pressure to bring yourself wholeheartedly awake to the grief you have carried for so long and the vastness which awaits a merciful awareness.

One of the remarkable qualities of this meditation is that when you have completed your process and take your finger away, you may still feel very distinct sensations where the grief point has become the touch point for the heart. And you continue to breathe compassion in and out of the newly opened channel.

This meditation on our ordinary grief is one of those practices you do alone so you can be together—with each other, your loved ones, even your children.

FIND A COMFORTABLE place to sit in a quiet room and settle in there.

Take a few moments to just feel this quiet.

In this stillness so many voices, so many feelings and sensations.

Notice in the body, at the center of the chest, the numbness or ache that so expresses these feelings.

Gradually bring your attention to this ache, this place of high sensitivity.

It is the ache of our mental longing there at the center of the chest. Let awareness touch these sensations, this pain, this longing in the heart.

So many voices. So many images arising as we focus on the grief point there at the center of the chest.

Now with the thumb press gently into this point of grief and love that aches on the sternum, on the chest just above the heart. Press gently into this painful, this sensitive place. Gently now. Gently pushing into the pain. Letting the pain open to receive these sensations of touch.

Begin to exert some pressure on the grief point. Feel the sternum, the bone beneath, as though it was an armoring over the opening to your heart. Pushing into the sternum, relating gently, mercifully, steadily pushing into the blocked entrance to our spaciousness.

Slowly, without force, but with mercy and steadiness, push into that point. Let the pain into your heart. Press in. Breathe that pain in through the grief point.

Breathe that pain in. If it breaks your heart, let it break. Let go of the holding. Let go of the agony of separation from your pain. Let yourself in. Breathe that pain in through the grief point.

Push steadily without force into that ache. Awareness entering deeply through years of the accumulated sediment of unfelt, unexpressed, unexamined feelings. Penetrating the exhaustion of our everyday ordinary grief, compressed hard as rock: the armoring of the heart.

Push into the pain. Push past the resistance, the resistance to life. The resistance to death. Past the fear, the self-doubt, the distrust. Past feelings of being unsafe, draw this pain into your heart. Let the armoring melt. Let the pain in, past all that holding around being unloved. Past the ten thousand moments of putting yourself out of your heart. Past the judgment, the longing, the anger, the fear.

Breathe the pain into your heart. Let it in. Let it be in the heart of mercy, in the heart of healing. Breathe the pain in, past years of hidden grief, past the shame and secret fears and unrequited love spoken of to no one.

Past our posturing and our fear. Past the pain that frightens us so, entering the mercy of the heart that has room for all this pain. The mind can't handle it. The body is burdened. But in the heart, just beyond our armoring, our fear of all this pain, lies our healing.

Breathe the pain. Let it in. Have mercy on you. Feel all that you feel, drawn in through the grief point. Breathe into the enormity of the heart. Have mercy on yourself. Let it in past the holdings and armorings of a lifetime. Let it in. Let it in at last.

Let your heart break. All the losses, all the injuries, all the grief of a lifetime layered there, holding you back from your life, holding you out of your heart.

Push into that point. Breathe that into your heart. So little room in our minds, in our bodies, for our pain. So much room in the heart. The heart has room for it all.

Receiving the pain with mercy instead of fear or judgment, cradle your pain in your heart. Let each breath gently rock that cradle. All that pain you have tried so long not to feel, now drawn in with each breath.

All the news of the suffering world, the world on fire with pain and confusion. Breathe it in. Breathe it in. Our grief is immense.

Our grief for the past, our fear of the future, felt in our body and our heart. The pain of separation. The longing to connect just once more. Let the heart open to receive this pain. Breathe it in.

We've lived our lives attempting to elude the pain of our daily grief. Our daily fears, our daily anger, our daily sense of isolation. This is the grief of a lifetime, focused at the center of the chest.

Feel the sensations pulsating in the grief point. Breathing mercy through the pain into the touch point of the heart. Letting the pain in. Meeting it with softness, with kindness. Even with gratitude, knowing all that we love lasts only a moment.

Let the heart open to embrace the pain. Breathe it in. Breathe it in. This is the pain that ends suffering.

Let the mind sink into the heart. Let the fear, the loneliness, the guilt, the sense of loss, even the illusions of failure, let them float in the heart. Make room in your heart for your pain.

Let it in. The voices, the memories. Let them into your heart. Don't confine them to the past. Let them into the presence of your heart. In the heart you have room even for this pain. Let it break.

Let yourself be in mercy and loving kindness. Let the mind of grief sink into the heart of healing. Let it all float in the vast spaciousness of your deathless nature, your true nature, the vastness beyond the body.

Sense the space this pain is floating in. Enormous as it is, sense the space. Feel its edgelessness. Float in mercy for yourself and all sentient beings.

Let go of the holding with each exhalation. Breathing through the grief point into the touch point of the heart. Breathing out a blessing. A breath of thanks shared.

May all beings be free of suffering. May all beings be at peace.

May all beings meet their pain with mercy and loving kindness. May all beings make room in their heart for their pain and the pain of all sentient beings who, too, want only to be free.

III

~

THE SOLID
GROUND
OF THE PATH

CHAPTER 25

~

HAVING
CHILDREN,
CHILDREN
HAVING YOU

S PEAKING OF OUR ordinary grief and extraordinary joy, twenty-
seven years ago, while working in Mexico on a book to be
illustrated and published there, I received a terrifying phone
call. I was about to become a father! When my artist friend Felipe, a
father of two, heard the news, he leaned back in his chair and
laughed wildly. "Well, Stephen, it looks like you're no longer the
center of the universe!" I was frightened. I was angry. Who would I
be in the midst of another's needs, in the midst of no control?
Felipe laughed louder.

Small mind reeled in its tiny cell. No control!? Not the center of
the universe?!

It was several difficult minutes before big mind could catch its
breath sufficiently even to acknowledge the states of mind racing
through. But within an hour or two the message reached the heart,
which laughed like Felipe, and whispered, "Ah, no longer responsible for the entire universe. What a relief! Only responsible to 'just
this much.' Soon the cervix will stretch to allow heaven to pass. Be
there for it! Be there completely for it!"

Even after ten years of work on myself, it was the coming of my first child that woke the "me," greedy for spiritual experience and still nearly wholly self-centered, to the possibilities of a yoga-be-yond-my-choosing, baby yoga. Or what a friend calls "saint school," remarking that a colicky infant is a teaching in boundless compassion.

When I received that phone call, my mind spun like a top. I had enough difficulty attempting to keep up with my life without hav-ing to be responsible for another's. I felt my life was out of control. And that feeling has kept me in good stead ever since. It had always been easy to appear "the lover" when I felt I was in control, but now any attempt at control caused me unbearable suffering, which insisted I let go. And I thought I heard my daughter's embryonic heart pumping toward the light.

Even in the midst of fearful insecurities, it taught me I didn't have to be the center of the universe, or have things on my own terms, in order for the heart to be open.

Children are a teaching in helplessness. A teaching that deepens our compassion and keeps it wakeful and responsive even in mo-ments of helplessness and hopelessness. It teaches the heart to stay present even while the mind is still agitated with strategies for escape. It teaches us to keep the heart open even in hell, the uncon-trollable.

Many people, as they become spiritual, seek what is called "self-less service" in order to deepen their practice. But if you want selfless service, all you need do is have children. When Mother Teresa is speaking to the wealthy matrons who have gathered to support her work, she tells them that before they think of feeding the starving, and clothing and housing the poor, they should first look to their own family. She asks if their families are in harmony. "Before you go out into the world to serve others, how is *your* home?" And several of the matrons look helplessly at each other, perhaps having discovered that being married with children can be more painfully confusing than even helping the dying abandoned on the streets of Calcutta. That it is easier to "march for peace" than maintain a peaceful family. That it is often easier to imagine the Beloved in some graven image (mental or physical) than to recog-nize it at the breakfast table.

When Mother Teresa said she did not see that person dying on the pavement as a tragedy, but instead as "Jesus in his distressing disguise," she was teaching us all to see our lover, our partner, our parents, even our children, as the Beloved in its sometimes distressing disguise. Seeing your beloved as the Beloved allows you to see behind your mask as well as theirs. The only teaching is to be. The rest is all words—self-flattery and unresolved grief.

A Zen student we know, wishing to study with his teacher's teacher, went to his monastery in Kyoto, Japan. Meeting him, he was very moved by the teacher's deep, soft presence. When the teacher asked him, "What kind of work do you do?" he replied, "I do service work." To which the old man queried, "And what do you mean by service work?" To which the fellow replied, "I work with schizophrenic teenagers." "That is good work, but it is not service work," replied the Zen master. "The only service you can do for anyone is remind them of their true nature." The greatest service we can offer anyone is to mirror their true heart.

Such teachings have been a guiding light in our attempts at child rearing. Recognizing children as a gift, not a possession, we have attempted, when mindful, to direct them inward, toward the source of ultimate happiness. And when all our hearts met, more often than not there was more than just a parent/child relationship. There was the Beloved in us all embracing the Narcissus in each. A beloved relationship filled with laughter and hugs and tears and whispers and reassurances. Most of the time, even when our three children were teenagers (a time we had often been warned about), we found life quite exciting and exceptionally heartful. The love in the house was palpable and healing to most who entered. Indeed, our home became the hangout for our oldest son's wrestling team fellowship. And for our daughter's giggling girlfriends, and our youngest son's green-haired, spike-headed chums. And there were a few who stayed over even when our children were away. It was the circus of the Beloved.

At other times when hindrances and hormones limited communication, the continuum of seeing each other as the Beloved most often broke through with surprising ease. One day our oldest son, the state wrestling champion, came into our bedroom after wrestling practice while we were watching the evening news. He was walking testosterone ready for a face-off. After a few rather pointed remarks, we said to him, "We're not in the mood for this right now. We don't really feel like being abused at the moment. Why don't you go in the other room for a while and abuse your brother and sister." To which he laughed and responded, "Abuse you?! I'm not abusing you. I know when you want to be abused!" And the shadows in the room turned gold as he leaned over and gave us a kiss and went whistling off to his siblings. There's nothing like humor to turn small mind to big mind with children, much less the child in each of us. Our children have learned to use it well. Trying to impress that same older son one day, watching the news on television we noticed a commentator from Beirut sitting before a bookcase with one of our books prominently displayed. "Look, James," I said, still somewhat auditioning, "there's one of our books on the bookshelf behind the announcer." To which James joyously replied, "Yeah, yeah. They only read your stuff in war zones!"

It is said that your parents can push your buttons because they installed them. But your children seem to have a game board all their own. They often recognize your holdings better than you. But, when the priority is to let go, whatever points out those holdings is useful.

One of our children's favorite buttons on their game board was to mimic us. And they did it perfectly. Often when we went out to dinner with the children, our oldest boy and daughter would sit in the backseat and pretend they were Stephen and Ondrea teaching. They were a cartoon of us, sometimes so accurate we had to soften our belly to hear. We would all be laughing so hard, it was difficult to drive. Like meditation, they were teaching us we were not the mind. They were reminding us only the Beloved would do.

And though we both resisted having children, it is children that have been perhaps the greatest teaching in compassion and awareness in our lives. We know a Buddhist teacher who says we should add children to the traditional "illness, old age and death" that are said to test our practice and challenge the heart. Indeed, the clearhearted poet Gary Snyder said, soon after the birth of his first child, that it was like living with a Zen master in the house. It requires your whole attention and all the patience and selflessness you can muster.

Each of our three children is very different. Each has a different temperament. Each differs in preferences and prejudices, priorities and goals. Though all were raised around meditation and service work, each has related to "the work" in a very different manner. At times they were chagrined by our "laid-backness." They said we were different than their friends' parents. They wished we were a bit more clothes-conscious, complaining that we "looked like we dressed from the free box." But when we would ask them if they would rather we didn't meditate or do service work, all would chime in chorus, "No!" Though they wanted us to "be like everyone else," their friends seemed to be drawn to our "weirdness" like a magnet. Anything could be said in our home. And when someone was in trouble and could not speak about it to their parents, it was brought first to our home. We thought our children were a bit weird too, and loved it. Sometimes the Beloved's just a little weird, but never less than remarkable.

In dozens of workshops, when we ask thousands, "How many of you were born into your own family?"—a family that wanted and cared for you, that supported and listened, a family that wished you well even in your most individualistic endeavors, a family that loved and honored themselves—only a smattering of hands are raised. Truly, this is more easily said than done and we are still learning. But in no group has there been more than five percent who raised unwounded hands. The *Bhagavad Gita* states that a being who has lived a life of wholesome devotion and deep exploration will be "born into the womb of perfect yogis." Spiritual initiates as parents! Love and wisdom the medium of expression. Deep listening. Deep caring. Support on the heart's path. So few hands raised.

It might be added here that it is this longing for our true family that sometimes draws us into spiritual groups. Often that drive creates a family of the spirit which encourages the heart and deepens participation in the whole. But sometimes that desire for community draws us toward unwholesome teachers and unskillful teachings, which offer a kind of togetherness in which everyone outside of that circle is "other." And then it is our family against their family. Holy war. Rivalry and abuse.

Recognizing the painful truth of how many leave home to find their family—gone into the world so very incomplete and vulnerable to confusion—we have shared with our children, as we have learned ourselves, that to be responsible for one's life is to cultivate the ability to respond instead of the compulsion to react. That response-ability is not a matter of blame, but rather a process of expanding our capacity to respond, fully alive and completely awake. We have tried to break the addiction to a world of excuses, theirs and our own. We have tried to break the conspiracy of isolated indifference that the world so lauds in the poverty of success. To not settle for anything less than their true heart. And to break the clanism of small mind: bigotry, sexism, insensitivity, conformity to the destructive old-mind tendencies which denude the planet. Instead, we have encouraged them to be wild and generous, investigative and experimental, kind and resourceful. We have reminded our children, when they see injustice, to fight, without injury, for what they believe, and trust their great spirit.

Ah, the teachings! Imagine the quality of reactiveness while attempting to teach our daughter to take responsibility, saying to her, "Well, if the shoe fits . . ." And she completes the sentence, "—buy it!" Or when I forget for a moment that she, too, is the Beloved and go a bit on automatic, slipping into "the lecture material," and Tara looks up and winks, saying, "Put it on tape!" Ah, another opportunity to soften the belly and let go into the Beloved.

As our youngest child, Noah, dutifully rebelled, he rejected "meditation and the lot." Having mutinied with considerable energy and originality in our youth, we could not imagine how he might "get us" as we had "gotten" our parents. What was he going to do? Grow his hair long? Listen to rock music at hormonal decibel levels? We had done it all. What, indeed, could he do that would surprise us?

Until the afternoon he came home from school with a tattoo and nailed me. He got me right where I lived, right where my mindfulness was weakest and my conceptions strongest. My button got stuck. I was certain he had made a mistake. He was certain I was mistaken. Our only meeting of minds was that the other was way off the mark.

Although the tattoo caught me for a while, it didn't disturb Ondrea in the least. She just saw Noah as the tattooed Beloved. He was just doodling in form and I had to let go of many long-held prejudices and scriptural confusions to see with the heart.

Because we did not lose our original minds when he came home with a tattoo (and gradually acquired others), the heart did not close to small mind's insistence that another be different. Instead, Ondrea and I involved ourselves in his interest, speaking with him about Oriental, and particularly Japanese "skin art," reading and researching with him the exceptional tattoo aesthetic of Asia. Gradually he became curious about "things Oriental." Taking classes in Japanese culture in college, a spontaneous attraction arose, which has now, some years later, developed into an occasional interest in "going to Thailand and becoming a Buddhist monk." In the meantime, he follows an interest in acupuncture and meditation. His practice is strengthening daily: a practice he approached on his own two feet from his own ground. His own practice, not his parents'.

The teaching in helplessness which was Noah's tattoo was quite wonderful.

At this moment in time, all three children show considerable disparity in their manner of seeking the Beloved. One quests in meditation and service. Another demonstrates it in extraordinary acts of generosity and loyalty to his friends. And the third in her ebullient search for self and a loving partner "able to go the distance." Each demonstrates remarkable capacities of the heart in very different ways. Each perfect to their process. Each teaching us that we are not the center of the Universe but just a simple heart longing for the Beloved.

CHAPTER 26

A WHOLE FAMILY

WHEN OUR FAMILY formed, my son was seven, my daughter nine, and Ondrea's boy was eleven. I had been a single parent for much of the last five years. Ondrea had been a single parent for ten years. In combining into a single family there was fear and joy, expectation and disappointment, anger and love. When families combine there is another form of triangulation. Each individual ascending toward a whole family. But when families come together, there may be a complex mixture of aversions as well as attractions. (Not that such energies do not reveal themselves in all relationships, but in a combined family, they may be evident from the outset.) Each child and parent, like each couple, has bonded in their own unique manner. Each has found a *valence*. Valence is a term used in chemistry for the "combination potential" of any two elements. It is a measure of the capacity to unite. To be exact, it is a calculation of the openness to connect with another in the outer ring of any atom. In individuals it is the ability to go beyond "the calcified outer ring of thought" that maintains small mind. It is the ability to become larger. It is the "chemistry" so long referred to in the meeting of hearts. The particularistic capacity to join individual elements into a whole new substance.

Each parent and child has found valence points where deep interconnecting roots have become established. Each has their own formula for connection. But when two families come together, their valences may have developed very differently. If two individuals, whether adult or child, display the same mental proclivities, similar holdings particular to their personality and temperament, then there may be more a clashing of swords than a perfect fit. However, if one cultivates a receptivity to the other's opposition, there may develop an interlocking, an experience of interbeing, which unites the two and constructs a triangle for future growth and healing. Valence is the "bonding quotient," the capacity to allow another's mind into your heart.

It may take a combined family months, or even years, for their valences to evolve and accommodate "a whole family." To meet equal-heartedly on the common ground of our triumphs and despairs, griefs and joys.

There was a period about a year into my relationship with our oldest son where, lost in concepts of what "an oldest son" was supposed to be and do, I became rather judgmental and somewhat "authoritarian." In a not-infrequent moment when mindfulness was weak, we would sit at the breakfast table in silent, rigid disagreement. But one day, in the kitchen across the table from each other, it was just too much. It was so evident what we were missing by continuing to allow fear and judgment to separate us that I looked into his eyes softly, probably almost pleadingly, and said to him, "James, this is just too painful to bear. How long is this going to go on? How long are we going to push each other away when we really want to love each other so much?" He didn't say a word, but the bow of his head signaled the beginning of the end of our agonizing separation.

As our connection developed, he allowed me to adopt him legally. We became as close as hearts become when the willingness to love expresses itself. About a year after that conversation, playing basketball with James and some of his high school friends, my smooth sneakers slipped in the dust and I fell flat to the ground.

James' friends of course laughed, as they would had any one of them fallen flat on their face. But in an instant, James was beside me, pushing them away. Telling them to shut up! Standing guard over me like a samurai, helping me gently to my feet like Mother Teresa, brushing me off like my oldest son.

When I asked James that morning at the table how long would this go on, how long could we stand to maintain this separateness, it broke the mind and displayed the valence of our hearts. In the years since those hard openings, our relationship couldn't be better. I am at least his father. He is at least my son. I cannot see him without recognizing the Beloved. He sends me a Mother's Day card every year.

To transform a combined family into a whole family, it is not only the parents who need to find the valences for relationship; the children need do this work as well. And the braille method once again becomes the only true way. Feeling our way a moment at a time. The children testing, laughing, joking, teasing each other. Discovering who these other beings might be. Wrestling. Vying for pecking order. Stealing each other's dessert. Flushing the toilet while the other is in the shower. Water fights. Working together on common projects. Gossiping. Gossiping. Gossiping. Discovering a family in each other. Insecurities turned to confidences. Trust becoming the context even for moments of suspected untrustworthiness. And in the years they lived together, they couldn't have been more sibling-like (with all its ups and downs, ins and outs) than if they had been born into the same family. And as they each migrated away from home, they eventually ended up in the same small California town. Each with their own apartment, seeing each other regularly, growing in relationship.

It is perhaps here that we might address the obsession with "blood." We hear many in a combined family speak of their biological children as "blood" and the other children, one step removed, as "stepchildren." This always saddens us. To be "blood" is to share a gene pool; a pool in which many, like Narcissus, seek primarily their own reflection. They are obviously still missing the point. They are not paying attention, either to the heart needs of their new children or the poverty of relations with their original family.

Here again is the confusion between given relationships and acquired relationships. We believe that if someone is "blood," only they are a given in our life and must be treated with preferential respect. But our combined families, our new children, are not acquired, they are a given in our deep commitment to a new life. There is no "blood" in the heart of the Beloved: everyone is a fellow traveler in process on the way to the living truth. In truth, our combined family is more family than we were born into. There is more love, more true speech, more concern for each other's well-being than we have ever experienced.

To be attached to blood is the superstition of ignorance. To imagine your new children as any less a part of your life momentum, your karma, is to miss completely the point of your incarnation and the healing you took birth for.

Because each generation, much less each individual, has its own taste in music, part of the combining of our family was to find a place where our musical tastes overlapped. After hilariously mimicking us in the backseat, often all would begin to sing Steve Miller's "Fly like an Eagle." Our five "unique" voices rising into a single chorus of laughter and song, reaching all the way to the heart of the Beloved in each who heard it, in each who sang.

In case all this leaves you feeling that Ondrea and I had some mystical connection with the children that always cut through difficulties, let us dissuade you from that notion. Our attunement and interventions were often a good deal more practical than you might imagine. When, for instance, the new siblings fell into an evening's bickering joust, having long since found that even our most skilled interventions usually created only a momentary quietude, we chose another modality. Because our home is heated by wood, it was a simple matter to walk over to the stove unnoticed and throw another log or two on the fire. Half an hour later, when we came back into the room, now at about a hundred degrees, everyone was either asleep or stupefied to the point of less arduous communication.

We know from counseling so many that often, even with the

most intense desire to communicate, there can be the armored residues of so much wounding that there is more a sense of frustration than completion. We are grateful for the grace that has allowed us each and all to go beyond our boundaries and fortifications to enter together a whole family.

Once we went to psychiatrists
to confess we hated our parents—
now we go to admit
we love them.

Our parents are a teaching
in forgiveness—
at least that's what
we tell our children.

CHAPTER 27

~

LEARNING
TO LOVE
YOUR PARENTS

I WAS BROUGHT up in a loud, angry household. Ondrea was raised in a "serious," quiet home. Emotional expressions in both households were limited to unresolved grief. Thus our "styles of loving" were somewhat different. When we met, though Ondrea and I had many previous relationships "under our belts," clearly we had come together to learn how to love. For both of us this was "the last relationship."

Obviously we had to transform the ways we had learned to love, *to uncondition our love,* to send forgiveness and gratitude to those who taught us about love, beyond the limitations of our early conditioning.

Part of our practice of simply learning to love, and love simply, was to focus on any distancing from our parents. The renewal of love with our parents a repeated theme in our work together to clear the mind and open the heart.

My father was angry and frightened. He treated my mother quite badly at times. But even before I came to love him again—in the decades I despised his bigotry and loud confusion—I always appreciated his enormous laugh. He was a very mixed bag. Sweet and sour. Watch your step! Indeed, until my late twenties I cannot recall loving my father. But when it began to arise in moments here and there, in a kind reflection, in forgiveness and self-acceptance, there was more room in my heart for love itself.

When I was a raucous, teen-aged black-leather-jacketed, "hot-rod delinquent," during my occasional scrapes with the law and my ongoing war with my father, my mother used to say, "I should only live to see the day!"

In my late twenties, having not visited in many years, I returned home to introduce my parents to Tara, their first grandchild. Having already established some foundation practice in meditation, I was more present and attentive than I may have been previously.

But my father was extremely aggressive and unkind to all at the dinner table. Picking on my brother, ordering my mother about, he turned his fire toward me—my long-hair-spirituality-poetry-family. But as he was attacking I softened my belly and saw him perhaps for the first time as the wounded love that he was. With genuine care I listened and did not react. His pain was so evident. His fear so blatant. And I looked into those hazel eyes I had seen so often with hatred, at last with love. Because I was not holding to our separation there was no one opposing him for him to demean. And he softened and relented and told a joke. And my mother turned to me and said, "Well, I've lived to see the day!"

This finishing of business with our parents is a noticeable aspect of our coming into our own that provides the ground for healthy, conscious relationship.

In Ondrea's home, though quite liberal and generous, there was very little group consciousness or "together action." She left feeling a need to touch, to communicate, to play, to laugh. And she thanked her parents, from a distance, for the "isolating silence" which sharpened her inner senses: "the gift in the wound," as Ondrea says. The gift of healing that exists within the heart of each and every injury. The forced quiet became a stillness within which she had to listen if there was to be any contact with the family at all. Which she says, half kidding, was the training for what has become her widely acknowledged work with patients in coma. Gradually, the healing gift at the center of the wound became an increasing capacity available to others and herself.

Extending a tendril across the miles and years, Ondrea began to reestablish contact through dozens of phone calls. Reaching out across the abyss, opening to embrace her parents. A renewing.

When Ondrea's parents attended their first workshop fifteen years into this process of reconnecting, her father found it "quite interesting" and said he had "probably meditated." Her mother was excited at the "wonderful process." It took forty-six years for her parents to acknowledge her gifts. Their hearts more open now than ever, healing the past into the present, leaving room for more.

Ondrea's rapprochement with her parents was so deep that they are planning to move out to be near her. Indeed, yesterday her mom asked if they could come to another workshop.

During the last decade both of my parents died. In each case there was nothing left unsaid and our connection at the time of their death was profound. Ondrea and I share a deep wish that when her parents approach their deathbed we will be able to be there for them during that horrible/wonderful time.

Ondrea speaks about how our true family—those who teach us to live—appears and disappears around the corners turned in one's life. She speaks of the aunt she visited for just two weeks during her early adolescence who embraced her in the shmaltz of a Brooklyn Jewish adoration that drowned her in a loving she never knew existed. How some of our true family passed through so quickly, like the lonely old gentleman who lived down the block by himself in the dilapidated Victorian whose top floor was a ballroom with a polished floor, mirrors and music. And how she and he waltzed, abandoned to kindness, for an hour. An hour of kindness, two weeks of merciful love, and she knew. She knew there was more to the heart than she knew.

Robert Bly said he didn't write a poem to his father until he was forty-six. I was fifty-three and my father had just died a week before.

At twelve I refused to kiss my father goodbye at summer camp. And he congratulated me. He patted me on the back for "growing up and not needing that kissing stuff." I was rewarded for distancing. I was confused all that summer.

When I was seventeen, returning home a little drunk from a friend's funeral, my father made a crack about my friend's "unimportant death," and I told him to go fuck himself. He swung, but I caught his wrists and looked him hard in the eyes and told him if he ever hit me or anyone else in the house ever again, I'd knock him on his ass. And called him names I think he'd never heard before. My older brother nearly swooned in appreciation and dismay—disoriented to hear his secret thoughts dumped on his father.

But in those later years, even after the forgiveness and laughter, something else happened I can't explain—we connected in the intuitive heart. And shared events beyond the mind in territory only the heart can reach.

At eighty-six, a year after my mother's death, he had a stroke and went into a coma. Called by my brother to come across the country to be by my father's bedside, I sat down in meditation that evening before the flight and attempted to make contact with my father in whatever space was available. We spoke of life and death.

When I got to the Long Island hospital, breathing with him at his bedside, his eyes opened, and this man who never spoke of God except to curse, whose main preoccupation had been his small factory, said, "I met the Lord. He runs the place. But I think we can do business." Also acknowledging what we had shared when I was in meditation and he said he was "somewhere out there." Later that day I asked him why, if the Lord was so friendly, he came back. And he looked up at me and said, "Stevie needed me." I thought he was disoriented, that he'd mistaken our meeting in "other spaces" as some call from me to return to his pained old body. I thought he was confused and hoped I had done no harm by encountering him in realms with which he was unfamiliar.

But perhaps he was not mistaken. He taught me more about courage and kindness in those last three years—coming out of himself in the nursing home, serving so many around him—than he may have thwarted in the first three. He became a *mensch,* a whole person. But he was in such pain. He had always wanted to be Thomas Alva Edison but he had become Willie Loman.

He lived until he was ninety, and I never heard him say a nice word about his father except, "He cut a good suit!" I hope our love has stopped the conspiracy before my children need to write such a poem.

The last words he said to me were, "I love you." After years of healing, a few minutes after we spoke on the phone, he lay down and died.

That summer I was a bit less confused, and capable perhaps of just a bit more love.

CHAPTER 28

DESIRE

ELATIONSHIP IS the interaction of two desire systems. A desire system is the matrix of likes and dislikes, attractions and aversions, preference, perception, and judgment which comprise the superstructure of the personality. Comprehending the nature of desire is fundamental to progress on the path.

If you have a desire system—as everyone who takes birth seems to—then you have the basis for disagreement. In the beginning of relationship when desire systems are well coordinated and the energies reside mostly on the physical and emotional levels, each person wakes up and together they "want a blue one." But one morning, as nature would have it, each wakes with a different desire in mind. One wants a red; the other wants a green. Conflict.

Out of dissatisfaction, the frustration of desire, comes resentment. It is a natural by-product of our wanting. Indeed, it is said, "If you don't have room for resentment, you don't have room for relationship!" This conflict of desires strains relationship. Narcissus gets anxious when his image is not reflected by the world. To protect our desires is the foundation of our fears and multileveled defensiveness. Attachment to these desires is a source of suffering in our lives. And in the lives of all we know and love. It keeps us fragile and guarded.

Resentment is not a sign that a relationship isn't working. It is only an invitation to the work that is to be done.

Desire is very inconvenient. It keeps getting in the way of what we really want. Desire is a restlessness in the mind. A leaning out of this moment into the next in which some imagined satisfaction might be acquired. Desire is the skeleton in our closet around which our body and personality form. Indeed, each person is a desire system as complex in its cosmic inner workings as the interplanetary gravitation which both attracts and repels celestial objects, keeping them in their uneven orbits, creating a universe. Actually what we call the personality, indeed, what we call the person, is somewhere between a coping mechanism and a connect-the-dots portrait of our likes and dislikes. In each moment of perception, our conditioning reacts with approval or disapproval. This patterning of perception and desire is the personality. It is ironic how little we have to say about what conditioning gets imprinted on us and how it acts itself out. Yet we take the personality so personally that its tendency toward judgment is turned back on itself. We are constantly at the mercy of the mercilessness of desire.

It is the mindlessness of desire, its automatic quality, that calls out most for mindfulness. The compulsive reaction to desire and the mechanical momentum it unleashes keeps the mind small. It experiences itself only as dissatisfied longing. But it is the merciful, nonjudgmental observation of these phenomena which expands the mind.

Because of our Judeo-Christian, Old Testament conditioning, it is important to note here that desire is not "wrong" or "bad," only painful. To desire the present, which does not offer the object-of-desire, is unsatisfactory. Indeed, the nature of desire is the quality of unsatisfactoriness itself. Desire longs for what it does not have. The moment is not enough. The nature of wanting is the experience of not having. Clearing any old mind cobwebs, let us reassert that one is not punished *for* desire; one is punished *by* desire.

Ironically it is not the object-of-desire we so long for, but rather the experience we call "satisfaction." We are addicted to satisfaction. We use all our cleverness and guile to allay our grief at the absence of essential satisfaction in our lives. Perhaps that is why so many settle for "bad relationships": because they cannot have what they really want, the source rather than the reflection of satisfaction.

The irony of desire is that the moment of satisfaction is literally only a moment. The nature of desire is such that only in the millisecond of "getting" does satisfaction arise. For a moment, the unpleasant experience of wanting what one does not possess or cannot control abates. Satisfaction is not part of the "having" so much as in the relieving of the painfulness of not having. In that moment of getting what you want there is the experience of the absence of desire—the clouds roll back to reveal the sun. In that moment of getting, satisfaction arises because for a moment desire is absent from the mind. Satisfaction is a glimpse of our true nature beyond the agitated mind. Satisfaction reveals itself easily in a mind unclouded by the commotion of desire. But the absence of desire endures only a moment before we then wish to protect that object-of-desire. And when desire once again coagulates around its object, satisfaction instantly disappears. What was, a moment before, an object-of-satisfaction instantly becomes an object-of-dissatisfaction.

Desire, longing for control, often feels out of control, helpless and angry.

Recognizing that desire is not wrong but only painful, we focus a merciful awareness on its inner workings. To watch that feeling of incompletion that arises with desire until the object-of-desire is acquired, to watch desire bending the mind, leaning out of this moment, longing for a satisfaction that exists in the unknown future. Observing the hard belly of desire. Observing the subtle panic that permeates the mind, as the fear of not-having presents itself. Watching the grief of desire.

Watching how satisfactory it is to meet the unsatisfactory with clear mercy, with a mind that longs only to be present, we come to recognize that a satisfactory mind is not necessarily even a mind from which desire is absent. When we want to be free (the Beloved) even more than we want temporary pleasures (Narcissus), when the source of satisfaction rather than its mirror reflection is our goal, we will begin to focus on the intentions that precede every action. We begin to explore the chain of events by which desire acts itself out. Watching the mechanics of desire moment to moment to investigate how the energy inherent in desire is transferred from the wanting mind to the active body. Watching the chain of events link by link, instant to instant, as it draws desire into action, creating unconscious, automatic activity. Recognizing that when we are not aware of this process, we are dragged through our life by our senses. We live outside ourselves.

Mindful how each link in the chain conveys the energy from unconscious desire to unconscious activity, we learn to unhook desire from mechanical action without suppressing or denying anything. Breaking the chains of unconscious action driven by unexplored desire, we lighten to the task.

Acting from the appropriateness of the heart, we are freed from the neediness of the mind.

We are not helpless, only habitual. Awareness melts holding. We have the capacity to watch the chain of events from its very inception. Watching the reception of sensory input—moments of hearing, thinking, seeing—we notice, almost before we can name it, a flash of memory informing the mind if that object is pleasant or unpleasant, liked or disliked. If pleasant, a leaning toward occurs; if unpleasant, a leaning away. Each is active desire. Clinging is a wanting attachment, condemning is an averse attachment.

When desire forms in the mind, it inspires an intention. This intention motivates the body to move toward or away from that object in an attempt to grasp or control it. This volition projects the body of our imaginings toward imagined satisfaction. It is a mechanical process, but one which can, like eating or breathing, be received in a clear awareness, where conditioning is no longer "on automatic pilot."

Observing how perception creates name and form, how memory produces inclination, we watch the chain grow as liking and disliking stimulate desire. And we watch the capacity of desire to move us unwittingly toward what may be unskillful or even injurious action. In this seeing we discover a way to play a bit more lightly with desire. Another opportunity to be a bit more fully alive.

Exploring moment by moment this process, we discover that intention is the weak link in the chain. That desire seems uninvited and quite compulsive in its leanings. And note the voice which says we must act on each wanting. Although the contents and the "logic" of desire are quite seductive, when we are relating *to* desire rather than *from* it, its process becomes painfully evident. Interrupting intention by holding it up to the memory of mindfulness, though perhaps a bit disquieting at first, leads to a satisfaction so deep that rather than judging or punishing "the desirer," we embrace Narcissus. Being mindful of intention—the "will toward action" which precedes every activity—the mind hardened by desire, in time softens into the heart flowing with compassion.

When intention is recognized wholeheartedly, explored in its texture and tone, it is released from small mind into something considerably larger. Floating in awareness itself, there is no compulsion to act, nor sense of deprivation. Indeed, great satisfaction arises in watching the dissatisfactory in such an acceptable manner. When the heart touches the disheartened, the moment is enough. All that we seek is present: the Beloved.

It is said that all karma is based on intention, the motivation behind the act. When motivations are deeply explored, and compulsions floated, our karma is more *in* our hands than *on* our hands. We have what seems to be free choice. That which connects the "involuntary" (desire) with the "uninvited" (unconscious activity) is greatly diminished.

As we quiet a bit, the subtler whispers of the mind become more audible and before we speak, before we take a step, before we sit down at the breakfast table, the intention that motivates that action is noted clearly. And its mechanics observed. Desire is like gravity —it keeps us stuck where we are while intensifying a fear of falling. Like gravity, desire can either destroy when it is released from a great height, or at ground level can keep our tires on the road. In fact, it is desire that takes us beyond desire itself.

It is the desire to understand the nature of desire that motivates a mindfulness of intention which brings subtler motivations into view. We start to get our life back. Mindful of intention, we dehabituate.

Exploring the urge for lesser satisfactions, we experience the Great Satisfaction. To be free from compulsive desire, we need to desire the end of compulsivity. This is called the last desire, the

Great Desire, the will toward nothing less than the living truth. This Great Desire for the truth, which is even greater than our desire for our beloved, is the solid ground on which our relationship becomes wholly possible.

Because our deep desire for completion goes unsatisfied for so long, we settle for success, or food, or sex, or intoxicants. But none satisfies the profoundly unsatisfied for *long*. We settle for such small desires and just create more of the same. But our deepest desire will not be compromised, it will not settle for lesser gratifications. Only the truth that goes beyond understanding will do. All other desires are consumed by the Great Desire, a yearning for the end of confusion and dull indifference. The Great Desire eats other desires. It has no table manners. It plays with its food.

The Great Desire teaches us to play gently with lesser leanings. Its priority is a letting go of all that limits letting go. And eventually dissolves happily into the heart.

This is no grim relinquishment of pleasure. This is not the end of play but its beginning. This is the path of joy. It allows even desire to float lightly in the vastness of being. It recognizes desire as a given, an uninvited guest with which we share our daily lives.

In fact, it is not even desire that is the cause of our pain, but identification with it as our only alternative. When desire is held to, all else is lost, but when it is allowed to float, like any other natural phenomenon, in vast *amness,* insight rather than difficulties arise. When it's *my* desire, it's *my* suffering, *my* deepening wound. But when it's *the* desire, it's *the* pain, *the* deepening healing.

At yet another level, the investigation of the nature of desire becomes an opening into "the heart of giving and receiving." It becomes the basis of compassionate service to others, to our beloved, to ourselves. It does not punish us for waves of greed or lust but softens its belly to receive even the hardest moments. Opens the heart to heal judgment. Clears the mind to peer beneath what it thinks it wants, to what it really needs. The Beloved.

So, when the mind says, "I want a hot fudge sundae," it enjoys each mouthful wholeheartedly while staying tuned for "recent developments," unsurprised when the mind turns back on itself five minutes later and says, "I wouldn't have done that if I were you!" Big heart whispering in response, "No wonder the world has gone crazy with the heat—the heat of desire and burning judgments too cruel to nurture. Let go and let be."

In time we learn, with exploration and joy, that when we go out for an ice cream cone and the store is closed, not to panic. We watch the repeated waves of desire pounding on a barren beach. We soften to the moment. We have yogurt.

~

WHAT DO YOU WANT?

A CONTEMPLATION

A S YOU READ this book, put it down for a moment and close your eyes. Just sit for a moment with the mind. Don't use some technique for watching the breath or use a mantra or a visualization technique. Just simply sit. Just sit, and watch the mind. Notice that soon there arises a thought or feeling of something wanted. Perhaps you want to get back to the book. Or you want an object of desire to arise so you can watch it. Or you want the chair to be more comfortable. Or you want something to eat. Or you want the noise outside to diminish. Or you want the noise inside to diminish. Or you want this meditation to end. Or you want your knee not to be so sore. Or you want to be enlightened. Or you want to be better than you are. Or you want to know God. Or you want to stop drinking. Or you want to be more loved. Or you want all this wanting to end. In rondo after rondo of spiraling desire.

Just watch wanting. Nothing to do about it. Simply allow a noninterfering, nondesirous awareness to receive this energy as it presents itself. Noting its imagery and assertions, watch its process unfolding. Watch the chain of events that leads from a flickering thought, a momentary liking or disliking, to a momentous activity (which encourages more of the same in the future). Watch desire play itself out in consciousness.

Now take five minutes, eyes closed, watching the flow of consciousness, and count the number of desires that arise uninvited. Count the moments of wanting things to be otherwise, wanting something to come closer or move farther away, wanting more of this or less of that. Wanting not to want, wanting to be able to do this meditation. Wanting to be perfect.

What is desire?

How is something as fragile as a thought, a bubble floating in space, capable of creating a new life or ruining an old one?

How can mindfulness of lesser desires lead to the heartfulness of the Great Desire? How do we begin relating *to* instead of *from* desire?

How in a world of incessant change, constant impermanence, can any desire satisfy for long? And how does the Great Desire stir all the smaller desires into the stew of liberation, into the fire which is water? How does it float Narcissus on the ocean of compassion?

CHAPTER 29

~

SEXUALITY

T HERE IS NOTHING like making love with the Beloved. Nothing like the boundaryless heart to make us edgeless and agile. The Beloved embraces old fears and strategies, dissolving lovers into oneness. In the *shared body* two aspects of the identical primal energy intertwine like a double helix. Our lovemaking decoding the genetics of form—meeting at the boundary of formlessness, love becomes the catalyst for creation. When the formless makes love in form, we are present at the Creation.

Making love in the shared body is the natural expression of living in the shared heart. Such boundaryless interaction is called "sacred sexuality." This quality of making love with the Beloved is delightfully reflected in a line from Kabir: "If you make love with the Divine now, in the next life you will have the face of satisfied desire." And if you do not, he says, you may just end up with an empty apartment in the City of Death.

Indeed, the levels of commitment in an evolving relationship are usually manifest in gradually opening levels of intimacy. One expands from the awkward touch of powerful desire filled with self-consciousness and anticipation, past the history of previous lovers, our life flashing before our eyes, so to speak, as we join toward what seems a mystical connection.

In the beginning of a sexual relationship, each stays in his own body. Rubbing at his edges. Bouncing on his boundaries. It is two individuals separately having sex, together. If there evolves a meeting of the minds in the body, and the other levels of relationship are in sync with sympathetic intensity, the boundaries break and we pour into each other's space. At this point the levels of attraction have deepened to the possibility of bonded commitment. And the quality of tenderness in lovemaking increases. Touch sending waves of energy through the body/mind into the spirit. And a sense of the Beloved and the potentials of triangulation arise.

It is at this stage that *monogamy becomes an absolute necessity for further ascension.* It is here, as contracts are considered and vows contemplated, that we enter the shared heart which gradually manifests as the shared body. The remarkable, nearly mystical experience of the space dissolving in space, of edgelessness dissolving into the grace-filled body of the Beloved. This mystical union gives breath to the scriptural image mentioned earlier, of experiencing oneself as a cell in the body of Christ. As a thought floating free in the mind of a Buddha. Each of us, a cell in the body of the Beloved, an equal part of the enormity, the one body we all share, the heart.

At this level such differentiations as male and female, and I and *other,* disintegrate. Making love in the shared body, we often cannot tell whether we are male or female. One is just beingness in connection; physically, mentally and spiritually. In truth, we never realized there was so much to be experienced in sexuality until we brought the Beloved into bed with us.

Indeed there is beyond even orgasm a potential for a high-energy ecstasy, a rapture, that develops naturally, gradually, from a moment to moment attention to sensation and a one-pointed transmission of energy from the heart through the body. We have received so much insight from mindful, heart-filled sexuality that we have come to recognize considerable possibilities of mind/body healing from this much consciousness in an area so cluttered with old mechanics and mental debris. Indeed about a week ago after having a tooth pulled, throwing off my bite, chomping the inside of my cheek a few times—the soft tissue slightly torn and raised—we made love. Afterward the empty tooth socket had stopped bleeding. The inside of the cheek smooth and healed.

Moving through these stages together, we have discovered a spirituality and sensuality in sexuality we had never before experienced. In the magnificent Hindu holy book the *Ramayana,* Hanuman, the perfect servant and ally of the Beloved, says to Ram, the Beloved, "When I do not know who I am, I serve you. When I know who I am, I am you." Such are the levels available in the shared body to the shared heart. Before we know who we are, we make love to another. When we know who we are, we are that other—love itself.

Sometimes in lovemaking we have a sense of ourselves disappearing into the other. A sense of ecstatic oneness. Just energy unfolding within the shared spaciousness of being. No *I* or *other.* Nothing separate. It is a kind of nondual sexuality. It is this breaking of duality, this shared oneness, that Sita, the beloved of the Beloved, refers to when she says, "Sometimes I am Sita, sometimes I am Ram."

In such nondual sexuality, the opportunity for mystical union exists which powers inner practice and reaffirms the spirit. It has taken sexuality from what we had previously experienced as a relatively low level on the consciousness ladder, and brought it into the realm of the sacred. Now sexuality is no less fulfilling or insightful than meditation. Indeed, sexuality has moved from one of the more agitating, "lesser" desires (enormous though it may have been at times) into the realm of the Great Desire, the longing for the Beloved.

Many have heard about the practice of celibacy in certain spiritual disciplines as a means of raising "spirit power" and clearing the mind of the emotional upwelling that attends our lust. It settles the mind, decreasing agitation, attending to the desires which cause such discomfort to ourselves and others in this often confusing, desire-driven world.

A period of celibacy can be quite helpful in realigning sexual priorities and the sense that the lover we have so longed for is the Beloved. It creates one-pointedness, a wholehearted commitment to freeing ourselves from imagining another as "other": an object in our mind rather than the subject of our heart. It forces us to relate deeper than the body, to the heart of the matter. A few weeks or months or even years of celibacy can be very fruitful, particularly between relationships, as a means of deepening potentials. Even in a committed relationship, some period of celibacy can propel one into the next stage of unity and commitment. It is an interesting experiment in consciousness.

One of our teachers used to say, "You can be celibate with one person." That one could gain the power and clarity of celibacy in a heart-committed monogamy. He said the power of commitment to only one intensified the power of commitment to the One and only. He said that in high monogamy was all the power of high celibacy.

Infidelity breaks the contract. Infidelity flattens the triangle.

We are not saying that a committed sexual relationship is the only level on which sexuality can be a wholesome interaction. We are simply suggesting that if one wants to go for broke, commit-ment on every level is required. Until the Beloved is discovered in a partner, other levels of communication and connectedness can still be quite healing when honesty and sensitivity are the context. The problem is that often desire makes us stupid. We act in ways we often sense as unwholesome, creating pain in seeking pleasure. Right speech flies out the window. We'll say anything to get our lust satisfied. We'll do almost anything to get out of such pain.

It is in this realm of unexplored, uncommitted sexuality that so much suffering is caused. It is the "slippery slope" on which even spiritual teachers have "fallen." It is a fragile area in many psyches, a quicksand into which so many have disappeared like Narcissus in his own reflection, in her own longing.

Until we experience completely our true heart, the mind is sus-ceptible to sexual power games. As one teacher said, even a ninety-year-old sage is vulnerable to the unexplored.

To intensify our commitment, one of our practices is "the with-drawal of the senses." If my attention falls on any object that could engender lust, awareness mindfully diverts. Withdrawal of the senses is a "turning away" from objects of desire. Changing the channel on anything that conditioning might find in the least erotic. Reconditioning the senses—sight, smell, hearing and even thought—to turn aside whenever the sexual aesthetic, for anyone other than Ondrea, is in the least stimulated. If perfume wafts my way, I am mindful moment to moment of any tendency to visualize the source of the fragrance. I do not allow my attention to rest on any object that could lead to a mind-moment of sexual desire. Even in my dreams, if a sexually motivated person approaches, I watch myself turn away saying that I'm in a committed relationship.

In this culture, such ideas as the withdrawal of the senses are met with nervous disapproval. To the degree we have been taught we are only the small body and the small mind, any discipline we fear will limit the "free" expression of our small sexuality threatens us considerably. But the withdrawal of the senses is not suppression, it's commitment. There is an enormous joy in going only to the Beloved, only to Ondrea. The resolve to merge solely with one other fuels the practice of self-discovery and healing.

When you no longer see others as sexual objects, there is a level at which you can be trusted by those who have, through sexual cruelty, learned to distrust. Perhaps that's why so many sexually abused men and women have offered Ondrea and me such a profound degree of confidence, and allowed us so deeply into their healing. Perhaps that's why, as the room emptied after a very intense grief workshop, a woman who had been severely abused approached me and asked if we could speak. She said she had not allowed a man to touch her, to literally *touch* her in any way, in more than seventeen years. "It's just too terrifying." She asked if I would just touch her hand. And then if I would hold it. And after a few minutes of quiet, she leaned into my arms and we rocked back and forth crying together for the pain we could hardly contain in the mind and only had room for in our hearts. "You're the first man I've let hold me since I've been an adult, since I left home!" Crying together with this woman, I looked toward Ondrea, a dozen feet away cradling in her arms a gay man who sobbed that his lover and more than fifty friends had died of AIDS, that his world was collapsing. He said he couldn't stand to take another breath, breathing softly into Ondrea's tear-soaked hair. The lack of any sexual intention emanating from us allowed a trust into which many released their fear and long-held grief. It was another example of how the work on ourselves is for the benefit of all sentient beings. Clearly, our practice of mindful retention of the senses has not suppressed or limited contact with others, but rather opened it to deeper levels of connection.

If, even after hearing the benefits of the practice of retention of the senses, the Freudian-suppressed small mind still shudders with a sense of loss of control and unfulfilled yearning, let me speak directly to that small mind: you have fears that such an exercise will be suppression, a limiting of the senses rather than an honoring of them. Let me suggest that what you imagine it might be is not at all its inner experience. Though in theory you may fear that such an exercise will be a limiting of the life force, in practice it is a focusing of that suchness. There is no violence in the swinging of the senses to a more heartful object of reflection. It is mindfulness of intention, with intention. As small mind expands to big mind, we are able to observe mercifully, and with a bit of humor, that which once so overwhelmed us. Mercifully watching our Narcissus huddling, libidinous, in the corner, bragging its birthright as if Casanova on a binge, when in truth it is just Little Orphan Annie born to find her eyes.

When we see all women as the divine mother and all men as the merciful father, everyone you meet is sacred. No one is an object of lust. When I see Ondrea as the Beloved, the Mother of Mercy, it is not difficult to see all women as aspects of the divine. When I see myself as the Beloved, it is possible to heal and forgive that in man, and in men, and in the human psyche, which has caused such violence and abuse in this tender world. When we see each other as amnesiacs of the divine, as lost as Narcissus in our smallness, evolving toward the Beloved, we honor the unlimited vastness of each being. Playing hide-and-seek with the Beloved, we expose ourselves to the sacred.

About ten years ago in a conscious living/conscious dying workshop, a casual question about sexuality brought a somewhat drowsy group to sharp attention. The room was no longer "too warm" or "too stuffy." You could hear a pin drop as we described, in answer to a question, that an often very satisfying and "spirit raising" position for lovemaking was the Tibetan posture called Yab-Yum. A practice in which traditionally a man and woman sit facing each other, she atop his lap straddling him, her legs crossed behind his back—his legs folded lotus-like beneath her, creating a pedestal on which the goddess sits—eyes open inches apart. When we sat on the floor to quickly demonstrate the position, everyone in the room stood on their chairs to see better, their interest never so great. And when we added that an extraordinary intensity could be brought to sexuality by practicing the coordinated Ah Breath breathing (described earlier in the Dyad Bonding Meditation), many asked if they could break early "to go home for lunch." Some returned shiny-eyed and hungry. Others did not return until the next day. A few mentioned that a new level of the shared body had been explored. Some, grateful that a disinterest in the "dualistic gravitations of old form sexuality" had found a new ground and interest in the merging and emerging of a nondual sexuality.

Many discover in an exploration of sexuality an expanded realm of the senses which has the power to lead them from the occasionally ridiculous to the often sublime. They recognize that the whole-hearted investigation of their sexuality is essential if their bond is to become a mystical union.

CHAPTER 30

~

THE
GREAT DESIRE

WE REPEAT THE following story because we trust the genuine heart which offered it, though when I mentioned it to Ram Dass, he asked if it was "real." To which I replied, "I don't know if it's real, but I think that it's true."

A year or so ago at a workshop in Monterey, California, a woman approached and asked if she might tell us a story. She was a therapist who for some years had been working with a client who had just given birth. Her client's three-year-old daughter had repeatedly asked over the last few months if she might be left alone with the baby. The mother and father had come to the therapist for a special session to inquire whether she thought it was a good idea given the possibilities and dreadful stories of sibling rivalry, which the mother had feared might be the case. The therapist, knowing the three-year-old as a seemingly well-adjusted, happy child who had not displayed untoward aggression in the past, sensed that the meeting with the infant would probably be just fine. "Remember, you have an intercom in the baby's room and one in your bedroom. Let your little girl go into the baby's room and be alone with her if she wishes, and go into your bedroom and listen. If there's any difficulty, you could be in the baby's room in a second. Give it a chance and see what occurs."

So the parents left the three-year-old daughter in the baby's room and went into their bedroom to listen. They heard the three-year-old close the door and walk slowly over to the infant. Leaning over the crib, they heard her say, "Baby, baby, tell me about God. I'm forgetting!"

Clearly we are born longing for completion, longing to experience our great nature. All our clumsy attempts to fulfill desire are a reflection of that longing, a fumbling for satisfaction, a sideways glance at our true nature, a groping for the spaciousness of satisfaction, a glimpse of our vastness. This process of seeking little objects to satisfy our enormous desire to capture a moment of peace leaves us dry of heart and addled of mind. It is our desire to see beyond desire, the absolute longing for the absolute satisfaction of our absolute nature.

The whole world, the universe, is composed of, and by, desire. Desire is the shape of the world. And only the Great Desire is large enough to absorb all the suffering it entails.

The Great Desire, our homesickness for God, the truth, wanders through the dark forest of the mind, seeking a clearing in the woods. Seeking not its reflection on the surface, but the cool depths of a still forest pool. It is not Narcissus' pond but that same pool to which the extraordinary meditation master Achaan Chah refers when he says, "Try to be mindful, and let things take their natural course. Then your mind will become still in any surroundings, like a still forest pool. All kinds of wonderful rare animals will come to drink at the pool, and you will clearly see the nature of all things. You will see many strange and wonderful things come and go, but you will be still. This is the happiness of the Buddha."

When the Great Desire sees its reflection it becomes the Great Satisfaction. When awareness meets itself, it becomes fully conscious. We discover what we have been looking for all our lives: the whole of us. When consciousness becomes more than a mere reflection of the light in the mind, the Beloved throws her blanket over us and we are absorbed in love.

Our homesickness for our true nature preexists our birth. We take birth to discover the Inseparable in the painful midst of the separate. Our whole life is a journey toward the Beloved. All we have ever wanted is that which wants, free of its wanting.

When one travels with one's beloved toward the Beloved, each step is perfect. Each moment of equanimity as well as disequilibrium received by a merciful awareness. Each step completely satisfying. Stumbling in the footsteps of the God-drunken poet Kabir, making love with the Divine now!

CHAPTER 31

~

UNFINISHED
BUSINESS

T HERE IS A popular phrase, "unfinished business," which describes the degree of separation and unattended grief that distances the partners in any relationship. It is a manifestation of our fear and distrust, the armored heart running relationships like a business. A constant trade-off of affections and tentative support. Something forever feeling cheated within our psyche—oh, poor Narcissus—loathes giving more than it imagines receiving. The doorway to the heart narrows, the cost of admission increases.

But obviously, the unfinished business of relationship is just a projection of business long unfinished with ourselves. Our unfinished business with ourselves is the healing we took birth for, the wholeness approaching. This unfinished business is what Buddha called "the work to be done." The work to be completed on any level. Even for those "nearly complete" in their expansion, reveling in realms previously unimagined, unfinished business can still draw one back to the unexplored and unhealed. Even though the context may have been expanded to include more of us than we ever imagined existed, what remains undone has, even for a yogi in a cave, the power to pull us back to lower levels of consciousness that require completion. Perhaps that is why it is said that even a nearly enlightened being still needs to be very mindful of such things as sexuality, spiritual pride and the tendency to abstract the simple, to trade the living suchness for a comfortable concept. When there is unfinished business at any level, no matter how "high" one gets, no matter how clear, one still "comes down." How few, like the great saint Ramana Maharshi, having opened to the Beloved as life, as death, at seventeen and never closed, continue to expand unabated. Most expand gradually, healing the unhealed as it arises, carrying the light deeper into the unknown. Committed to the Beloved, even when mind reverts to shadow, residing in its least conscious, densest levels, there is still a flickering context of space in which what is incomplete can wholly dissolve. The Beloved present even when we aren't.

Because we have not wholly made peace with the past, allowing our personal history to remain unhealed, our Narcissus unembraced, sometimes the heart closes and the mind replays unfinished business. We may think we have "lost it," but in truth our direction has never been clearer. Never have the qualities of the heart been more longed for than in the agony of separation and dense-mindedness. Unskillful moments from the past come up. Glitches, perceptual warps, hidden insults and embarrassments arise and fill the mind and block the heart. But turning toward those obstacles instead of hiding from them, the pain becomes so evident that the heart just lets go into the oneness of simply being and being simply, and aligns us once again.

Indeed, unfinished business is the perceived inequity of our unfulfilled desire systems. This sense of incompleteness, of even "not enoughness," further cultivates the distrust and fear which demand control in order to feel safe. And tends to run relationships as though they were a business. I'll give you five if you give me five. But if you give me four, I'll give you three; and if you give me two, I'll take my marbles and go home. I won't play anymore. When relationships are run like some sort of commerce, a trade-off of minds rather than a coincidence of hearts, there of course always remains business uncompleted. It creates a disgruntled restlessness which waits for the other to give what it believes is its due. Unfinished business is the result of unfulfilled expectation and often unacknowledged personal need.

Having discovered in personal practice the power of mercy and awareness to heal the unhealed within, one instantly recognizes the power of forgiveness to call the wounded past into the healing present.

Forgiveness finishes unfinished business. When I take you into my heart "as is," when I unconditionally embrace you as the process you are on its way to the Beloved, then I no longer am angered by not receiving from you what I am unable to give myself.

When I forgive you, when you forgive me, our business is done. And we can just *be* together.

If you are waiting for your parents, your children, your ex-lovers, to accept you, good luck! You don't accept them. Why should they accept you? If you accepted them as is, you would not be discomforted by their nonacceptance of you. If you're waiting for them to say you're okay, if you're waiting for anyone to approve, how will you hear beyond such painful desires the still small voice within which whispers of your own great nature?

Talking things out can be very fruitful, but it seldom completes business so much as it renegotiates the past to fit neatly into a revised present. It is reassuring to hear that you are loved, but there's more assurance in the direct experience of loving kindness and forgiveness as it embraces those qualities in another we judge in ourselves. It makes room for the journey to the Beloved.

Unfinished business may be mollified, but is not completed even by apology, or "understanding." This is only the beginning of a communication which leads toward the heart. But it is the heart that must finish all that remains undone. The voice of the heart in the mind is loving kindness and forgiveness.

When I forgive you, when you forgive me, there is no waiting to be understood or even accepted. Only forgiveness will do. Only the mercy which allows the embrace of the Beloved.

Some of what we have learned about relationship has come during fifteen years of working together with dying patients. Watching the relationship process beside the deathbed, there is much insight to be gained observing the business, finished and unfinished, that provides the context in which a beloved physically departs a relationship.

Couple after couple have reminded us of what it takes to stay present with another and what is lost when we do not. Couples who find "time too short" to say all that has remained unsaid for so long. As well as those who need say nothing because it's all been said and a connection deeper than words allows transition to the next stage of their relationship, in or out of the body. Or the husband who visits his dying wife sporadically while cultivating the next relationship. And those who never shared their pain attempting so painfully to "keep up appearances" locking down on their fear, experiencing feelings of failure and isolation while dying alone at night. Maintaining the same old front. Their marriage in unspoken tatters. As well as couples who, as when they were pregnant, exquisitely attend to each other moment to moment through the process, even accompanying each other to the threshold of death over which only one might cross.

We have seen couples whose anger could not be contained any longer and spilled like fecal matter onto the deathbed. Couples who had left so much unresolved that there was no space for forgiveness or love. As well as couples who could barely stand the possibility of losing the contact with their heart that their partner had become. Those who would gladly, willingly die to save their loved one from "the long slow pain." Those so healed by the love around the deathbed that eventually they were able to share that healing with others.

CHAPTER 32

~

FORGIVENESS

ORGIVENESS IS the process that puts an end to the business of unfinished business. Forgiveness is a letting go of holding which lightens the load. Forgiveness is a giving that requires nothing in return. It has no business to transact. It offers well-being to the giver of forgiveness, and often to the receiver as well, depending on the readiness of the heart to begin anew.

Used skillfully, forgiveness is a very powerful tool. It has the capacity to lift painful resentments and allow us greater breadth of movement. It is a letting go of density around the heart, to allow its natural expanse.

Forgiveness has the power of reenergizing the numb areas in the mind and body. It has the potential of letting us take birth at last, fully alive. Belly soft. Heart open. Mind clear.

There is a quality to forgiveness, when done in a timely manner, that allows us to live our life lightly and more directly. But, before forgiveness of another can be practiced wholeheartedly, the unfinished business with ourselves that blocks forgiveness needs to be investigated. There may be anger, guilt, fear and distrust that fill the grief point and block the entrance to the heart. They are the hindrances to the heart, blockages to freedom.

To understand the nature of anger, the voice of so much unfinished business, we must continue to explore the nature of desire and its mechanics in the mind. When desire arises and is not fulfilled, whether it is desire for an ice cream cone, desire to be loved, or desire for God, frustration arises. Mindful of how blocked desire creates frustration, we watch dissatisfaction flip over into resentment and anger. Following the unfoldment of anger, recognizing its process as essentially impersonal, we watch the mental agitation and discomfort that proceed, punctuated by feelings of aggression and isolation. It requires all the mercy we can muster and as little judgment as we are capable of. Anger is a wound reaction. Forgiveness is a wound response.

When we come to see the nature of anger as a moment of desire blocked, resulting in a moment of frustration, resulting in a moment of confusion and aggression, we see that anger is not a single state of mind but a process of unfolding and interactiveness of one mental state after another. Only our drowsy blindness, only the way we usually relate to our mind as an otherness, missing the precise moment to moment process, sloppily labels it just anger. Actually, anger is a moment of holding, manifesting as fear, becoming a moment of pride, becoming a moment of doubt, becoming small mind dialogue, shadowboxing and fantasy, dissolving into a moment of distrust, cycling again into a moment of doubt, a moment of pride, fear, confusion. Again and again, states of mind dissolving one into the other. The process of anger, once recognized, receiving a new mercy that tends toward forgiveness. Then a remembering arises, a softening of the belly, an opening to what is. Kindness toward self and other. A nonjudgmental, noninterfering awareness meeting moment to moment states of mind in the very instant of change, process unfolding in space, and a subtle growing sense that you're not even the content (small mind) or the process (big mind). In truth, you are the space it's all happening in, the Beloved.

Then anger can be in the mind but you're not angry. It's just a passing show. Indeed, you may be more fascinated than anything else watching the ever-changing states of mind, the flow of consciousness.

In fact, joy may become the predominant state—a joyfulness at no longer being caught in old modalities and closed-heartedness.

When a teacher first said, "Anger, too, is God," I was confused. It was perhaps another five years before I truly understood the naturalness of the unfolding we call anger. Indeed, it has brought us to a place where we see there are not even skillful or unskillful, wholesome or unwholesome, states of mind, but simply wholesome or unwholesome, beneficial or unhealing, ways of relating to those states of mind. Anger can arise in the mind of space, its old momentum simply passing through. When there is no holding, there is little to promote identification, or any tightening around it. No need to solidify our pain or create suffering to make us feel more "real." Then there is anger, but no one angry. There is fear, but no one frightened. There is confusion, but no one confused.

Indeed, from big mind's perspective, there is delight in even normally afflictive emotions seen clearly—a great sigh of freedom from the suffering that attends our often dark identifications.

When anger and those qualities which block forgiveness have been well explored, forgiveness becomes quite appropriate. But because of the tendency of the heart once awakened to be drawn to forgiveness, we must be respectful of the pains that this forgiveness is intended to relieve. Like walking into a gymnasium, if you and I go directly to the three-hundred-pound weight and attempt to lift it, even together, we will not be able to do so. And it will just discourage us from ever lifting weights, from ever trying to develop our strength again. But you and I can work out all day long with the five- and ten-pound weights. It is suggested that you practice forgiveness in just the same manner. Do not go to the heaviest weight when you begin the practice. Please do not invite in the three-hundred-pounder—the rapist, the abuser, the cruel, the unjust—when the practice is in its infancy. Let the practice build over time to eventually touch these profound wounds with the deepest possible mercy.

Indeed, for many in relationship, forgiveness not only finishes unfinished business but keeps their business current. Opening slowly to the lesser holdings, we gradually expand to include in our heart even that which we had no room for in our mind. There is nothing like forgiveness to make the small mind big. And make the big enormous.

You cannot force forgiveness. Force closes the heart. And becomes just another way to be unforgiving of ourselves; to feel a failure. In general practice it is good to begin with the rude waiter, the forgetful lover, the confused co-workers or boss, the lighter weights. Take someone who for a moment forgot, who for a moment put you out of their heart, and was insensitive, and meet that pain-holding moment with this pain-releasing possibility.

Eventually those pains which took longer to accumulate, which lie deeper in the psyche and the body, may very skillfully be approached with forgiveness. To rush the process is to be unkind to oneself. To force forgiveness just creates more unfinished business with ourselves, more which calls out to be embraced by mercy and loving kindness.

And remember, too, that you are forgiving the *actor*, not the *action*. Forgiveness does not condone insensitivity, cruelty, or unkindness. You are simply opening your heart to those qualities in another that you find all too present in yourself. Opening with a mercy, forgiveness and kindness, which senses how another, too, might have gotten lost in the shadows of the frightened, angry mind.

The extraordinary Buddhist monk and meditation master Thich Nhat Hanh wrote a poem called "Call Me by My True Name." It is about the boat people escaping from Vietnam into the China Sea, where they are accosted by sea pirates who steal their belongings and rape an eleven-year-old girl. The young girl is humiliated beyond endurance and throws herself into the sea and drowns. In the poem he says that he is all—the bird, the ocean, the boat in which the people are attempting to escape, and the people themselves. He says that he is the young girl raped by a sea pirate and the sea pirate as well. He says, call me by my true names: I am she who threw herself overboard and drowned; and I am the sea pirate *"whose heart cannot yet see."* Here he has given us a key to the practice. He has allowed us to recognize that those who may have done us injury were those whose hearts could not yet see. He has allowed us to touch them with a moment of mercy, with a possibility of forgiveness. He is forgiving the actor, not the action.

In the context of relationship, the practice of forgiveness, besides being a means of keeping current, can also be used to clean up any loose ends from past relationships that intrude themselves into the present.

The process of the forgiveness meditation parallels the workings of the loving kindness practice. Each is a progressive opening into the heartful present. When the past is met in mercy, it no longer acts itself out. Becoming just another unfolding in consciousness, received by the heart. Forgiveness is a means toward an end: the end of separation.

Forgiveness is one of those qualities which one may well benefit from practicing individually as part of one's daily spiritual/meditation practice, as well as in a meditative dyad to define the openhearted communication between couples.

An interesting experiment in consciousness that many have found useful is to take on a mutual forgiveness practice for three days a week for a month. To practice forgiveness even with that person from whom no separation is particularly noticeable. It can be a profound uncovering of loose ends and whispered thoughts of desire and frustration. Even in the best of relationships, various levels of mind still present themselves, and whatever holding remains. It is a fascinating experiment in truth to send forgiveness toward those from whom you presume there is no separation. Where there is mind, there is a possibility of resentment. Where there is desire, there is frustration. Where there is frustration, anger follows naturally. When we are without desire, we will be without frustration or resentment. When we are without desire, forgiveness will be unnecessary. In the meantime. In between time. Forgiveness uncovers that which blocks the heart. And when well developed, becomes a spontaneous responder of the heart, automatically softening to the hardened. A natural osmosis that balances hearts, and connects beyond the mind.

We know no couple who would not benefit from a mutual forgiveness practice. If small mind says it's not necessary, forgive it its fear. Recognize it as an uninvited pain you need not suffer through.

Let this be an exploration of the possibilities of forgiveness and the enormous potential for healing. Begin lightly to lighten. Have mercy on you in this process.

AN INDIVIDUAL FORGIVENESS MEDITATION

Find a comfortable place to sit and settle in there.
And as you settle in, reflect for a moment on what forgiveness is.

What is forgiveness? What might it mean to bring forgiveness into your life?

Now invite into your mind the image, the sense, of someone you have resentment for. Someone who caused you pain. Someone you have, perhaps, put out of your heart. Just feel their presence in your mind, this person you have resentment for.

Now gently, just as an experiment in truth, invite that person from your mind into your heart. Feel their approach to your heart. Notice whatever blocks that approach. Fear, anger, distrust. Notice the qualities that block the entrances to the heart and just for this moment let that person through. Let them into your heart, this person you have resentment for. And in your heart, say to them, I forgive you.

I forgive you.

It's so painful to put someone out of your heart. For this moment, let them back in. And whisper to them silently, in your heart, I forgive you. I forgive you for whatever you may have done that caused me pain in the past, intentionally or unintentionally, through your words, through your action, even for your thoughts, however you hurt me. I forgive you. I forgive you.

Let go. It's so painful to hold onto the resentment. Let it go. Have mercy on you. Forgive them.

I forgive you for whatever you may have done in the past, intentionally or unintentionally, that caused me pain through your confusion, through your distrust, through your anger, through your separateness. However you caused me pain, I forgive you.

I forgive you. Allow them to be touched by the possibility of your forgiveness, by your mercy, by your kindness. Forgiving them, letting them back into your heart.

I forgive you. I know just as I wish only to be happy, so do you. I forgive your ignorance, your fear, your pain. I forgive you.

Now, having been touched by the possibility of your forgiveness, let them go on their way. Bid them farewell for now. Perhaps even touching them with a blessing as they depart. Let them go.

Now invite into your heart, into your mind, someone who has resentment for you. Someone who has, perhaps, put you out of their heart. Someone who has judged you, someone you have caused pain, and just invite them in. Let them into your heart for this moment, for this experiment in forgiveness. Let them in, this person who has resentment for you. Let them in.

Notice whatever limits or blocks their entrance to the heart. Your fear, your anger, your shame or guilt, your distrust of *I* and *other*. Just notice what blocks or limits forgiveness. No judgment. And invite this person into your heart.

And in your heart say to them, I ask your forgiveness. I ask for your forgiveness. However I may have hurt you, intentionally or unintentionally, through my confusion, through my fear, however I may have caused you pain, I ask now that you forgive me. I ask to be forgiven. Let it in. Let it in. Allow yourself to be free of it. Have mercy on you. Let it be so.

I ask your forgiveness for whatever I may have done that caused you pain through my forgetfulness, through my self-interest, through my fear. However I could not contain my pain and spilled it out on you, I ask your forgiveness.

I ask that you forgive me now. Allow yourself to be touched by the possibility of their forgiveness, by their mercy, by their healing. Let it in.

Allow yourself to be forgiven.

I ask for your forgiveness. I ask that you let me back into your heart. Let it be.

Allow it in, allow forgiveness.

Feel their forgiveness as a warmth, as a mercy, in your heart. Let them forgive you, that you might forgive yourself.

Now let them go. Let them be on their way. Perhaps touched with the possibility of a blessing given and received in mercy, in forgiveness. Let them go now. Let them be on their way.

And turn to yourself in your heart and say, I forgive you to you. I forgive you, to you. Have mercy on you. You've been carrying this baggage for so long, this self-negation, this ruthless self-judgment. Have mercy on you.

Have mercy on you.

Say I forgive you to yourself. Say I forgive you, to you. If the mind mercilessly tries to block such forgiveness, if it says self-forgiveness is self-indulgence, have mercy on this unkind mind. Touch it with forgiveness, holding so hard to its pain, turning it to suffering again and again. Have mercy on you.

Calling yourself by your own first name, say I forgive you to you.

Say I forgive you, to you. Letting yourself back into your heart, whatever parts of yourself you have pushed away, you've judged, you've abused. Let yourself back in. Let yourself be embraced by your mercy and loving kindness.

Let your mind, let your body, let your heart be filled with this mercy, with this loving kindness for yourself and for everyone else, too, who wants only to be free of their pain, wants only to be at peace.

Let this mercy radiate from you, expanding outward to touch all those you love that they, too, may forgive themselves and all else in healing mercy, in kindness.

Let this loving kindness expand outward to include all the

planet, all the creatures, all the hearts, all the minds, all the pain of sentient beings everywhere, touched by your mercy, by your loving kindness.

Letting this mercy expand outward, the whole planet like a bubble floating in your heart.

The whole planet like a bubble floating in the ocean of compassion.

May all beings be free of suffering. May all beings be at peace.

Letting this mercy, this forgiveness, expand out into the universe to touch all sentient beings everywhere on every plane of existence, seen and unseen. May they be free of suffering. May they be at peace.

May all beings unto the last blade of grass be free of suffering. May all beings know the absolute joy of their absolute nature. May all beings be at peace.

May all beings be at peace.

DYAD FORGIVENESS MEDITATION

S it facing your partner and focus on their presence.

Look into your partner's eyes. And as you look into their eyes—soft eyes—reflect on what it might mean in your relationship if forgiveness was a stronger quality for both of you, both the ability to give as well as receive forgiveness.

What might it mean in your relationship if forgiveness were a stronger presence? That quality of letting go of resentment. The quality of accepting our resentment and letting ourselves into another's heart as well.

And in your heart, silently say to your partner, I forgive you. I forgive you.

Notice what blocks that forgiveness, what distracts it as well as what allows it.

Soft eyes, not staring, just allowing contact at that level where you don't pull away. Where you go beyond the old, the hard, the forgetfulness, and merge with the being beyond personal histories.

Allowing forgiveness to open the way.

I forgive you for whatever you may have done in the past that caused me pain, however I was insulted or hurt or injured by you, intentionally or unintentionally. In this moment at least I touch you with the possibility of forgiveness. Just for this millisecond allow the possibility of forgiveness.

Fear, distrust, anger, expectation, joy, relief—all coming and going, allowing contact, breaking contact, moment to moment forgiveness swelling in the heart.

I forgive you.

I forgive you. It's so painful to put you out of my heart. It happens all by itself so often. Nothing's worth it. Nothing's worth it. I forgive you.

I forgive you.

Let it be. Let them be forgiven. Breathe them into your heart.

Let your breath draw your partner into your heart in forgiveness and mercy, to embrace them in loving kindness and care. In forgiveness. In acceptance of their pain out of which insult or confusion may have arisen.

Let them be in your heart as is, floating in the ocean of loving kindness and forgiveness.

Have mercy on them. Have mercy on you. Let them be touched by the possibility of your forgiveness.

Let go of the need to control noticed in the breath. Don't even try to appear loving. Let go of all that separates, that "thinks" that other person.

Die into that being. Let go into loving kindness.

Such pain this separation, this thinking them instead of being them.

Forgiveness connects. The bridge between hearts. Let them in as is. I forgive you. I forgive you.

Now let your eyes close. Let your eyes rest for a moment. And just feel that being, not as a visual image, but as a presence in your heart.

Feel the connectedness of forgiveness.

Each breath draws them into your heart. Let them float there in mercy and loving kindness. To heal them. To heal you in mercy and compassion and forgiveness.

Now gently let your eyes open and look into your partner's

face once again, into their eyes. Take a moment for your eyes to adjust.

Soft eyes.

And then let your eyes merge and in your heart say to your partner, I ask for your forgiveness. I ask that you forgive me for whatever I may have done that caused you pain, intentionally or unintentionally. I ask not in guilt or shame, but just in wisdom, in wanting to start anew.

I ask that you forgive me for whatever I may have done to cause you pain. Through my forgetfulness, my anger, my distrust, my impatience, however I caused you pain. I ask that you forgive me.

It's so painful to put someone out of our heart. We can hardly stand it. It's so painful to be put out of someone's heart, to feel we're not wholly accepted there. So alone. Such grief. I ask that you forgive me. I ask that in any way, even any minor way that I'm excluded from your heart, I ask that you breathe me into your heart, that you take me as is with my pain and with my joy. I ask that you forgive me.

Notice whatever blocks your ability to receive that forgiveness from that other person. Let yourself be forgiven. Let it in. Receive their forgiveness in your heart. I ask that you forgive me. I ask to be forgiven, however I may have caused you distress. Just as I wish to be happy, I know that you, too, wish only to be happy.

Let it in. Breathe their forgiveness into your heart. Let it break your heart. Let yourself be forgiven.

And let your eyes close. In your heart, turn to yourself and say, I forgive you—to you. Let it in. Watch whatever the mind might bring up to block forgiveness of yourself.

If the mind says self-forgiveness is self-indulgent, see this merciless mind that separates you from yourself and all you love. The unkind mind. And let it too melt in self-forgiveness.

In your heart say I forgive you to you. I forgive you to you. It's the only voice we have ever wanted to hear "I love you" spoken in. Your own voice. We've been waiting our whole lives to hear that from ourselves.

Call out to yourself in your heart, call yourself by your own first name and say, I forgive you to you. Let it in. Have mercy on you.

Another sentient being who so longs to be free. Have mercy. Allow yourself to be breathed into your own heart.

Make room in your heart for you. All of you. Angry you, frightened you, impatient you, doubting you. Make room.

Let yourself in. Have mercy on you. Feel yourself breathed into your own heart in forgiveness and loving kindness. Let yourself float in the luminosity of your own great being.

Now let your eyes open and look at this incredible being you're with. Know that they, too, have longed to die and longed to be born. That we're all in it together and that to the degree we acknowledge our grief, we acknowledge the enormity of our heart to go beyond even this conditioned separation. To break the old.

You are looking into the eyes of the Beloved. These are sacred eyes. You may kiss the bride.

CHAPTER 33

KARMA SAVINGS AND LOAN

I F WE MAY be allowed some metaphor play, let us explore business-laden relationships with the image of Karma Savings and Loan. As one comes to understand that karma is not punishment but just momentum—more evident in the perception of events than in the events themselves—it is a great teacher in balance. It whispers "go right" as we tilt left—it keeps us centered. Karma is the ground beneath our feet. It is a form of teaching grace. Does a river have a "dreaded case of karma" or does it just flow in accordance with gravity and conditions?

Each brings to relationship personal accounts: unfinished business and accumulated wisdom, the stage of their growth, the healings completed and those yet to be undertaken, triumphs and tribulations. Each brings to their account a momentum begun at least at birth, their principles and compounded interests. Their life equity. All the work on themselves up to that moment.

When two momentums intersect in a committed relationship, their personal holdings are offered into a newly opened, joint account at Karma Savings and Loan. Each contributes, for the benefit of the whole: their ambitions, dreams, talents, wounds, and strategies for healing.

Deposits are a moment of kindness, of supportive surrender, of mutual investigation, of oneness, of another step on the tandem climb in the ascent toward the truth. Withdrawals come from the closedness of our hearts, moments of dishonesty, passive aggression or cold indifference.

Although such joint accounts can reinforce trust, they can also maintain the tendency to insist the deposits be equal, checking the statement at the end of each month to see how each contributed. It is the nature of the all-too-conditioned mind, distrusting the process, to put on the green visor of the accountant and the black robes of the judge to review these accounts.

But when small mind holdings (the accountant) meets a big mind willingness not to suffer, we touch with forgiveness those who so often forgot their true healing, and our business is finished. We are no longer waiting for them to make a giant deposit to counterbalance what we imagine is their preponderance of withdrawals.

Karma Savings and Loan is not protected by the Federal Deposit Insurance Corporation. It offers no assurances. It can only keep your account intact until you, together, can discover a more profitable means of investment.

To go beyond the numerology of separation is to enter the realm of the awakened and lightened. To begin to see as the Beloved sees, with forgiveness and a mercy that watches in another as in oneself how anger and fear can accumulate around the precious heart.

Open a joint account at Karma Savings and Loan today. They're offering metaphors and premiums: a two-slice toaster.

CHAPTER 34

~

PASSIVE AGGRESSION

ONE OF OUR teachers used to say, "Be like Gandhi!" but in relationship this could be bad advice. Because, on the path to peace, even "peaceful aggression" must be watched for closely.

When Mahatma Gandhi was asked about the nature of the "passive resistance" for which he was so highly regarded, he answered, "There is nothing passive about our resistance. It's just nonviolent!"

Though such controlled expressions of hostility may be an effective political strategy, as a means of dealing with unfinished business across the breakfast table, they are a catastrophe.

When we turn toward the heart and attempt to practice peace, part of the mind sighs in relief. But part of it stiffens to hold its ground. Narcissus is not so quick to relinquish his abode. He said moving is too much of a hassle and besides, he's got *so much* to move. So, Narcissus, gritting his teeth, smiles obsequiously to mimic acceptance. But there's more going on than meets the eye. Unacknowledged desire creates unacknowledged resentment. Unfinished business continues submerged, rearing its angry head only occasionally, and with such guile as to be easily denied. This quality of residual holding, of unresolved grief, manifests as a hundred "playful" barbs, followed by "just kidding." It is clever and unkind. It employs language as a subtle irritant. It attempts to push your buttons.

It is also the anger of omission, of nonsupport, of subtly pulling the ground out from under another. It may be the three-month procrastination in fixing the screen door. Or forgetting you don't like parsley. Or showing up late for an appointment. Or not reinforcing a fragile line of inspiration as it arises in an exploratory conversation. Or letting a person "just hang" with their confusion a moment longer than is kind. It is the withheld touch, the unsaid word, the hard belly.

When we say that relationship is among the hardest spiritual work we have ever done, it is because of the work it requires to uncover that which we have long attempted to hide. It is because of the investigation of just such qualities as passive aggression, and the owning up to our hidden incompletions, that such work is threatening and has let our suffering remain so long unattended. It is in the investigation of such qualities as passive aggression that the pain and difficulty of acknowledgment, approach, investigation and letting go of such a state is most evident. It is here, the hard work of uncovering our less than perfect attributes and mental constructs, that we abjure for simpler tasks.

Our cold indifference, our anger, our righteousness, our fear, guarded so adroitly by the doubt and distrust that waylay mercy on the way in. They plead, cajole and threaten to remain disguised. They riffle the surface from which Narcissus demands a perfect reflection.

Before we go much further with the exploration of passive aggression, let us explore the term itself. Passive aggression is aggression in its most subdued, even suppressed, form. It can be very subtle and extremely tricky. It is an uneasy feeling of powerlessness, of helplessness, which cultivates a hidden agenda. It is a grief reaction.

When exploring this quality of residual holding which gives rise to aggression, it is very important to maintain a nonjudgmental, merciful awareness of the passing show. It is very much in the nature of unsuccessfully suppressed anger to respond favorably to unabashed kindness. Nothing less spacious is safe enough to open into. Narcissus doesn't like the situation one bit. It makes him angry.

Robert Bly said something to the effect that if you yell at the average man, he will just roll over in his crib and turn his face to the wall. Many fear anger even more than that which they are angry at. Anger fears itself coming out of hiding almost as much as it harangues itself for hiding in the first place. Passive aggression is often an angry fear.

Active aggression strikes its object and stands back white-knuckled, threatening more. Soft aggression, containing an added element of deceit, passively attacks, tripping another, insisting it was an accident. In hard aggression, one is struck with the closed fist. In soft aggression, one is struck with the open hand, which on the backswing caresses and further confuses.

As fear and a lack of self-investigation allow the original objects of our frustration to submerge below awareness, our aggression becomes less specific. As our grief remains unexplored and unintegrated, our aggression becomes more generic and we find the guarded mind leaning toward such self-centricisms as nationalism, racism, sexism and a thousand holy wars at the office, at the dinner table and across the soft sarcophagus of the bed.

When one feels even little frustrations cannot be safely expressed, that frustration builds. When one feels unable to confront the object of that discomfort because of a position of imagined power or an imagined position of weakness, or any of a number of censors on emotions, the aggression doesn't just go away. It goes deeper, awaiting the next available target, which usually turns out to be you.

When this anger, aggression, dismay, frustration, resentment, can find no adequate or appropriate means of expression, it is often turned inward. In its milder form we notice it as varying severities of self-judgment. Such inward-turned aggression often displays itself as a sense of guilt. And a general unkindness toward Narcissus, yours and mine.

All states of mind, every emotion, have a wide breadth of expression. Each has an active and passive aspect. An external and internal enactment. It is said that the right hand of fear is aggression and the left hand is pretense. Active fear attacks, passive hides, but in each the goal is the same. Active doubt pulls back while passive says yes with no intention of carrying through. Each has a goal of eluding the present. Active love embraces; passive love lets go. In each case its goal is to cross the abyss that separates hearts.

When passive aggression is observed in a nonaggressive mindfulness that receives with mercy even our occasional mercilessness, noninjury becomes a possibility. When we observe with forgiveness how many parts of ourselves we have suppressed in order to maintain our self-image, our frustration discovers another path. A path of mercy and healing. Exploring with a merciful awareness our passive aggression, we come across feelings of helplessness and a sensed inability to express frustration without fear of retaliation. We enter directly the frustration with a moment to moment awareness of its process, perhaps employing the Meditation on Afflictive Emotions in Chapter 49A. Observing frustration transform into aggression, passive and overt, that if left uninvestigated, gets displaced on the next being down the pecking order. Dumped perhaps on your beloved or anyone seen momentarily as "other," or kicking the family wolf. And recognize with the irony that wisdom often provides, that passive aggression is really just a sense of helplessness which defends offensively.

In the investigation of how our frustration has become conditioned toward war or peace, there is a fascinating juncture in the coincidence of suppressed aggression and forced passivity. For instance, in most cultures women have been more forced than persuaded to suppress frustrations and be passive. Any anger investigated and embraced gives one a deeper sense of coming into one's own. Forced passivity often gives rise to suppressed aggression.

The sense of forced passivity imposed by family, education, social status and conditioning in general creates a certain unease. As does the constant disappointment of unfulfilled desire and uncontrollable happenstance which causes even the best-laid plans of mice and men to often go astray. This anxious discomfiture is smoldering somewhere within most minds. A sense of being oppressed by God and circumstances that leads to the angry dismay and restlessness we call *angst*. This discomfort with our lives, this repression of its natural expression, leads to a frightened anxiety which grieves its lack of wholeness. It makes us nervous and aggressive. It causes us, like Narcissus, to test the waters constantly, to insist on a world made safe by our fear.

In the space between *I* and *other,* in the distance from *I* to *amness,* is all the work to be done in the mind fields of relationship. The natural tension between individual psyches is an echo of our separation from our true nature.

On the acrobatic swing between *I* and *amness* is the ongoing work of taking responsibility for birth at last. For making peace, perhaps, where others have made war. In the distance between I and amness are constructed all the barriers wrought in the shadowy chambers of complaint and imagined insult.

We learn to be loving by watching how unloving we are. And this "how unloving we are" is precisely what is observed in the painful exploration of our passive aggression. There are many parts of us, wounded and unwilling to expose themselves, fearful of infection, which resist the next step of letting go, the next level of our healing. There are aspects of the psyche embittered with distrust and satisfactions too infrequent to allay isolation. In this unresolved grief that isolates and angers us, we discover another facet of the resentment which arises when two desire systems pass within each other's gravitational pull. We would like to imagine that if our desire systems don't coincide, they are at worst but ships passing in the night. But this is wishful thinking. Opposing desire systems are more like the *Titanic* meets its iceberg. We don't react well at not getting what we want. Dissatisfaction coils at the base of the skull waiting to strike. And the heart is withdrawn.

This "how unloving we are" is quite painful to watch in its momentary reaction and vaguely insensitive responses. It is an expression of the natural resentment that arises when Narcissus feels cheated or misused. It is another teaching that the way to Narcissus' heart is through his soft belly. Only by embracing with mercy that which withdraws in anger can we make peace in ourselves and peace in the world. The profound exploration of our passive aggression leads to an ever-expanding experience of active compassion.

This emptying of the space between *I* and *other* is like the story by Chuang Tzu of the fisherman crossing the river at dawn, hearing another boat approaching through the fog. Concerned that it will collide with his, he yells to the person in the other boat to steer away. But the boat continues to approach through the mist, as he curses the person navigating for not being more attentive. As the boat floats near he sees that there is no one in the boat. It has slipped its moorings and floats empty in the waters. His anger vanishes when he discovers there is no one opposing him. He maneuvers gently past the empty boat. Just so, our teacher often would say, "Empty your boat!" In the empty boat, in the spacious mind, in the vast spirit, there is nothing separate from essential love. And all that is must be taken into our enormous heart.

CHAPTER 35

THE
HIGH-WIRE
ACT

RELATIONSHIP IS a high-wire act. To the left is the irretrievable past—your personal history, your previous relationships, your triumphs and your grief, the momentum which mechanically seeks to repeat itself, your helplessness. To the right is the uncontrollable future—your expectations and fears, a thousand desires yet unfulfilled, fading dreams, your hopelessness. That is perhaps why Buddhist practices are called the Middle Way: a balancing of the heart and mind to enable unimpeded forward movement. Lean too far to the left and we become lost in guilt, anger, fear, self-protection and cleverness. Lean too far to the right and we disappear into romantic fantasy, superstition, magic thinking and a self-punishing sentimentality. The tightrope is the present moment, this very instant in which we attempt to maintain some balance between aspects of the underdream. When the balance is perfect, grace and disgrace dissolve equally into unconditioned love.

But in truth, relationship is the art of falling down. Or more accurately, the art of picking oneself up lightly. In those moments when mindfulness and heartfulness are not in balance, there is the tendency to trip over one's feet. To fall, once again, into old patterns, to be confused and unhappy. Our fear of falling automatically activates the "grasping reaction," only to find that we land on another high wire—that we fall from tightrope to tightrope, from moment to moment as the path continues. Our growth is measured in the lightness of the fall and the tenderness of our resurrection.

Buddha said, "It doesn't matter how long you forget, only how soon you remember!"

Though each time we lose our footing we may imagine it is "a fall *from* grace," in truth, it is a fall *through* grace.

On the high wire, the balancing pole is our mindfulness, our practice, spiritual and psychological, the inner work which allows progress from moment to moment. This balancing rod is what the remarkable teacher Ramana Maharshi called the "great staff": the last as well as the first desire, the Great Desire, which stirs the fire of liberation in which lesser desires are toasted to a golden hue.

When two commit to such an acrobatic act, each provides balance and perspective for the other. Seeing a loved one leaning a bit to the right in fantasy and projection, the lover whispers, "A bit to the left, a bit to the left," bringing the other back to the present. Seeing the loved one tilting too far left, heavy with the past, the lover gestures, "Lean right, lean right," returning with the loved one to the center. Each brings an added depth of field to the balancing act.

And when one trips, there, waiting on the new wire, is your collaborator to stabilize the fall.

Balanced on the high wire, we see clearly on the left the multiple layers of conditioning and personal history which form the armoring over the heart. Entering the touch point of the heart through the grief point, we encounter a broader sense of being, no longer limited by, or to, the experiences of the past. Mindfulness lets us live this moment fully alive. It allows us to, as one Zen master said, "just go straight." Not wandering to the right, projecting anxious possibilities, grasping so imperfectly at possible perfections, daydreaming the night—forgetting the process is not to become someone or to get something more, but simply to *be* completely present. When the mind is no longer devising the future and the past, it resides in the immediate present. The moment we were born for. The space between thoughts.

Discovering the path beneath your feet is mindfulness. Walking that path with your beloved is heartfulness. When mindfulness becomes refined, heartfulness takes care of itself. Nothing obstructs it. The least disturbance of the space becomes instantly noticeable. The first tremor of any afflictive mental state noticed in its first arisal. Noting its first tightening as "fear," dozens of mind moments before identification becomes afraid. Naming that first sense of *otherness* as "anger" long before one is lost in being angry. Mindfulness, knowing that force just closes the heart, makes the moment more manageable by not attempting to manage the moment. Mindfulness creates a merciful space for new alternatives, while heartfulness receives it all with a wink and a nod and a knowing glance as *other* becomes the Beloved, closer to the heart than even your idea of yourself.

Mindfulness offers itself to the heart like a bouquet laid at the feet of the Beloved.

CHAPTER 36

~

LOVING KINDNESS

M ANY SPEAK OF the "path with a heart." Carlos Castaneda and a generation of longing find these words both inspiring and comforting. It is the path discovered as we turn inward toward the heart. It is the way of loving kindness. Many seeking their true heart, the Beloved, have walked this path before us. Each step a trailblazing. Entering the moment afire, seeking the oceanic heart.

Loving kindness is the effortless expression of the heart reflected in a state of mind. Like any state of mind from joy to terror, it can be cultivated and encouraged to blossom. Like all states of mind, "by their fruits ye shall know them." The fruits of fear are isolation and war. The fruits of loving kindness are communion with mercy and peace.

The cultivation, the ongoing practice of loving kindness, often resonates with and parallels the deepening levels of consciousness that are reflected in the stages of commitment in a wholehearted relationship. Opening first to the mind/body most deserving of mercy—yourself. Recalling with a deep sigh Buddha's statement that "You can look the whole world over and never find anyone more deserving of love than yourself." Deepening the soft mercy in which the exploration of the primary levels of existence, physical and mental, are received. And mindfully, mercifully, explored.

Opening to this mind/body in which we find ourselves (so to speak), all that is disheartened is welcomed in the heart. We meet ourselves with a mercy and loving kindness that sends wishes of well-being to our self. It is a healing of the primary levels of our existence: the body flooded with a kindness seldom imagined; the mind immersed in an ocean of compassion. Its grief and joy welcomed by the mercy, forgiveness and patience it has perhaps never known. It is the essence of healing—entering with mercy and loving kindness that which has been withdrawn from in judgment and condemnation.

In the Loving Kindness Meditation one addresses oneself first, sending wishes for one's well-being to oneself. Speaking to oneself as to a loved one, observing the aversions and long-conditioned self-negations that arise to limit such an expression of self-care and mercy. Watching how merciless we are with ourselves. Discovering that, to the judging mind, all is *other*, including itself. Observing how the small mind obstructs our great heart, prosecuting much that comes within its view. Condemning this "me-thinking" mind to a hell constructed from its own images and likenesses.

Deepening this stage, one turns to oneself as if to *other* and calling to oneself by one's first name, sends waves of mercy and care. It is a momentous move. It embraces distress before it contracts into the resistance we call suffering. Loving kindness resists nothing. It opens to the long-closed. It gives the tightened fist of small mind an opportunity to let go. Looking on yourself as on your only child, the self-image is allowed to float in mercy instead of drown in self-judgment. We embrace Narcissus. We call her out of her prison. We beseech him to be kind to himself.

As this process deepens, there may even be glimpses of the long-conditioned dualities which cleave the living truth into the acceptable (the liked) and the unacceptable (the disliked), exchanging boundless *amness* for a two-dimensional identity. At this level where images of self are seen to be less than the living truth, *I* and *other* are recognized simply as concepts awash in the often-unloved.

And an expansive mercy arises that does not attempt to control or destroy such insubstantial mental constructs, but invites this conditioning gently into the unconditioned, undifferentiated heart of loving kindness.

As *I* and *other* become more a mystery than a fact, mercy begins to extend outward. And one begins to focus loving kindness meditation on the beloveds of one's life—friends, teachers, mates. Because of the previous stage of the meditation, whenever that loved one is seen as *other,* they are also recognized as *self. Other* and *self* experienced as aspects of the same fearful underdream that scrambles to make itself solid, panicking for "someone to be" in the midst of the flow of consciousness and change.

Bringing that loved one to heart, one sends wave after wave of wishes for their well-being with each breath. "May you be happy. May you be free from suffering. May you discover the absolute joy of your absolute nature." And all that separates, all the anxious territory between *I* and *other* is filled with the loving kindness that displaces fear. Generating deeper and deeper levels of care, narrowing the "no person's land" between hearts, relationship expands to new possibilities. The distance between self and other diminishes. The distance between mind and heart decreases. And less is other than the Beloved.

As the loving kindness practice continues to develop, this focused energy for the well-being of others is directed toward yet another friend. Perhaps someone in a less intense relationship than with your loved ones, but an ally nonetheless, who has touched your heart. "May you be happy. May you be healed. May you be free from suffering. May you be at peace." Each breath connecting. Each inhalation drawing the other in. Each exhalation sending waves of gratitude and blessing to this friend. Dissolving like salt in a salty sea. Oneness. This is the depth of loving kindness which reflects the level of consciousness we call the heart. It is the Angelic Stage of growth.

Eventually one expands this circle of loving kindness to include those who are neither friend nor foe, perhaps simply a casual acquaintance or even a stranger on the street. Sending wave after wave of loving kindness from your heart to theirs. Discovering there is no such thing as a stranger, but only ourselves in other mental and physical garb. Each essentially the same. Each self-image exhumed from the disregarded flow of consciousness, from which small mind picks and chooses who it imagines it should be that day, and suffers the consequences. Each wishing only to be happy, only to be free of suffering. And the heart embraces even the "casual stranger." Walking down the street, everywhere we look, we see the Beloved. And no other.

In time, as this loving kindness practice expands, it may naturally come to embrace even those whom we thought of previously as enemies. This is the last stage of personal loving kindness. The last duality. The first level of undifferentiated consciousness we call the mystery.

Here the right hand of the Beloved has met with the left in a prayerful bow to those parts of ourselves numbed and ostracized, chided and abused, which seek only to be whole. Loving kindness, mercy and forgiveness flow naturally from such an open state.

And eventually there is no *I* and no *other,* only love. *I* and *other* are seen as figments of the unsure mind, the mind scrambling to be real in the midst of the surreal. And that in "reality," there is no one separate to relate to, but only the heart of the Beloved to relate from. And we become the Beloved bowing to itself.

When Narcissus practices loving kindness, his self-hatred becomes less clever. She navigates less by the mind. He discovers the heart, the reflection she was always seeking, her true self, worthy of praise without ending and gratitude beyond expression. And a happiness that does not differentiate between inner and outer. Between self and other. Between letting go and letting be.

And we come to the vast spaciousness in which we hear one of our teachers saying once again, "Your only friend is God." Reminding us once again that all that we love is the Beloved.

The following Loving Kindness Meditation uses the conceptual word-oriented mindscape in perhaps its most skillful manner. It turns a hindrance into an ally. It introduces Narcissus, and all his loves and losses, to the Beloved. It heals the mind while opening the heart.

~

LOVING KINDNESS MEDITATION

Sitting comfortably, allow the attention to come gradually
to the breath.
The breath coming and going all by itself deep within the
body.

Take a few moments to allow the attention to gather within the
even rhythm of the breath.

Turning gently within, begin to direct, toward yourself, care for
your own well-being.

Begin to look on yourself as though you were your only child.
Have mercy on you.

Silently in the heart say, "May I be free from suffering. May I
be at peace."

Just feel the breath breathing into the heart space as we relate to ourselves with kindness and care.

Allow the heart, silently, to whisper the words of mercy that
heal, that open. "May I be free from suffering. May I be at
peace."

Allow yourself to be healed.

Whispering to yourself, send wishes for your own well-being. "May I be free from suffering. May I be at peace."

Repeat gently with each in-breath. "May I be free from suffering."

Repeat gently with each out-breath. "May I be at peace."

Repeat these words slowly and gently with each in-breath, with each out-breath. Not as a prayer but as the extending of loving care to yourself.

Notice whatever limits this love, this mercy, this willingness to be whole, to be healed.

"May I be free from suffering. May I be at peace."

Continue with this rhythm, this deepening of merciful joy and loving kindness drawn in with each breath, expanding with each exhalation.

"May I be free from suffering. May I be at peace."

Let the breath continue naturally, as mercy for yourself, your only child, for this being within.

Though at first these may only feel like words echoing from the mind, gently continue. There can be no force here. Force closes the heart. Let the heart receive the mind in a new tenderness and mercy.

"May I be free from suffering. May I be at peace."

Each breath deepening the nurturing warmth of relating to oneself with loving kindness and compassion. Each exhalation deepening in peace, expanding into the spaciousness of being, developing the deep patience that does not wait for things to be otherwise, but relates with loving kindness to things as they are.

"May I be free from suffering. May I be at peace."

Allow the healing in with each breath. Allow your true spacious nature.

Continue for a few breaths more this drawing in, this opening to, loving kindness. Relating to yourself with great tenderness, sending well-being into your mind and body, embrace yourself with these gentle words of healing.

Now gently bring to mind someone for whom you have a feeling of warmth and kindness. Perhaps a loved one or teacher or friend.

Picture this loved one in your heart. With each in-breath

whisper to them, "May you be free from suffering. May you be at peace."

With each breath draw that loved one into your heart. "May you be free from suffering."

With each out-breath fill them with your loving kindness. "May you be at peace."

With the next inhalation draw their heart closer to yours. "May you be free from suffering."

With the following out-breath extend to the loved one a wish for their well-being. "May you be at peace."

Continue the gentle breath of connection, the gentle wish for their happiness and wholeness.

Let the breath be breathed naturally, softly, lovingly into the heart, coordinated with your words, with your concentrated feelings of loving kindness and care.

"May you be free of any suffering. May you know the deepest levels of peace."

Send them your love, your compassion, your care.

Breathing them in and through your heart.

"May you be free from suffering. May you know your deepest joy, your greatest peace."

And as you sense them in your heart, sense this whole world that wishes so to be healed, to know its true nature, to be at peace.

Say to yourself, "Just as I wish to be happy, so do all sentient beings."

And in your heart, with each in-breath, with each out-breath, whisper, "May all beings be free of suffering. May all beings be at peace."

Let your loving kindness reach out to all beings as it did to your loved one, sensing all beings in need of healing, in need of the peace of their true nature.

"May all beings be at peace. May they be free of suffering."

"May all sentient beings, to the most recently born, be free of fear, free of pain. May all beings heal into their true nature. May all beings know the absolute joy of absolute being."

"May all beings everywhere be at peace. May all beings be free of suffering."

The whole planet like a bubble floating in the ocean of your heart.

Each breath drawing in the love that heals the world, that deepens the peace we all seek.

Each breath feeding the world with the mercy and compassion, the warmth and patience that quiets the mind and opens the heart.

"May all beings be free from suffering. May all beings be at peace."

Let the breath come softly. Let the breath go gently. Wishes of well-being and mercy, of care and loving kindness, extended to this world we all share.

"May all beings be free of suffering. May all beings dwell in the heart of healing. May all beings be at peace."

IV

~

A CERTAIN
CLARITY

CHAPTER 37

~

MEETING
THE BUDDHA

THE BUDDHA'S Buddha was mindfulness. After almost two decades of immersing himself in the various spiritual and yogic practices of his time, developing enormous concentration, patience, willingness, discriminating wisdom and profound insight, he sat beneath the bodhi tree, touched the earth and vowed not to move from that spot until he received full enlightenment. He later taught a mindfulness meditation, Vipassana (seeing clearly), which his enlightenment had revealed as a direct path through the mind to the truth beyond. He suggested that this mindfulness practice was the path of insight that leads to the heart of the matter. He offered in the *Satipattana Sutra* the practice of observing the various levels of consciousness—physical, mental, emotional and spatial— the play of the senses, the unfolding of thought, emotion and sensation, and the ever-changing states of mind, which have become more a conditioned dream than any sort of healing wakefulness. He implored us to know ourselves and be free.

I began spiritual practice when I was nineteen years old. Coming across *The Compassionate Buddha,* an early Buddhist treatise by A. E. Burt, I scanned the pages with a deep sigh and purchased the book, even though I felt it was "already too late" for me. I was clutching at straws. The pain of being, or actually not being, was getting a bit much to bear. I could just as well have picked up a bottle of pills that day as brought home the Buddha.

After reading the book in agonizing judgment of my "unenlightenment," I looked about for a teacher. In 1956 there were very few meditation masters available in America. But then I met and studied with a fellow named Rudi sitting outside his oriental art store on Seventh Avenue in New York City, learning about the heart and mind by his focusing me on the states of mind of the individuals passing by. But then I went west. For the next few years I practiced alone. I worked for several years with the *Bhagavad Gita* and Hindu heart meditations that seemed intuitively appropriate. Sitting each morning with three different translations of the *Gita,* I would attempt to find the truth somewhere in the space between subtly varying interpretations. These heart practices drew me further into the exploration and, for a period, the sacred heart presented itself in the practice of the Jesus Prayer and a sense of the suffering to be served in the often indifferent world. Returning again and again to the absolute clarity of the Buddha, I was longing somehow to actualize this vision when an old friend returned from Burma after three years as a monk, with the instructions in mindfulness as presented by the great Burmese meditation master Mahasi Sayadaw. It was the complete instruction in Vipassana (mindfulness) as offered in the monastery to those committed to long periods of silent practice. For two years I practiced Vipassana as best I could without a teacher.

Then, twenty years ago, after five years of taking many teachings but never a teacher, I met Sujata, a young Buddhist monk, who had recently returned from Asia. I was employed to work with him on his book for the Mindfulness Series published by Unity Press. He soon became a primary influence. He edited me more than I edited his manuscript. Repeatedly insisting I let go of thinking I was my thought. "You are not the mind!" he chided each time I would spin off into random thinking. "Don't think Buddhism, practice it."

Some years later when Joseph Goldstein, a meditation teacher of considerable depth and commitment, quoted his teacher saying, "Don't be a Buddhist. Be a Buddha!" it completed that particular circle. (Indeed, since then I have been corrected once again, "Don't be Buddha, just be.")

For that first year I reminded myself again and again that I was not the mind. Much confusion, much conditioned mind, arose to meet this shocking revelation and blatant deconditioning. The mind had lots to say, but the heart nodded wisely. As small mind attachment to everything it thought and felt was challenged, its authority, its dominion, began to diminish. Big mind opened to small mind. And at last small mind could be seen with some big mind mercy. I began to embrace my Narcissus. And Narcissus looked up from its own reflection and wept with joy to be cared for that much—and surrendered into the arms of that clear mercy. When old mind beleaguered itself, I reminded it once again it was process only. Reasserting again and again that there was more to mind than its conditioning left it with nowhere to stand and nothing to stand on. The insecurity which arises in the shadow of deepening experiences of emptiness repeatedly presenting itself. Demanding to know, if it wasn't the mind, then who the hell was it! Agitated Narcissus. Frightened Narcissus. But it was becoming increasingly clear that even this insecurity was what those who have gone beyond such entanglements call "mind only." And all that separated us from our true nature, too, was mind only. All that was other than the heart was mind only.

And I came to see that the mind has a mind of its own. That thoughts think themselves. That feelings feel themselves. That sensations sense themselves. That the whole process we are constantly calling I is simply the unfolding of *amness*. That when we say, *I am,* it is the *amness* that does all the work, while the me-thinking mind attempts to take credit and is thus discredited.

Recognizing that the whole world was "mind only" at the same time I was experiencing that I was not only the mind, a greatly expanded sense of I and *other* ensued. Knowing I was not the mind, neither was anyone else. Neither were my lovers, nor my children, nor my parents, nor even my teachers. And the more profoundly this truth was experienced, the less I mistook my friends' or lovers' minds for their true hearts. And levels of relationship so subtle that the mind had never considered them possible arose in a merciful awareness that experienced itself with fascination and considerable satisfaction.

The same tradition that offers the concepts of "big mind," "small mind" and "mind only" also speaks in terms of "no mind." No mind is the mind before thinking big or small. It is the presence in presence, the breath inside the breath. No mind is all heart. Such concepts as small mind and big mind are mind only. Just varying solidities of the same vastness. To employ such concepts without mindfulness of the undifferentiated vastness of our underlying reality is like drawing concentric circles in a sandstorm. As relative points, they are useful to our absolute understanding. In the small is personal identification with self. In the big is impersonal identification with selflessness. Each relates to the same content, but identifies differently. One sees content as *my* thought; the other as *the* process. But eventually deeper experiences of our largeness cause even such skillful concepts as these to dissolve in the essence of mind. Mind only turning its insides outward becomes no mind. Mind only is the world as thought and thinking. No mind is the heart without obstructions.

This identification, big or small, is not unlike the conflict in Buddhism between the School of the Elders called Theravada, or derogatorily by some, "the Lesser Vehicle," and the more recent schools of Buddhism, Mahayana, called by themselves "the Greater Vehicle." Each at times derides the other for being too small or too big. But as Joseph Goldstein wrote, having practiced extensively in both schools, "Greater vehicle, lesser vehicle. All vehicles will be towed away at the owner's expense!"

Even terms such as "small mind" and "big mind" can be used by the insecure politics of the mind to convince another that *their* way is *the* way. You are not small-minded if relationship just doesn't suit your needs and circumstances at the moment. Nor are you big-minded if you allow yourself to deny the truth of our frequent small-mindedness. Big mind is in relationship to all as it is. Small mind simply relates to itself: Narcissus does what it does best, it thinks about itself. It is mind only.

It might be added, since I have told a bit of my story, that

Ondrea met the Buddha in a very different manner. She didn't go looking for him. He was just there one day as a spontaneous experience of her great nature that has illuminated her life ever since.

Now we ascend together past even Buddha and the golden noose of such concepts, to our original birth in buddha nature. Resting in being.

CHAPTER 38

~

MY MIND,
YOUR MIND,
NO MIND

THE NEXT TIME comparing mind distances from an *other* in judgment, rather than identify with the mind's uninvited complaints, "She did this!" or "He did that!," you might substitute the words "the mind" for the personal pronoun. Instead of playing pin the blame on the donkey; rather than the indictment, "He did that," perhaps see what the words "The mind did that" might reveal. Instead of "*He* created *my* pain," perhaps experiment with "*The* mind created *the* pain."

In the Zen tradition the concepts of "small mind," "big mind" and ultimately "no mind" continue the profound exploration of "mind only." It is mind—the cognitive capacity, long diminished by the deeply conditioned sense of self—that creates suffering. What keeps us apart: mind only. What creates the world: mind only. What creates suffering in the world: mind only. What blocks the heart: mind only. When we are enlightened, what are we enlightened of: mind only. Most of what we call our life is an afterthought: mind only.

It is said that the greatest "noting" is "mind only." When two people disagree, it is mind only. When two people make a case for being right, it is mind only. When either thinks the other wrong, it is mind only. When hearts feel inalterably separate, it is mind only. We think we are only what we think. Small mind only. But when the two see the process out of which separation arises, relating *to* that which isolates instead of *from* it, there is an inseparable relationship to the process unfolding. Big mind, wisdom mind. But still there may be a sense of "someone watching," a point of view capable of turning pain into suffering.

No mind displays how attachment even to big mind can be a trap; a big trap if it creates duality, preference and judgment. Attachment to big mind is small mind. It is like the story that Hui Neng, Fifth Zen Patriarch, tells of approaching two men arguing about the cause of a flag's fluttering. One says the wind is moving. The other insists the flag is moving. Hui Neng, Fifth Zen Patriarch, corrects each saying, "You're both mistaken. The mind is moving."

No mind is the stillness in which small mind flutters. Big mind is awareness of this process. In small mind, big duality. In big mind, a certain singularity. In no mind, no duality—not relating even *to* the space, but *as* the space (the nondual with no alternative) it's all happening in. We are the experiencing of being. These three stages of small mind, big mind and no mind in many ways represent the evolutionary stages of consciousness, the levels of commitment to the truth.

Small mind is our youth. We are the center of the universe. Big mind is our growth, our evolution onto land, the ability to take the small self into the big heart. Healing. No mind is the *Uh* in which nothing that passes through is more than a nano-bubble in the experience of boundaryless suchness.

And in time we discover we are not our personal history, only to uncover a step further in timelessness that we are not our personal present either. We are universal suchness wearing our old life like bandages, unwinding in layers to reveal our native skin to the warmth of the precious sun.

The three stages are: relating *from;* relating *to;* and being.

When we love "as is," there is no mind. Nothing old to separate. No place from which judgment originates. When the closed identifications of *small mind only* are recognized as the root of so much pain, that insight turns us toward expanded states of awareness that experience not only the cause of suffering as mind only but the end of suffering as well. The big mind that leads to no mind, which is the unobstructed heart.

On the level of physical and mental attachments, small mind predominates. On the heart level big mind is regularly present. And expands into the mystical level on which the mind and heart are inseparable. But on the fifth, no-mind nonlevel, that which separates vanishes and the wedding is complete. Nothing separate remains. Only being, being.

Small mind longs for the Beloved. Big mind relates from the Beloved. No mind is the Beloved.

CHAPTER 39

~

BEING
PRESENT

OST OF LIFE only lasts a moment. Then our life becomes a memory, a dream. We are only alive a millisecond at a time. This moment! Or as one teacher put it, holding his thumb and forefinger about a quarter inch apart, "All of life is only just this much—just a moment at a time." When we open to the very instant in which awareness produces consciousness, we are fully alive. Completely present. Big-minded.

To the degree we are present for "just this much," this living moment, we are alive. Otherwise we numb to the vibrancy and beg upon our deathbed for just one more chance.

Most think that living a "full life" means living into old age. But if you are not alive this moment, what makes you think you'll be alive then? To live fully alive is to be filled with this moment. Present for this millisecond, this day, this week, this life.

We discover it is difficult to differentiate between one who is fully present and one who is *in* love. Presence and love are of the same etheric substance—an unobstructed awareness is an unobstructed heart.

Mindfulness is the art and science of being present. Its art arises from our intuitive will toward completion. Its science, from a daily meditation practice.

As we develop our mindfulness the mind realigns. There is an increase in the capacity to think clearly, to let thought pass gently and without judgment. And there is an increasing participation in our lives. It is the cultivation of a merciful awareness that meets whatever is happening in the moment of its unfolding. This ongoing mindfulness becomes a dear companion, a softener of pain, a deepener of wisdom, that accompanies us wherever the body/mind may go.

Mindfulness teaches us to trust our life. To take the teachings it provides, no matter how hard or seemingly facile, into our hearts. It reminds us that all we are missing is what we are missing. It suggests we pay attention.

This capacity to see clearly what is happening while it is happening, to experience our life directly, is greatly enhanced by a regular meditative investigation, alone in silence, of the passing show of consciousness in its most subtle detail.

Many say they would not leave the house in the morning without meditating any sooner than they would without brushing their teeth. And for many of the same reasons. Each morning they sit quietly, stilling the mind by first exploring the sensations that accompany each breath: mindfulness of breathing. Moment to moment they follow the sensations that accompany the beginning, middle and end of each inhalation, each exhalation. They focus on the field of sensation against which the least thought or feeling is instantly noticed. As their concentration on the natural flow of the breath is developed, any image or word, even the slightest movement of anything other than wordless sensation, is recognized at its inception. They don't get lost in thought, but simply watch how lost thought can become. They watch "the watcher." They relate *to* the mind rather than *from* it.

Often they employ the technique of a silent "noting" of the qualities of the mind as they pass through. This noting is an acknowledgment of where we are while we are still there. A silent noting of "anger" from the heart when the mind has become disturbed with aversion and judgment keeps them present. Keeps their business current. It is a labeling, a *naming* of the content of the moment. It has "the power of naming" to call the shadowed into the light. Through the day noting states of mind, they acknowledge their momentary presence. When anger arises, "anger." When doubt arises, "doubt." When fear arises, "fear." When joy arises, "joy." They see that when small mind acknowledges its contents heartfully, it becomes big mind.

Focusing on changing mental states, noting the contents passing through, enables them to see their process. It allows them to observe the constant unfolding of mental imagery with a soft-bellied mercy and absence of judgment which refines their capacity to see, to hear, to taste, to touch, to smell, to think, to love. Recognizing that each moment explored openheartedly, mindfully, has little to attract identification or suffering, they use noting as a constant means of staying present in meditation and throughout the day. Then "fear" does not frighten, "judgment" does not judge, "joy" does not leave us breathlessly grasping for more.

As their awareness explores the most noticeable activities of the mind/body, it gradually becomes refined, able to hear the subtlest whispers of thought, feeling and sensation. Able to discover the breath inside the breath, the thought within thinking, the feeling within feelings. Breaking the illusion of Narcissus, they uproot the "ownership of thought," observing that the idea of something, someone, separate thinking, is just that—only a thought, the next bubble on the breeze.

As they separately meditate together each morning, each partner gently returns their wandering attention back to the breath again and again, acknowledging and noting all that arises. Not surprised by the subtle fears and doubts that flicker through. Developing courage and patience, concentration and honesty, openness and clarity. Deepening the capacity to relate with each other by opening to themselves.

Each investigates together old-mind tendencies toward control. Each recognizing that what blocks access to their own heart blocks access to their loved one's. Committed to a mindfulness of self which includes the benefit of another. Learning to relate to the delicacies of the ever-changing breath in the same manner as they might the subtle alterations in another's consciousness. Tuning to the immediate present in which relationships may meet in a mystical union.

Exploring the moment to moment process of their ordinary grief and extraordinary joy, sudden wordless understandings arise, insights which break their addiction to the mind and enables them to appreciate their own true light reflected back from consciousness. Not mistaking awareness for the objects of awareness, they do not suffer from the mistaken identity that all they are is the mind, recognizing they are the awareness which produces this consciousness. Becoming conscious of awareness itself, the space it's all happening in, the identification that keeps objects trapped in small mind dissipates. They allow thoughts to dissolve in a process floating in space. Like one who has discovered that the moon is but the reflected sun, they divine their original nature.

Small mind may argue that an ongoing mindfulness of the passing show will suppress spontaneity. But much of what we call spontaneity is actually a compulsive twitch. When we are wholly present, unsuspected alternatives arise that increase the breadth of action rather than narrow it. To small mind there are few possibilities, to big mind many. It is not, as fear might suggest, a kind of hypnosis, but rather as Achaan Cha says, a "de-hypnosis." Although it may sound as though one would "flatten" experience, in truth, one opens to yet subtler levels of being, discovering that what we always supposed to be the "aliveness of thought" is actually the magnificent scintillation of the awareness which receives it.

The unconscious becomes conscious when nothing censors even the least arising of suppressed material. When nothing is eluded or left unexamined, that which lies hidden—from the terrifyingly personal to the rapturously universal—comes into the healing light of an effortless awareness. No words can describe the absolute joy, freedom and peace of a liberated mind. It is synonymous with the open heart. Nothing obstructs it, no one suffering.

Many couples in developing relationships have told us that "watch breath, soften belly, open heart" has become almost a mantra, a sacred repetition, a wake-up call for mindfulness and mercy; that it has taken them beyond old mind/body interaction into a deeper peace and an ever-present healing.

Mindfulness is the ultimate responder. It is the responder that ends reactiveness. It is the responder that can end the need for responders. It fulfills the Great Desire which eats lesser desires. It is the big mind context in which anything smaller than the Beloved floats to the surface.

This moment to moment attentiveness, encouraged and focused, allows one to meet pleasure and pain in the mind/body, and participate directly without fear. It is looking oneself directly in the eye, meeting oneself as if for the first time, each time. It means entering directly the flow of a constantly changing consciousness. It is an investigation of sensation, thought and feeling, as they are generated at the point of inquiry. It is a probing of the very nature of the experience we call life. It is an examination of perception itself. It means approaching life directly, without models or preconceptions. It means entering the moment with a choiceless, merciful awareness, an openhanded receptivity which seeks nothing but to experience the moment as it is.

It means approaching the present at the ground zero of "don't know": open to any possibility. Letting go of preconceived attitudes, the colored lenses through which we have only dimly perceived for so long. Seeing and examining seeing. Feeling and examining feeling. Watching and examining the watcher. Entering directly into one's life. It means watching unconditionally the conditioned. We watch the mind seeing who we are not from the mystery of who we might be. Observing the conditioned in the unconditioned vastness which is the heart of the Beloved.

Seeing things as they are, the cloying identifications of old mind diminish. More and more the process of consciousness simply floats in clear awareness. Less and less its contents are mistaken for all that we are. Gradually, awareness itself may be directly experienced. When awareness takes itself as its object, going to the very root out of which consciousness is produced, we meet at last our primordial nature.

When we see how difficult it is to "just watch it," we see the nature of what many call monkey mind. Like a monkey swinging through the trees, propelled by desire from limb to limb, the unintended mind flits by, reaching out for the next object to grasp—the exquisite beauty of the forest canopy a blur, indistinct, unknown.

Much that makes it difficult to "just watch it" is our incessant rumination on unfinished business.

When awareness is gently encouraged to return to the moment, it looks straight ahead and all is seen arising and passing away. All we have been grasping at, at last recognized in its most minute and impermanent detail. Without the least need to change our way of being, awareness changes it all by itself and a new path arises to meet each step.

As mindfulness develops, awareness receives previously unnoticed realms of being. Then the journey together seems not somewhere we are going, but an increasing appreciation of where we are.

Old mind is monkey mind. Old mind is small mind thinking. Old mind is compulsive reaction to unexplored stimuli. It is the uninvited, the mechanical, the moment as dream, as a blur of confusion and suffering. New mind is "just this much." It is a new heartfulness in which the mind need not be sacrificed, but embraced with kind attention.

What we are suggesting is a soft-bellied mindfulness. An incorporation of soft belly into the practice of letting go each time awareness is brought back into the present when holding has caused identification with a passing thought or feeling. The use of soft belly in moments of letting go reinforces that process. It provides a physical correlation for a mental reconditioning. A space into which to let go. In meditation, as in the rest of life, when awareness is noticed straying from the present, lost in daydream and rumination, as we let go to return to the moment, soft belly becomes a physical trigger for that mental release. Soft belly and let-go-mind are part of an interactive whole. When the mind contracts in anger or fear and begins to spin out in reaction to pride and confusion, in that big mind glimpse of small mind suffering, the belly softens in compassion and wisdom as the mind/body emits the great sigh of letting go.

When soft belly is coordinated with a willingness to soften mentally, the process of letting go is reinforced and supported on many levels. Then our letting go is not, even in small mind, confused with suppression. There is no restriction of awareness, there is a going beyond, an opening into.

Letting go is a willingness not to suffer. An ever-increasing capacity to meet the moment spaciously, softly, recognizing that letting go is actually *letting be*. When the conditioned mind is not grasping, it is freed. It allows the passing show to unfold as it will without any attempt to control or contain it. It simply meets the moment as it is, openly and at ease.

Mindfulness is a means to heartfulness in the same way as heartfulness is a means to the Beloved. Without mindfulness, one is liable to repeat another mindless relationship. Another forgetfulness of being.

Following are two guided meditations on mindfulness. The first is the Meditation on Mindfulness of Breath, which focuses the attention on the sensations that accompany the breath. Noting all else that arises in the meditative mind. The second is a Meditation on Mindfulness of Process, which focuses on the breath to stabilize awareness and then expands that awareness to include not just the content but the process of the mind as well. It is a letting go into being. Many have also used the meditations as a Letting Go of Control or a Surrendering to Process Meditation.

Like the Grieving Heart Meditation, which is done alone so that we can be together, the mindfulness meditations, as well as Soft Belly and Forgiveness Meditations, are done silently, within oneself. Although they may well affect considerably the world in which this mind floats, they are the solitary preoccupation of the heart. Meditations such as the dyad practices in which two people face each other in order to cultivate a deeper sense of connection and encourage wholesome states of mind are often most effective when each has committed first to these solitary meditations. Once again we see that the work we do on ourselves is the potential we bring to relationship, the foundation for the triangle within which we collaborate toward our truest natures.

~

A MEDITATION
ON
MINDFULNESS
OF BREATH

F ind a comfortable place to sit, and settle in there. And let
your attention come into this body you sit in.

Let awareness come to the level of sensation in the body.
Feel this body vibrating with sensation. Certain sensations predominate. The sensation of gravity pulling on the body, sensations of pressure in the buttocks or as the feet are drawn to the
floor. Pressure. Sensation.

The sensations of breath in the body. Chest expanding with
each inhalation, sensation arising. Chest contracting with each
exhalation.

Sensation arising. And in the belly, each breath expanding
and contracting the belly. Belly rising with each inhalation. Sensations of stretching or filling. Belly falling with each exhalation.
Sensations of emptying or letting go. Rising and falling belly.
The sensations of the breath in the body.

Each breath filled with sensation. Moment to moment changing flow of sensation accompanying each inhalation, each exhalation. Awareness focused in the belly receiving moment to mo-

ment sensation arising in each breath. Moment to moment awareness, moment to moment sensation in the belly as it fills, as it empties.

Mindfulness of breathing. Mindfulness of breathing. If the mind wanders off sensation, gently bring it back to the moment to moment unfolding of sensation in each inhalation, in each exhalation.

Soften the belly to receive the breath fully, completely. Not controlling the breath. Just receiving it as sensation in soft belly. Softening the belly, receiving life as sensation in the softness.

If thoughts arise, let them come. Let them go. Just bubbles floating in the softness. And return awareness to the sensations that accompany each inhalation, each exhalation.

Even expectation can harden the belly, can leave so little room for thoughts and sensations to just float in awareness.

Fear. Pride. Anger. Doubt. States of mind arising and dissolving in the vast softness of a spacious awareness. With attention, come back to the sensations that accompany the breath simply noting whatever else arises, not holding. Letting it come. Letting it go.

Letting go. Returning again and again to the sensations that accompany each breath. Holding nowhere. Simply being breath breathing itself in soft belly. Letting go of whatever arises, softening the belly, returning to the breath.

Softening the belly. Returning to the breath. Notice the very beginning of each inhalation. Notice the space between and the very beginning of each exhalation. Observing the end of each exhalation as well.

Notice the moment when the breath stops and is drawn back in again. Notice that point where the exhalation ends and the inhalation begins.

Awareness and sensation meeting moment to moment in soft belly. The breath breathes itself. Let it come. Let it go in awareness.

If the attention wanders to thinking, memories, feelings, daydreaming, just watch it all come, and watch it all go. And return gently without the least judgment, to the sensations of the breath.

If the mind wanders, simply note the thinking, feeling, memories, which have drawn awareness away from sensation of the breath and gently return first to soft belly and then to the sensations arising with each inhalation, with each exhalation.

Note the very beginning, middle and end of each inhalation. Notice the space between. Notice the very beginning, middle and end of each exhalation. Sensations floating in soft belly.

Stay present. If the mind wanders after two or three breaths, be merciful. Bring it back to awareness of sensations in soft belly.

Boredom, expectation, wondering, arise and dissolve. Feelings, thoughts, arise uninvited. Simply noting movement, change. And return to the breath.

Moment to moment sensation. Moment to moment awareness. The very beginning, middle and end of each inhalation, the space between. The very beginning, middle and end of each exhalation, and the moment when the exhaled breath turns into the inhaled breath. Very minute attention to subtler and subtler sensations arising with each breath.

Mindfulness of breathing. Belly rising. Belly falling. Sensations arise in clear awareness. Breath breathing itself in soft belly.

Each breath so precious, filled with the changing flow of sensation. If the mind wanders, bring it back to soft belly and focus on the sensations floating inside that belly. Moment to moment sensation, moment to moment awareness.

Now let your attention come back to the full body. Let the attention expand from just the belly to include all the sensations arising in this body you sit in. Feel this whole body breathing, sitting, being. Moment to moment awareness of moment to moment being in the body. Breath coming and going, sensations arising all by themselves in clear awareness.

Mindfulness resting in being.

And gently let your eyes open. Mindful of seeing, of feeling, of hearing, of tasting, of touching, of thinking. Mindful of being.

Moment to moment awareness. Moment to moment aliveness. Mindfulness of being. Mindfulness of breath.

~

A MEDITATION
ON
MINDFULNESS
OF PROCESS

*This may also be used as a Letting Go of Control
or Surrendering to Process Meditation.*

Find a comfortable place to sit and settle in there. And let your attention come to the level of sensation. Feel this body you sit in.

Let awareness and sensation meet in the body. And gradually bring your attention to the abdomen moving with each breath. Let awareness come to the level of sensation generated by the breath in the belly.

With each inhalation the belly expands, sensations arising. With each exhalation the belly contracts, sensations arising.

Feel the breath breathing itself in the belly. Multiple changing sensations. Mindfulness of breathing in the belly.

And soften the belly to receive life, sensation, awareness. Softening the belly. Receiving the breath as sensation.

Breathing in, belly expanding. Breathing out, belly contracting. Let the breath breathe itself. All by itself in soft belly.

Let go of any attempt at controlling the breath. Trust it. Let it breathe itself in soft belly.

If the breath is long, let it be long. If the breath is short, let it

227

be short. Just awareness of breathing. Just sensations and awareness meeting moment to moment.

Thoughts arise. Let them come. Let them go in soft belly. Let them float like bubbles, arising and dissolving in space. Soft belly.

Let go of any control of the breath. Let it breathe itself in soft belly.

If you notice even the least tendency to hold or shape the breath, let it go. Trust the process. Let the breath breathe itself in soft belly.

Let go of control. Let go of holding thoughts, of shaping thoughts, of controlling thoughts. Let thought think itself.

Just trust the process. Trust that the next breath will come. Completely let go of control of the breath. Trust the breath to come.

Hard belly is filled with control. Soft belly has room for it all. Trust the process.

If you notice any resistance or holding pushing against the moment, just let it in. Just let it float in a soft mercy and awareness.

Letting go of control. Opening into this spaciousness of soft belly. Receiving each breath as it breathes itself in awareness. Moment to moment sensation unfolding in the vast spaciousness of soft belly.

The breath smooth and easy. Breathing itself in space. Sensations unfolding in the vastness. In the spaciousness of soft belly.

Thoughts float through like bubbles. Rising. Dissolving in the softness. In the space of just being.

Soft belly. Sensations floating in space. Breath breathing itself. All by itself. In awareness.

Feelings, emotions, pass through like clouds. Thin at the edge, becoming dense toward the middle. And passing through again.

Emotion, expectation, fear, doubt, pride. One dissolving into the next. Clouds dissolving in space. Let them come. Let them go. In soft belly. Even a moment of holding tightens the belly, obscures the breath. Let go and gently return to the sensations of the breath, floating in soft belly.

Stay present. Let the breath breathe itself. Let thoughts come. Let thoughts go. No control. No holding anywhere. Just awareness and process unfolding as it will in the spaciousness of soft belly. In the vast spaciousness of awareness. Process unfolding in space.

A moment of hearing. A moment of remembering. And coming back to the breath. Thought arising once again. Feeling, seeing, thinking—rising and dissolving one into the next. Process unfolding in space.

No control. No holding. Let fear float—rising and dissolving. No holding. No posturing. No control. The process unfolding all by itself in spacious awareness.

Just being.

Moment to moment being unfolding in consciousness. A moment of sensation. A moment of thinking. A moment of remembering. Moment to moment change. Moment to moment awareness.

Just watch thoughts end. Moment to moment change. Moment to moment thought arising and dissolving in space.

Dissolving. One after the other. Bubbles dissolving in space. Incessant change, the flow of consciousness.

A moment of seeing. A moment of hearing. A moment of feeling. One dissolving into the next. Process unfolding in space.

Just watch thoughts end. Moment to moment.

Just being. Just consciousness unfolding moment to moment in the vast spaciousness of awareness.

Just being. Moment to moment unfolding in consciousness.

Notice the very beginning, middle and end of each thought. Of each sensation. Of each feeling. Arising and dissolving in space.

Content dissolving into process. Dissolving moment to moment. Thought becomes thinking. A moment of emotion becomes a feeling. A moment of hearing becomes memory, daydream. Moment to moment process unfolding.

Process floating in space. Pure awareness receiving the moment to moment unfolding of consciousness. Resting in being.

Breath breathing itself in soft belly. Mind unfolding. Consciousness changing instant to instant. Flowing in space.

Consciousness unfolding in space. Moment to moment. Process changing moment to moment. Moment to moment change floating in moment to moment awareness.

And return to the sensations of the breath. Floating in soft belly. Moment to moment breath. Moment to moment sensation. Each inhalation, sensation. Each exhalation, sensation. Floating in space. Unfolding in consciousness.

Mindfulness of breath. Mindfulness of process. Mindfulness of the spaciousness in which it all floats.

Mindfulness of feeling, of thinking, of hearing.

Being unfolding in the boundaryless spaciousness of awareness.

CHAPTER 40

~

AN EXPERIMENT IN CONSCIOUSNESS

A CLASSICAL ACT
OF MINDFULNESS

ET THE FIRST wave pass. Notice thoughts, feelings, memories, reactions, stimulus and response, in their first arisal.

See the "original thought," the first wave that stimulates thinking. Notice the first frame in the film that sets the stage for the story to unfold. Noticing clearly the first mind-moment that is of sufficient allure to create a thought. And the attachment that dwells on that thought turning it to thinking.

That "original thought," when seen at its inception, keeps our business "current" before it even becomes business. We have never been so alive or abreast of ourselves, never quite so much a part of our own process, as when mindfulness takes the mind to heart.

Let each wave pass, acknowledge its presence. Noting it clearly, naming it softly in the mind: "fear fear," "anger anger," "joy joy," "doubt doubt." Knowing we cannot let go of anything we do not accept, embrace whatever arises. Even afflictive emotions. Meet that first thought with mercy and awareness.

Observe each original thought arise and dissolve. Notice how the least holding to that thought—how any comment, even liking or disliking—causes the mind to spin out in random thinking and furtive fantasy.

Watch small mind deny or accept that first wave. Notice any "business" it has with that original impression as it turns it to dream. Observe the tendency to trade the mystery for a thought bubble floating in that vastness.

In big mind, each thought is first thought. The next moment in the process.

Chogyan Trungpa, the Tibetan meditation teacher who instructed so many of our contemporaries in the process of deep watching, used to say, "First thought, best thought!" In this instance, he was referring to the creative process, and poetry in particular. But he was also speaking of making an art of life. Of meeting that first thought so wholeheartedly, so wide awake, that our response has the lyrical quality of song.

Imagine if your mind just thought and never got distracted thinking. If it just received the senses moment to moment in clarity. Exploring the process. Imagine living so much in the present that Narcissus didn't need to be "lost in thought" in order to prove he existed.

CHAPTER 41

~

LIVING
IN THE LAB

URING THE COURSE of Ondrea's acquiring and healing various
illnesses, as what appears to be part of her "healer's training," ten years after our collaboration on her cancer, she
received a diagnosis of lupus disease. It was on the morning of the
day we gave that healing talk which became our first public exploration of what we had so long referred to privately as the Beloved. A
doctor friend, heavy with concern, had called us in our hotel room
in San Francisco to confirm that the blood work done a few days
earlier indeed displayed what he had suspected, lupus disease—the
illness that had just months before killed Ondrea's aunt.

Having gone through the near fatal aftermath of her cancer side
by side, at times breath by breath, nonetheless I had a sense that I
could participate even more profoundly in her lupus. In meditation, just this side of the mystery, I committed to her healing in a
way I was perhaps unprepared for ten years earlier in the union.
Letting go of the last vestiges of whatever might wish to protect
itself from the pain or process of another, I pledged my whole

heart. Opening fully to experience her pain so as to have a healing access to it, even share her death if that was the case. Nothing was held in reserve. Nothing was protected from even the most physically discomforting harmonic. Nothing was protected from the consequences of love.

With the cancer I committed my mind and heart, but now there was as much a *willingness* to go through everything she was experiencing as there was a *will* to cure.

And miracles began to happen. I have never felt physically worse in my life. Experiencing her body in mine—the burning, numbness, tingling, cramping, shooting pains, joint locking, muscle contractions, nausea, dizziness, weakness and fatigue. But something else began to be felt as well—enormous waves of energy began to course through both our systems. It was like putting two hundred and twenty volts through a hundred-and-ten-volt circuit. We had to surrender into it or blow a fuse. We had to make room for what felt like a highly amplified surge of the life force. Our essential life energy, or what some call "kundalini," opened with considerable intensity, immersing us in a sense of wholeness, of directly participating in the cosmos as never before. Levels of consciousness known only fleetingly in meditation began to establish themselves with considerable regularity. About a year and a half into this process these states of clarity, energy and rapture began subtly to displace the symptoms. The body discomforts gradually diminished as the periods of inordinate lucidity persisted. Clearly it was time to check back with the local physician who two years before had corroborated the original diagnosis. Sharing just enough of our miraculous process not to frighten her we asked for tests that might display just how deeply this healing may have entered. A week later she called back and almost whispered, "I don't know what's going on with you two, but there's no lupus here!"

Some dynamic grace had allowed the heart to permeate the body. A growing sense of the mystery embracing all that was silhouetted against the enormous energy of healing.

What began as an evening's spontaneous vision and clarity extended to days and even months. Disoriented by its enormity at times, it was our love which again and again became the ground on which was being enacted the "great don't know" healing of her body.

Now a few years later, the lupus, like the cancer, has retreated from her body, and all we are left with is the mystery and the love that goes beyond fear or "knowing."

Mystical Wedding

There is a silence between births
when the heart becomes a sacred flame
and the belly uncoils
which reminds me
of how remarkable it is
to awake beside you another day.

Between deaths we've met
between breaths
in that stillness which
has joined us ever since.

In that first breath
we entered each other—
never exhaled—
and danced unnoticed
through the void.

There is a path in the woods
which opens into a green clearing—
there are bear scat there
and lion tracks
and pools cradled in the rocks
where we go for a cool drink
from Buddha's belly.

Every once in a while,
stiller than air
an old ponderosa whispers,
"You are the bride of the Beloved."
The sacred everywhere we turn
and turn again—
an intermingling of our senses
which reveals ourselves in each other
at the far end of perception
where the mind becomes the heart

and form dissolves so generously
it offers entrance to the mystery.

When you are eaten alive
by the Beloved
you are wed again
with nothing left to do
but be
there for each other,
here in each other.

At this wedding there is nowhere to stand
where you are not beside me
where you do not accompany me
within.

CHAPTER 42

~

WATCHING
IN ANOTHER

F IFTEEN YEARS AGO when I asked my teacher how falling in love
and committing to Ondrea might affect my practice, he
turned laughing and said quite incredulously, "Affect your
practice! It is your practice. Remember, your partner is your practice." It reminded me of what that other meditation master had said
about the true test of spiritual practice being illness and relationship. Each attracts grief and old small mind momentum. Each requires our whole attention and as much mercy as we can muster.
Each requires a mindful watching and a heartful embrace.

It reminded me, too, of what Buddha stated in his mindfulness
instructions: that we can learn almost as much about the nature of
mind by "watching in another" as by "watching in oneself." That
mindfulness of oneself, one's thoughts, actions, desires, is not the
only means of insight. He suggested we should explore each other
with the same keen mindfulness as one investigates oneself, observing states of mind changing in each. It breaks the near primal
identification with mind as being our experience alone, expanding
from *my* mind to *the* mind, from the personal to the universal.

There are multiple levels of connectedness, healing and insight available from the practice of *watching in another*. At first as we attempt to observe with a merciful awareness the actions of our partner, our parents, our children, our co-workers, it may not be so easy to maintain the merciful aspect of clear observation. The long-conditioned compulsion to judge may, indeed, be the first quality clearly noticed. At first blush, the watching in another is a seeing of yourself. The small mind watcher we call Narcissus becomes the first object of big mind observation.

It is important to recognize that the first mind you watch in the practice of watching another is the mind that is watching. Your expectations, perceptions, comments, fears, confusion, anger, desires, intention, need be acknowledged before they taint and interpret what is received in the watching of the simple truth of the senses. We need watch the watcher.

Before you can recognize another's physical body language, you must explore the mental body linguistics. The first step of seeing into another is the capacity to see into oneself. To not be limited by old ways of seeing, entering directly the reality of what is, as it is.

As the capacity for judgment to float in a nonjudgmental awareness increases, not even judging judgment, *their* mind and *your* mind will simply be received as *the* mind. And just as you have noticed in yourself, you will notice in another, the places that call for harmony and healing. Those areas cramped by holding and numbed by pain. Those aspects of the psyche which have gone long uninvestigated and unhealed. Fears and doubts, anger and mistrust, self-pity and greed. For some, recognizing such "stuck places" in their partner makes them feel threatened and inadequate, desirous of withdrawal to protect their all-too-human flesh and mind. But for the true lover, it is an invitation to the dance.

If we can't share our suffering, if we can't swim in the reservoir of each other's grief, the levels of connection in relationship will be relatively shallow and its potential for healing of little note.

At first we notice that other person as the words that come from their mouth, the gestures that arise in their body. We see them as thoughts and emotions, desires and needs. As the intention to truly know that person deepens, so do the levels and acuity of the watching.

You are not watching like a Peeping Tom with a secretive agenda, but rather as one of two beings in a room, in a world, in a mind often laden with limitations and pain, and a heart longing to be free. One is not staring at the other's psyche or sitting "silent as a judge" appraising the other's value. We look toward our beloved as if gazing into a mirror. We receive them with soft eyes. Not encouraging this watching to reinforce any sense of separateness across which it must leap. Indeed, mindfulness of self and mindfulness of other, if not entered heartfully, can just create more concepts of *I* and *other*. In truth, mindfulness just meets the moment as is, whether the object of the moment is my imaginings of myself or my imaginings of yourself. It illuminates the underdream.

When we recognize the healing potential in mindfulness for ourselves and another, the process takes on a life of its own.

As this merciful watching, this receiving of another, deepens, each is seen as more than just their actions and thoughts. We experience them as constantly evolving process. And there is less of a tendency to judge the unfolding. Instead there is just a simple clear observation from the heart. Watching your child, your lover, your brother, your sister, your mother, your father, yourself, as process, small mind tends to melt at the edge. *I* and *other* is seen as just a way of seeing. The courtroom is closed.

Watching small mind in another from small mind in ourselves, nothing much is furthered. In fact, this is the history of most relationships—the judging mind reacting to judgment, the frightened mind tensed by another's fear, the angry mind agitated by another's disgruntlement. When we relate small mind to small mind, we have a small relationship. The sphere of possibilities is quite limited. But when we relate *to* small mind in ourselves or in another, *from* big mind, unlimited possibilities arise, cultivating deeper levels of understanding and forgiveness, insight and connectedness.

To focus gently on another in this moment to moment openness parallels in many ways the Ah-Breath connectedness of the Bonding Meditation. Watching in another with mercy and loving kindness is yet a deeper, ongoing level of commitment and bonding.

It takes a while. The capacity to see another clearly is predicated on our progressive clarity seeing in, and of, ourselves. As these levels of connectedness present themselves we find, quite amazingly and mysteriously, a capacity to participate in that "other's space." A mystical union naturally occurs, where at times we are actually able to enter their consciousness, to see as they see, feel as they feel, hear as they hear, think as they think. As this capacity to experience another wholeheartedly increases, a considerable amount of mutual healing occurs spontaneously.

Over the years of watching Ondrea from my heart, I came to recognize certain patterns to her process. Observing the physical gestures and words that accompanied various mental states allowed me to join her in a healing she had long been awaiting. Noticing periods of very skillfully disguised disorientation and a certain self-negation when becoming lost even in familiar environments, or having difficulty on an escalator or in elevators, we discovered she had an inner ear imbalance. And eventually this investigation of her spatial disorientation, manifested ever so subtly in the confounding of prepositions, difficulty with linear directions and a certain discomfort around complex definitions, led to the recognition of previously undiagnosed dyslexia. A condition which had grieved her life with memory and comprehension difficulties and a nagging sense of not-enoughness when everyone around her seemed to understand but she. Discovering this opened up a whole new world of mercy and compassion for herself. It was the great sigh of self-acceptance. Like our friend Jerry Jampolsky, who founded the Centers for Attitudinal Healing, when he first entered medical school and at last discovered he was dyslexic, an enormous amount of healing occurred. No one was "stupid" after all. The judging mind bowed and touched its forehead to these new feet, on this new solid ground of understanding and self-mercy.

Once again, we learned together that the mind has a mind of its own and that only by relating to it heartfully and with some clarity could its suffering be released.

As this ability to watch in another evolves into the capacity to participate in another, levels of relationship previously unimagined become readily available.

In Ondrea's ability to enter with mercy and awareness the pain generated in my body by a congenital spinal condition, she was able to aid greatly in its healing. As when we focused together and pulverized my kidney stone. When two beings concentrate their beingness on the pain in either, the potential for healing increases manifoldly. The combined focus of energy and loving kindness on the cancer and later the lupus in Ondrea's body seems to have somehow propelled the healings considered remarkable by her physicians. Such meta-rational, heartborne experiments in consciousness recognize that to be in relationship is to share the mystery.

We have spoken about what occurs when small mind meets small mind (not much or too much), and about when big mind meets small mind—mindfulness. But we have just begun to touch on what it might be like when big minds meet. When big minds meet, there is but one heart.

At first we are watching another's mind. But watching mind with mind, what becomes evident is *mind only.* When we see mind only clearly, without judgment, without desperation or alarm, then even any separateness which arises does not separate. Then it is not *my* mind against *your* mind, but rather *the* mind floating in *the* heart. Then even the previously small-minded unworkabilities become largely workable.

Tuning to your partner, you watch how each state of mind prepares the way for the next. You notice in the middle of a sentence the word on which the mind turns. You come to know their process so well, their patterns and inclinations, that on occasion you can predict the next state of mind, perhaps even before they are aware of its potential arising. You are able to hear in a half-halted inhalation the difficulties of the heart. You sense in their anger the instant when letting go is possible and a responder gestures itself acknowledging that space between thoughts.

Remember always that this is a soft-bellied mindfulness. This is not a hard watching of the other. It is a simple noting, naming, of states of mind, a whisper in the heart. One does not try to precisely label each mental state, just acknowledge them. It is another opportunity for insight into the process, and perhaps even the space in which it is all floating.

This level of paying attention to another may become so refined that your body/mind becomes a diagnostic instrument which empathetically resonates with the conditions in another. You experience how the meal did not sit well in their stomach. How the sunset reminded them of that summer on the Cape. How their mind may be struggling with a certain issue. How their body may be dealing with pain.

Clearly one of the by-products of refining the practice of watching in another over the years leads to a kind of psychic interpenetration. At this level of connectedness, *I* and *other* dissolve into a mystical union, resting in the shared *Uh* of being.

In the process of watching another, qualities not fully recognized in oneself may be seen acting themselves out. One watches with care the effects of afflictive emotion, and how dense states of mind sculpt the body, observing the unique personality of each mental state. The body language, intonation and vocabulary of each emotion. And how intense desire loses any larger context, forgetful of the Beloved.

Watching with a merciful awareness the subtle emanations of another's body, their momentary awkwardness of movement, the slightly distended arch of their neck, the tilt of their head, the coloration of their skin, the tension around the mouth, the positioning of the hands and legs—in the changing of mind and body postures—the heart of each receives the process of the other.

Connecting in another, we see random acts of kindness spontaneously appear as the mind and heart pass within each other's gravitational pull and produce a gentle touch, a deep smile, a meal imbued with love, a child held, a brother comforted—a heart exposed. In such love, a dish washed, an engine fixed, a life lived.

When your beloved becomes the subject of your heart, rather than just an object in your mind, you tune to subtleties previously unnoticed watching their breath with moment to moment sensitivity as you enter your beloved's respiration. Watching the breath breathing itself, changing in quality from emotion to emotion. Entering their breath completely to sense the body/mind flow unfolding, volumes are spoken of the breather. Keeping the flow of their breath as close to you as your own allows the heart to receive your beloved on many levels.

Watching the ever-changing content of each other's process is a key to the experience of the vastness in which they float, which our consciousness exploration might name "emptiness"; and our devotional aspect might label "the sacred." But which, in the coincidence of these paths in relationship, is expressed by the mind, from the heart, as "sacred emptiness." This "Absolute emptiness" is the essence of the Beloved.

CHAPTER 43

~

SOME
THOUGHTS
ABOUT
THINKING

S OME YEARS AGO during an extended period of meditation, a few weeks into the process, the mundane mind began strongly to reassert its old-mind self. It kept repeating the same phrase over and over again. It went on and on. It wouldn't stop. And what was more disconcerting was that the sentence was a line from a Bob Dylan song. My mind was like a broken record repeating, ironically enough, "Don't think twice. It's all right!" The light seemed far away. My resistance increased my restlessness. I wanted it to stop. It fed on that wanting. It continued for hours. Exhausted with resistance and self-judgment, I went to my teacher, beseeching him to give me some means of stopping the incessant repetition in my mind. But instead of giving me a way out, he pushed me in, saying, "If you can't be bored, you can't meditate!"

Reminded that Fritz Perls had said that boredom was just a lack of attention, I focused a nonresistant awareness on resistance consciousness, boredom itself. Indeed, opening to boredom was fascinating and not at all boring, offering insight into the curative power of focused awareness. And the heart whispered to the mind, "You can think twice. It's all right. Just do it mindfully."

In the same way that you can't meditate if you can't be bored, we have come to realize you can't be in a bonded conscious relationship if you can't be occasionally dissatisfied.

Or unheard.

Or the object of another's grief.

Or confused.

Or insulted.

Or bored.

Or embarrassed.

Or forgiven.

It is hard to maintain contact if you can't let the first wave of any mental state, from fear to ecstasy, pass.

Or be mindful lightly of the darkness.

Or be steady in the face of uncertainty.

Or love another more than yourself—here a quality that leads to self-suppression in a codependent relationship leads to liberation and boundarylessness in a bonded commitment.

Or triangulate beyond your truth to *the truth*.

Or have a bad day well.

Or be held in another's heart in such purity that their love disorients your negative self-image.

Or let Narcissus come out to play—with the Beloved.

But there is something within, some "not enoughness," that believes it is not up to the game. Like the fellow who came to Maharaji and begged for his help because he was "so impure," we doubt our capacities and gifts. Maharaji looked at this fellow for a while, then walked around him poking him in his belly, looking under his hair, walking in a circle prodding him, looking under his arms, peering into his mouth and finally, laughing, said, "I see no impurities anywhere." It is from the greatness of such a great heart that we learn there is nothing that needs to be judged, only embraced. It is from prolonged contact with a heart that never closes, that sees no impurities anywhere, that our capacity to love has matured. To let yourself be loved that much teaches you to love.

It is from experiencing unconditioned love of this magnitude that the mind is called out of hiding, and mercy and awareness become as natural as the breath. When we see beyond our imagined self, imagined impurities dissolve in the vast perfection beyond superficial inconsistencies. When you let yourself be loved that much, you almost begin to see as God sees. Distrust atrophies. Even our infant paranoia is put to rest. We merge at last in the shared heart. Our wildest dreams come true. The tandem climb continues.

We are Adam and Eve, us all, searching together beyond even Eden for the essential energy which animates all consciousness, every electron, each distant star. The essence, rather than the forms, of paradise.

Love takes the mind beyond its self. Love transmutes small mind attachments into big mind commitments. Small mind is constantly shopping for "something in its size," but in big mind one size fits all.

Such love offers Narcissus exactly the safe territory he imagines she needs to "come out of the cold" of his well-defended isolation . . . The play of light and shadow observed equal-mindedly, openheartedly, moment to moment. The mind-show passing by, the process unfolding in mercy and awareness.

V

~

FINE
TUNING

CHAPTER 44

~

COMPARING
MIND

T HE ASPECT OF mind which drifts toward comparison is called the comparing mind. Comparing mind never lets us *be*. Comparing mind is judging mind. A symptom of our destabilizing imperative to accept and imprint conflicting conditioning. And to relate alternately from those differing points of view. Confusion.

Comparing mind is complaining mind. It's too big! It's too small! Narcissus does not know, or remember, what he wants. She only knows what she doesn't want. And he doesn't like anything without a shiny surface in which he can appraise his reflection. If she can't drown in it, if he can't lose himself in it, it simply won't do. But, of course, what she imagines is water is actually fire.

In Buddhism the definition of ignorance is to think you are only what you think. To believe you are only the conditioned mind and body. To forget the whole universe. To lose context. To compare yourself only to what you have thought in the past. To be your conditioning, deaf to the roar of your own great nature.

To comparing mind, the grass is always greener in the other hemisphere of the brain. It is never satisfied. It is desire fracturing the moment into fleeting acceptabilities. Comparing mind keeps us small. It compartmentalizes the vastness into *I* and *other,* acceptance and rejection, love and hate, peace and war.

Comparing mind is aching to get it right and often feels wronged. It is the auditor of our unfinished business.

Comparing mind imagines something better just around the corner. It leans into the next moment. It is seldom present.

Comparing mind is the perfectionist's addiction. It keeps us from discovering the whole truth. It is incapable of seeing perfection.

If we cannot see the perfection of this moment, now, what makes us think we will recognize it later? Each moment is a perfect opportunity to discover the perfection of the process unfolding moment to moment in the enormity always available, the ever-shining.

When we explore the self-condemnation at the core of our perfectionism, we no longer consider the comparing mind a skillful adviser. It delays grace. It keeps us stuck in judgment and negation of our perfection. Indeed, cutting through the comparing mind brings great joy and insight.

Just so, Ondrea and I have discovered that the perfect relationship does not come from finding the "perfect person," but from finding a person perfect for you. Neither of us is perfected, but we are perfect for each other.

And when the comparing mind, in a moment of fatigue or mindlessness, comments on the other's obvious holdings or "imperfections," the heart just watches the mind like a grandmother sitting by the crib of a feverish child. Soothing its brow. Singing to it of love.

When both relate *to* the separatist, comparing aspects of the mind, instead of *from* them, there is the experience of inner unity. Relating to small mind; relating from big mind.

Of course, when it comes to "big mind" and "small mind," comparing mind can have a field day. Indeed, it is wise to be mindful of such terms because of the way small mind interprets them. Big mind does not interpret. It is only experiencing. It does not judge or compare, it just receives "the relative" in the universal.

Comparing mind is the psychological correlation and demonstration of the theory in analytic physics which suggests that we alter what we measure by measuring it. It alters what we judge by judging it. Comparing mind is "a worm's-eye view" of the world. Big mind perhaps "a bird's-eye view." Come spring, big mind eats small mind.

When the comparing mind compares itself to a mind free of such agitation, it swoons with dissatisfaction. And the absence of our inherent joy startles us. We awaken from the underdream willing at last to be free. And focusing on the grief at the center of the chest, where judgment, fear and separation are fused into a dense armoring over the heart, we begin to let go of old-mind strategies and allow the comparing mind to float in the Incomparable.

CHAPTER 45

~

COMMUNICATION

S UJATA USED TO say, "Let it go! But if you can't let it go, I guess
you'll just have to communicate."
Communication is a crossing of our boundaries. At best, it
attempts to transmit the heart. At least, it attempts understanding.

Because everyone seems to be born with perceptual quirks
unique to their personality, or what some call "karma," misunder-
standing naturally arises between somewhat different "realities."
When this occurs, communication becomes a peacemaker, an attempt at understanding sent out by carrier pigeon over the fortress
walls. We think the moat of our affected indifference will protect
us. But our castles are burning. And in our confusion, we try to
hide the smoke instead of extinguish the fire. Much of our "communication" is an attempt at smoke control. Much comes from the
fear that another will see us as we fear we really are—confused and
clever, hidden and theatrical, self-interested, angry, distrustful. We
are afraid to share our grief, so little of ourselves have we surrendered to its healing. We weigh our words. No one says quite what

they mean. We bargain for love in dulcet tones like a cat wrapping itself, purring, around our ankles.

Most use language the way a sightless person uses a cane: to clear the path ahead, a kind of emotional sonar to test for safe ground. Reacting as much to tone as to meaning. Speech for most is not so much a form of communication as a proclamation of self, a marking of territory, pissing on the bushes to let those who follow know who went before. It is a declaration of dominion. Going off a few paces, lifting our leg, philosophizing.

But true communication comes out of a powerful willingness not to protect oneself or even to be right. It comes from a longing for the truth, as painful as that may be at times. It comes out of direct perception. Out of a big mindfulness of the process comes an increasing capacity to reveal blockages and embrace this unique other as is.

Communication, like relationship itself, is the art of space. It is a sense of timeliness and an ongoing exploration of the intention to communicate. It is a deep questioning of what, indeed, communicates.

It is said that Jesus, asked about acceptable eating practices, replied, "Don't worry about what goes into your mouth, worry about what comes out of it." Perhaps he recognized that, in either case, we are often most asleep when our mouth is open. So much of what passes for communication is not much more than a mumbling in our sleep. Seldom are we so mechanical or unaware as when we are telling someone who we think we are.

To small mind, communication keeps the world orderly and maintains its horizons. To big mind, communication is that which connects the heart with the disheartened. To the little mind, communication gets you what you want. To the great heart, communication is the ability to commune in beingness itself.

CHAPTER 46

~

RESPONDERS

W E HAVE BEEN speaking in the previous chapter of communication as the art of space, words that fill the gulf between the mind and the heart with healing and a gentle investigation of what maintains separateness. We have mentioned that although communication may not complete unfinished business, an ongoing communication can keep our business current.

To keep present takes more than words. Because there is within us a place which fears the beloved *other*. The slightest gesture or nuance—a wrinkled brow, a slightly squinting eye, a held breath—may overwhelm us with fear of being judged or excluded from the heart of another. We fear that others may have spied our secret and recognized how unloving and unlovable we may be.

To keep our business current we need to honor the truth. To honor each gesture and posture. To recognize that every movement is a form of communication: either an opening, a deepening of attention; or a closing, a withdrawal of presence.

To be this awake to what our body might be communicating from below the level of ordinary awareness, we need be mindful of the sensations that comprise each posture: sitting, standing, walking, lying down. And to attend very precisely to the sensations that accompany all "transitory movements" between each of these positions. To be mindful of sensation, to be present in the body, as a means of directly experiencing the states of mind which gesture communicates.

Because the body, at some levels, is just solidified mind, it is very important to be aware of the body's language. Even the best constructed words are negated by a body which says otherwise. When you say you love me but your arms and legs are crossed and your body is slightly turned away, what is the heart to believe? If you say you are speaking to me from your heart, but I notice an unusual tension around your eyes and an intermittent swallowing—a hidden agenda displayed in a holding around the jaws and hands, in the hard-bellied crossing of the legs—the meaning of your words will not compare to the nonverbal communication that warns otherwise.

Indeed, each state of mind has its own personality and corresponding body pattern, its own physical and mental tone. Each mental state has its own language and speech patterns, as well as physical and body patterns. The body pattern that accompanies each state of mind is recognized by investigating it at its inception, in its primary arising. We learn with the body, as we have with the mind, to not say anything we do not mean. We attempt to be truthful at every level, verbal and nonverbal.

Some years ago, because of our interest in animal behavior, we were quite deeply involved in the works of the extraordinary animal behaviorist Konrad Lorenz. Lorenz speaks in detail of the nonverbal language of animals. In particular he speaks of the wolf's capacity, even in major altercations, not to cause injury to the other. He speaks of the wolf's evolutionary development, of what he calls "responders": the apparently innate ability of the wolf to limit aggression with certain bodily gestures. For instance, in the midst of even the most ferocious challenges, if one wolf bows his head and shows his neck to the other, the violence instantly ceases. Displaying the neck is a responder for peace, a sign of submission. A willingness to stop there; a discontinuance of resistance.

It has occurred to us that another way the human mind has

remained unevolved is in its general lack of deep responders, its capacity to violate another without mercy or any natural limitation of heartless behavior. What we have of human responders is pretty superficial—limited mostly to "social graces." The handshake displays a weaponless nonaggression and is a form of vulnerability. The smile is a sign that there is no blood and hair in our teeth from previous predations, a display of the absence of predatory salivation. The wink, also, is a responder, but because of the multilayered conditioning of the human mind, it can be interpreted in various ways. It can be a responder of reassurance and even collaboration, or a responder for romantic or sexual attraction, or a conspiratorial acknowledgment of dishonesty (somewhat like crossed fingers behind the back), or even a challenge. But when responders have been consciously developed, there is no arbitrary quality. They, in fact, clarify such confusions, leaving a clear path to the heart.

Perhaps it is because the human mind is so enamored with itself —unable to look up from its reflection to see all the wonderful beasts that have gathered at twilight to sip of the pure waters—that responders which end miscommunication and violence haven't become woven into our genes in the same manner enjoyed by some animal species.

Recognizing the exquisite capacity of responders to keep business current in relationship, we began experimenting. We began by intentionally clearing the space across which responders were to be established. To deepen our capacity to stay present to whatever changes, expected or unexpected, might be occurring in the moment, we began working/playing with an eye-to-eye exercise. Using at first the formality of an openhearted dyad meditation, we soon brought "the shared space" into our daily process. Throughout the day whenever our eyes would make contact, unless we were involved in a demanding task, we would let go wholly of what we were doing and "die" into each other's eyes. Potting plants, walking in the woods, watching television, if one should look over and momentarily catch the other's eye, each would surrender completely into that open space. It was a practice of being instantly available to another. It was no longer a distance that could separate hearts, but the space in which they met. If I was washing dishes and Ondrea was vacuuming and our eyes met, the vacuum remained purring, the suds continued sputtering, as our eyes entered each other for several minutes, surrendering any urgencies we might imagine more important than this uniquely precious moment. Then letting go of even this exercise in letting go, our eyes gently blinking, the pupils remoisturizing, smiling, we returned to the task at hand. There is no staring in this practice, no unblinking ferocity, but only the meeting of soft eyes in the intuitive moment. Gently ending the exercise with an intuitive wink. This willingness to let go of what we were doing and attend wholly to the other, while allowing complete access to ourselves, became a very solid/spacious basis for yet subtler levels of verbal and body communication.

When we began this practice, our eyes meeting a few times a day, it was painfully noticeable how much self was being sent and how little else was being received in our desire to be seen. Or at least partially seen, still filtering just behind the eyes all that we feared might escape from our hidden thoughts. Small mind longing to be acknowledged, dissolving at its edges. Soft eyes meeting in big space.

As "the space" became readily available, various responders developed. If either slipped into "automatic," talking *at* the other, some subtle gesture arose to clear the space—a touching of the heart or a holding up of two fingers in the peace gesture. Occasionally we would make the Zen circle in the air with a flourish of the wrist as a symbol of our willingness to let go and experience the whole.

Responders are an alternative to reaction. They often signify a flipping from small mind to big mind. They breed confidence in our capacity to let go and let be. They represent the deeper levels of communication unique to each relationship.

Responders establish subtle harmonious connections that refine the rarefied interface of hearts. Recognizing a level of self-protective verbiage all too familiar in its power to separate, it departs from old reactors. Sensing the absence of another's heart—the furrowed brow, the clenched jaw, the tightened belly, the distracted glance—it softens, smiles slightly and displays open palms. Honoring the power of the unspoken to displace fear with love, the disheartened with great heart.

Of course, in this culture, given more to reactors than respond-ers, there are several old-style gesticulations which the mind inter-prets as a challenge or threat, but the heart sees as just the painful separation of minds. Indeed, children stick their tongues out at each other to signify disdain. As adults we add a bit of karmic wind and blow a few choice insults off that symbolically extended tongue. From such signals of distress, we recognize the potential of other alternatives: the bowed head, hands raised in gratitude, arms extended in praise, the head placed on the shoulder of the beloved.

This realignment of priorities which responders display is illus-trated by the story a fellow told of walking down the streets of Taos with a friend when a car of teenage "ruffians" drove by and gave them the finger. He said he noticed his belly tightening in old-mind reaction. But his friend, softening, responded, "Toward the One!" as they sped on. He had developed a new response to old reactors. In reconditioning his fear he was experiencing his joy.

When we moved back into the woods for this relationship-ex-periment-turned-lifestyle, we thought our dogs might like a wolf friend. Certainly we would, so we bought a female timberwolf. Her steady amber eyes and exceptional communication skills had us completely bewitched within days. She was clearly the most intelli-gent and affectionate animal we had ever lived with. And she taught us to howl. Some evenings Ondrea and I, the three dogs and Em-mie the wolf would sit on the back porch, necks extended toward the bright sky, howling at the moon. A chorus of intertwined hearts illuminating the sky. Our night song interlaced with the shimmer-ing hum of stars, softening the belly of the night. It had a feeling of family no less intense than any we have experienced. She taught us to howl for the benefit of all sentient beings.

In the years since, in workshops, we have stopped suggesting "a group scream" to release grief. There's enough screaming in this poor world already. Instead, we have encouraged groups to howl as a means of expressing that profound desire for a loving interaction in the sweet song of the moment.

Howling has become a responder which we find very wonderful at times. It is capable of expressing the deepest lament as well as the greatest joy. Just as we have responded to the good fortune of a loved one with tears of sympathetic joy, so we have responded to the death or misfortune of loved ones with a long series of howls.

There is nothing like howling with our children on the first day or two of their week-long visits to reestablish clan. The family that howls together seems not to growl together. If one of our children hears us playing music they don't care for or some old comedy videotape, their howl from the next room is a mixture of mild disapproval and intense love. Indeed, many years ago when one of our sons was just beginning high school, he came home one day with a ring through his nose. When Ondrea and I saw the slender gold earring perforating one nostril, which he undoubtedly hoped would create a considerable reaction, we instead responded by howling. After a few howls, we didn't mention it to him again. But for the next few days when we passed in the house, we would howl on seeing the ring. Within ten days the ring disappeared. Within a month the perforation mark on his nose had healed as completely as the mind's momentary intention to create commotion. A few months later I asked him whatever became of his nose ring and he just smiled and tilted his head back and howled and then gave me a long hug.

In quickly touching on our deep love of wolves and some of what we have learned from their great intelligence and enormous heartfulness, I am reminded of my response when a friend sent us a copy of Clarissa Pinkola Estes' *Women Who Run with the Wolves*. Recalling Ondrea's silhouette running the ridges behind our home with the wolf beside her and the dog pack close behind, I momentarily thought the book was about her. And in some ways, it was.

Once a few simple responders have been developed within a relationship as a means of refining communication, they become an organic part of its living dynamic, changing with the times. For months one signal, such as touching the heart, signifies openness and a deep listening. In another moment, perhaps "the gesture of wholeness" in which the thumb and forefinger form a perfect circle. Gestures that represent surrender or anger or fear or confusion may change over the years, evolving with each being's capacity to receive subtler and subtler levels of communication. As this process of tuning to even nonverbal signals evolves, there is cultivated "a sign language of the heart" which deepens considerably the sense of connectedness.

What began perhaps as a simple gesture to clarify the moment gradually develops into a subtle multileveled language which, even from across the room, can make one laugh or cry.

To the degree each relationship differs, it requires different responders. To the degree that each relationship is the same, any responder which cuts through to the heart becomes a path of awakening.

Develop responders to fit your unique relationship and individual temperaments. Experiment gently, continuously, to find the space in which relationship can unfold unimpeded. Responding to that which hinders and reacts. Joining in the sacred rondo of humanity howling the Beloved.

Aaaahhhhhhh ooooooooooo.

CHAPTER 47

~

PERCEPTION

W E HARDLY EXPERIENCE the world, much less this moment of its unfolding. We dream the world. We imagine it. We interpret it. We perceive it.

What we call perception is a very subjective quality, not a direct experience of the moving world, but a personalization, a reconstruction of multileveled suchness into a flat earth over whose edge we are frantically attempting not to fall.

Perception does not so much receive as conceive the world. It does not drink directly from the cup, but draws it through the long straw of its conditioning, transferring it from *the* world to *our* world. Its temperature changes. Its effervescence is lost.

Little gives rise to more conflict than when two people's perception of the same object differs. When perception is questioned, the self-image becomes threatened. When two people perceive different realities from a single event, heaven and hell arise in the slipstream. Seldom do two people disagree so much as when they interpret differently the same situation. We say we are differing about reality, but actually we are differing about *our* realities.

Driving to a workshop through the Oregon woods one summer, Ondrea and I and the driver noticed some motion by the side of the road. It was a large bird with something in its mouth. I saw a tarantula in the bird's beak. Ondrea saw a frog. The driver saw a snake. Afterward, each remarked on the frog, snake, tarantula, we had just seen in the predator's grasp. Each looked incredulously at the other's "misperception." Each condescendingly said the other must be right, though not believing for a moment that their own view was incorrect. It was an awkward moment of sociable dishonesty. After a short self-conscious silence, mindfulness returned and we all laughed. We all acknowledged that honest agreement was not possible if we were to be "true" to our perceptions. But this "true to our perceptions" had left us in small mind with nothing bigger to relate from.

To this day when Ondrea and I notice different views or senses of the same events, often to break the egocentrism of our perceptions, one will say, "It's a frog!" And the other, "No, it's a tarantula!" And together, "No, it's a snake!"

When agreement on perceptions seems unlikely, we recall what the tiny door said to Alice in her gigantic wonderland when she asked to pass through to the other side, but then remarked, "Oh, but it's impossible!" to which the door replied, "Nothing is impossible. I'm just impassable." Although we may, at times, seem to be at an impasse about that which is to each so obvious, when we recognize the limits of conditioned perception, each approaches that which passes beyond conditioning and manifests unconditioned love.

There is no time when letting go is more appropriate than when contention arises about individual perceptions. At that point, only an opening into deep "don't know" will suffice and give rise to a willingness to investigate perception rather than defend it. As one comes to understand the nature of perception, one is no longer surprised by misperception.

Indeed, one can gain considerable insight into the nature of perception looking at a rose. When the heart is open and the mind is still, the rose is soft in texture, rich in fragrance and luminous in color. But if, in another mind-moment, in another state of perception, one observes that same rose from an agitated mind, the rose personifies dissatisfaction. It is all thorns and wilted edges. Same rose, different minds. Neither is right. Each is just the moment. Thich Nhat Hanh says, "When the flower is real, you are real." When we see the whole flower, we see from whole being. And when we go beyond our conditioned way of seeing, we become the rose.

When perception itself becomes the object of observation, we are one step closer to living beyond the perceived. Mindful of the process, we are no longer in the fragile stance of attempting to defend our limited perceptions.

We imagine that perception is "what is to be seen." But it is only "what we see" of what there is. What we imagined to be seen. The leap from retina to recognition traverses all our personal history, recreating it moment to moment, projecting it on the screen of the senses.

Perception of the present is conditioned by how we have perceived the past. It slaloms through labyrinths of partially recalled epiphanies and all-too-familiar demons. It is more an articulation of memory than a recording of the senses. In the instant between happenstance and recognition, the great lie—the illusion of our smallness—presents itself quite clearly. By the time an event is acknowledged by the mind, it has shrunk from its universal enormity to a tiny bubble of thought. It has lost its bliss. The ever-new has become infinitely old.

Direct perception is quite different. It is an entering into sensory consciousness without interpretation or translation altering what is into what we think it is. Direct perception arises out of the "don't know" investigation of perception itself. It is an unwillingness to take anything secondhand, even from the mind. A dissatisfaction with mere "understanding." Observing perception directly, we learn to perceive directly. Not just "hearing," but exploring sound at its very first brush with the eardrum. Watching the mind label it as bird or car or music. Observing that concept displace the song as it chooses sides. Small mind watched with a merciful awareness that makes it big mind. And we no longer see a world of shame or fear or doubt, we simply see the world. As big mind perception develops, you can observe the world originate moment to moment on the brink of creation as it leaps from the eyeball to realms of fantasy and myth. You can watch perception funneling the world into its image and likeness. Perception is the dream screen onto which we project our world view and blindness. Narcissus is our misperception of perception itself.

The investigation teaches us that long-conditioned thought is insufficient to see the truth. That small mind defines and defends its truths, while big mind opens to embrace Narcissus, holding steady the entrance to the heart.

Each person has a unique sensory attunement. In each temperament there is a particular grace: one sense is more available than the others to direct perception. In Buddhism, for instance, each bodhisattva is associated with a predominant "sense door." And so is each bodhisattva-in-process. I am most sensitively attuned to hearing. The unfolding of the nature of mind is most readily perceived when focused on the hearing process. Ondrea, on the other hand, is most attuned to seeing. She experiences the flow of consciousness and receives the resulting insights most directly from seeing "seeing" break into a shimmering veil of constituent particles. She is quite literally able to see a moment at a time.

It is of considerable importance to comprehend and explore the predominant sense door of your partner. If I am a "hearer" and my partner is a "seer," I need to hear how she sees. And she needs to see how I hear. The sensory terminology we use alerts our partner to the sense we are most embedded in. Directly perceiving their experience—as is possible with such practices as the watching in another and bonding exercises—we are able to comprehend the language within language. So, although we may disagree about individual perceptions, we never differ about the nature of perception itself. Or as one fellow put it, "We always agree about everything, just not always at the same time."

Ondrea and I have long had varying perceptions of the color I would call blue and she would call green. In a turquoise room our comparing minds could go crazy if we let them. I know it's blue. She thinks it's green. I am right. She is confused. Heaven and hell are set infinitely apart.

And Ondrea, sitting at the next desk, seeing this last line, turns to me and asks, "Are the walls in that heaven blue or green?" as a wisp of brimstone wafts through the room. Differing, we agree about the nature of disagreement, laughing that even when we wear matching shirts, the same color, we contend about what that color might be. At times it seems impossible for the undifferentiated heart to tell whether we are the same or different—such is the heart's boundaryless nature before the superimposure of small perceptions.

The Top 40

The mind is like an old Wurlitzer.

We are a jukebox
of personal history.
Press 2B and its story
automatically ensues—
oldies but goodies, the hit parade.

We have heard all each other's stories
a dozen times—
soften, how delightful
to be here together.

CHAPTER 48

~

WHO'S
IN CONTROL
HERE?

I T IS ONLY our sense of powerlessness which seeks power. In order
to hide the great insecurity that there's not really someone in here
as solid and stable as everyone insists there must be, we camou-
flage our feelings that something must be wrong with us, since no
one else is tipping their hand. We grasp at power to disguise what
sometimes seems a wild river within. We attempt to landscape the
banks of the raging torrent.

As infants, acquired control kept us from soiling our clothing. As
children, boundaries defined the uncontrollable. Born into uncontrollable impermanence, the conspiracy of fear insists we get the
upper hand. When we attempt to control the moment, it is pulled
beyond our grasp, leaving us with disappointment, distrust and
fear, engendering the need for safe territory in which to hide. When
we are out of safe territory, we often feel "out of control." As adults,
identifying with the powerlessness that demands control turns us
old. Our desire for control defines heaven and hell. We imagine
heaven as orderly and well controlled, the ultimate in safe territory.
And call the uncontrolled hell. Indeed, Sartre defined hell as *no exit,*

no control. Even in Dante's Inferno, over the archway that leads to the underworld is the inscription "Abandon all hope, ye who enter here." It is not a curse but a blessing capable of turning hell to heaven. It recommends the letting go which allows us a letting be. Recognizing that one of the afflictive states we sloppily label "hope" is actually a hopeless reaction to helplessness, a feeling of things being beyond our control, a distrust in the present which longs for a different future. But to relinquish hope based on fear, to move toward that which is founded in confidence, trust in the process, is to turn even the hellish into the divine.

To let go and trust the next millistep beyond our edge is to discover the living truth as it unfolds in great "don't know." It is to step from small mind distrust in what might be coming around the next unknown corner to big mind fascination with each unique unfolding. Small mind prays for control. But to big mind it is interference. Cultivating this "don't know" trust, we are perhaps graced with a glimpse of the enormous process out of which each thought and species arise. It gives us the confidence to go beyond control and enter heartfully even the fear that impotently demands dominion over impermanence.

A fascinating insight into the nature of the suffering that control creates can be directly perceived in working with physical pain.

When we attempt to control our pain, harden to it, force it from the body, our life becomes an emergency. Our pain turns to suffering. For many years we did an exercise in workshops where we directed the group into an exceptionally uncomfortable position and asked them to maintain it for five minutes. In the beginning, just as the discomfort was causing muscular tension and some pain, we told the group emphatically, "Fight it! Whatever you do, don't let it in. Push it out! Push it out!" As people tried their hardest to control the pain, the groans of discomfort in the room rose to become a chorus of fear and trembling. The attempt to control pain causing uncontrollable suffering . . . Then we said to the group, "Now soften. Now let go. Don't hold onto the pain. Don't push it away. Just let it be there. No attempt at control. Just let it be." And the chorus of distress softened into a great sigh of relief. As each softened to their pain, as each let go, the pain—a hard sensation softened to—became quite workable, not dragging suffering in its wake.

It would be unrealistic not to acknowledge that in some circumstances where we have no physical control, we may experience injury or accident. This is why the Zen master tells us to "watch our step." But generally, this is not the case, and our attempts at control are more on the mental than physical level and just close the heart, keeping us distant from that which we love. When we check back to soft belly and recognize the hardness floating there, there is a recognition of the trail of tears that our inadequate attempts at control have frozen in the body. And we soften and let go. We soften and let be at last. No one in control. Nowhere to go. Nothing to do. No one to be. Just beingness itself unfolding perfectly in the vastness of our truest nature.

When the mental superiority games and the physical hard-belly postures are at last released, when we eventually take a breath, all the control games are seen for what they are: a tyranny to the heart too painful to endure if we attempt to hold on, and almost too spacious to believe when we let go.

Sometimes a desire for control, arising from our sense of helplessness, leads to the subtle abuse of overpowering or disempowering another as a means of seeming more real to oneself. How often do we lose control of our desire for control and cause pain to another? Or ourselves?

Of course, letting go of control is easier said than done. It is a slow process of trusting the ground beneath our feet. A process of being willing, perhaps even before we are able, to begin to relinquish our grasp on the results of our long-rehearsed seeming spontaneity. Investigating the desire for power, we experience its origins in our unspeakable fright at existing in a world of incessant change that is well beyond our control. Entering directly this fear leads to a freedom as wild and unrestrained as the heart of the Beloved, as the Enormity itself.

One of the attributes of the true lover is this deep willingness to just *be* with another *as is* in the ongoing exploration of the heart.

We have found in our own process, having watched fear so deeply, so often, that this letting go of the need for control allowed a deeper sense of the interdependency and interrelatedness that we shared with each other and ultimately all sentient beings. When fear engendered controlling behavior, we noticed our heart close not only to the other but to itself. Never feeling quite so helpless as when directed to maintain control.

Thus, we have over the years discovered through mindfulness and various experiments in consciousness ways of working with and letting go of this profound need.

One of the first exercises which displayed for us a way of entering and healing this habitual insecurity occurred when we were dancing one day and experimented with switching leads. All of a sudden, I didn't know how to dance, stumbling over my feet when Ondrea led. I was so used to providing direction that I didn't know how to follow. We laughed, tears rolling down our cheeks, at the absolute absurdity of how synaptically habituated we had become to our roles. I only knew how to dance when I was in control. Ondrea had no difficulties . . . We recommend this practice to all. Allow the person who normally leads while dancing to follow. Keep letting go. Watch the mind's reaction to changing roles and the flickering sense of powerlessness which habituates toward power.

As an aside I might mention that it always struck us as odd that anyone would want to be President. Who would want such authority except one who has a profound sense of powerlessness? Perhaps that is why we elect politicians instead of leaders. We elect the most frightened of the lot: those who require power in order to maintain their fragile self-image. I wonder how George does when Barbara leads? Does it make him nervous and in need of being presidential?

A teacher once said if I listed all the places "I had it together," all the places I was in control, all my "powers" in the world, I would have a compendium of that which separated me from the Beloved. And added that most of the people he met who said they had their shit together were standing in it at the time. He recognized that letting go of power did not result in powerlessness, but instead in a sense of connectedness, of nonseparation, of interrelatedness. That surrender is not defeat but a letting go of resistance to the next perfect moment. And that, if on your list you included all of the times in your relationship you had "everything under control," were the leader in life strategies, the sole initiator of events, you might discover an enumeration of your fear of death, and of being fully alive.

If switching leads in the dancing experiment seems fruitful to define and let go of control, you might investigate other experiments in consciousness equally useful to "break ranks." To allow the person who is most often the follower, or facilitator of the other's vision, to be the visionary and leader, the next step might be an experiment in which the usual initiator practices helplessness by remaining completely still, arms at their sides, while their beloved spoon-feeds them. Notice how the hands wish to go up to wipe the soup from your chin. Watch how you are wondering how much longer this may have to go on. Watch the mixture of giddiness and terror at this ever becoming a lifestyle. Watch the fear of old age and the considerable desire for control that arise as your partner wipes your lips or picks a piece of spaghetti from the corner of your mouth. And how do you feel when they wipe your runny nose for you?

An excellent preparation for going deeper into this experiment in letting go of control is the Meditation on Mindfulness of Process where we allow the breath to just breathe itself. To completely and utterly let go of control of the breath and just trust the process. To not shape or hold the breath in even the slightest manner. Most discover they don't even trust the next breath. They feel the need to contain the breath in order to just keep breathing.

We don't even trust the next breath! We fear we will die if we are not in control. In letting go, however, in simply trusting the process of the breath breathing itself, the belly softens, the mind clears, the heart opens. Becoming familiar with our fear, having explored it from its inception, deep latent tendencies do not act themselves out. There is a sense of participating in this process without having to direct it. When mindfulness embraces this tendency toward control with mercy and awareness, it breaks its compulsive momentum. It is not that the desire for control or the feelings of helplessness do not appear, but they arise in a spaciousness that feels no urgency to act, much less react. Just a heartful recognition that these tendencies still exist as part of the passing show of old conditioning.

Just as in the dancing experiment—tripping over your own feet, no control, laughter where once there were tears. Soft belly where once there was hardness. Big mind where once there was small. Another practice in bonding play, in surrender and trust, is called "blind walking." Go into the backyard or even in your living room blindfolded and guided by your partner. Another experiment in helplessness and trust, another joy beyond description. Perhaps a few bruised shins as we discover the ground beneath our feet.

And perhaps of lesser intensity, but equal commitment to go beyond the old, is to practice "uncontrolled listening." One partner accepting responsibility to listen "without the least taint of reactivity" to all the other has to say for a prescribed period of time. Allowing them to share their secret heart without fear of being corrected or even interrupted. Or perhaps better than calling it "listening," it might be more accurate to call it simply a "hearing" of the other. Even listening denotes a certain duality across which this information must pass. But hearing is present, availability, receptivity without interpretation or judgment. Indeed, it may take a long time of listening to the other before you can truly hear them. Listening is between I and other. Hearing is in the moment. Small mind listens. Big mind hears.

To deepen our "don't know" trust in the process is to explore with intuitive joy the places we angle for control. Which for many brings us to sex.

The next step in this process of letting go of control for most may well be to focus on sexuality. Many old-mind control strategies and feelings of powerlessness can be discovered in mindful sexual activity. An investigation of deep-rooted feelings of power and powerlessness can be explored by changing the pattern and process of our often habitual sexuality. Again, switch leaders. Whoever normally initiates sex surrenders that initiatory power to their partner. If, for example, it is the man who usually initiates sex, the woman is given all the power to say when, where and how. In any relationship configuration it is not difficult to sense how this might be a profitable experiment in truth.

It is a new form of sexuality: instead of switching partners, you switch the ways of partnership. You break even the slightest sem-blance to a master-slave relationship. This is an interesting experi-ment for even limited periods of time. Experiment for a few days, a week, a few weeks or even a month, depending on your sense of the appropriateness of this practice to balance any controlling habitualities which may remain. Such experiments are a powerful way to watch desire and our all-too-unconscious addictions to sat-isfaction on our own terms.

The more you feel such exercises are not for you, the more they may be!

In conscious relationship, there really is no leader, just partners in a tandem climb. Thus any attempt at control must be acknowl-edged at its inception, perhaps with a responder, before that which connects two people in their climb is stretched to its maximum, taut and unyielding, more a bondage than a safety line.

As a friend said, "Even though you may think that God is in control, he is not! No one is in control—be like God, let go of control, don't be separate from anything."

CHAPTER 49

~

FEAR
OF . . .

W E CAN SAY we are afraid of commitment, or trusting, or vulnerability, or monogamy, but the problem is not commitment or monogamy—the problem is fear. As important as it is that we embrace the *objects* of our fear, mindfully investigating their draw on our consciousness, it is that much more important that we explore fear itself.

Not confined to its content, but open to its process, we meet fear as fear itself in the moment it arises before it is reflected off the objects that we fear. Buddha said that we can pick the leaves off a bush day after day but it will continue to sprout and regenerate more of the same, or we can finish it once and for all and "cut it at the root."

Fear is a growth inhibitor. It keeps us stuck at our edge. Unable to take a single step beyond safe territory into the Great Unknown of our deepest nature. It is fear that obscures the sun and generates what Saint John called "the dark night of the soul," when the old has fallen away and the new has not yet quite presented itself. In that grace which is not always pleasant but always brings us closer to our true nature, we surrender our fear, trusting something kinder. The fear of small mind responded to fearlessly in big mind. (To small mind there are big fears, but to big mind there are only little fears.) Opening to the frightful insistence that we escape immediately, we settle in observing the compulsion to suffer, our attachment to our fear. And let go lightly into the vastness in which its process is unfolding.

In any such profoundly growth-inducing work as relationship, fear will not be an unfamiliar visitation. Like resentment it arises naturally, though painfully, in whatever distance remains between the mind and the heart. Fear arises as we approach our edge, the place where all growth occurs. In the psychodynamics of growth, fear can be a signal that we are approaching the unknown, the wholly new. Indeed, one can only expand in direct proportion to one's capacity to let go of fear and take the next step.

Because we have an imagined self, we imagine we must defend it. But the self-image is easily insulted, and if we are not mindful we will be fearfully defending it all day long. As one teacher said, "The truth is just one insult after another."

To insult another intentionally is to create suffering, but to insult ourselves all we need be is truthful. This is perhaps why relationship work is one of the most difficult spiritual practices. Twenty-four hours a day, seven days a week, there is no escaping the truth. We are pledged to confront our shadows and accept our light. It means nothing less than letting go of our fear and suffering. It is the hardest work we will ever do.

It is perhaps fear that is the very basis of our unfinished business. Fear of not being loved, fear of not being able to love, fear of unkindness, fear of being misunderstood. Fear is the musculature of our grasping. To be in relationship is to have a spectacular opportunity to work on these muscles. Indeed, the person you love most might well also be the person you fear most. They have your self-image in the palm of their hand. They know you like no other and you may fear, in some paranoid hilarity echoed in the back wards of the mind, that they will tell the world what a fool you really are. It is the perfect helplessness of love. The considerable vulnerability of the unprotected mind when the heart takes precedence.

Fear taints what we love. When we look at a beautiful flower, our heart is filled with gratitude for its form and color, its fragrance and texture, and we long for that beauty to remain—and fear it will not. Even in states such as ecstasy, there can be a fearfulness that this wonder will not continue.

To be in a conscious committed relationship is to be at the center of the laboratory of our fear and greed, our distrust and doubt, our longing and joy. We can experiment with our fear of abandonment, of being unloved, of being misunderstood; our fear of the opposite sex, our fear of the same sex, our fearful resistance to things as they are, and the dreadful need to change another into our image and unlikeness. Investigating our attachment to fear, we can analyze all the fears of a lifetime without gaining much insight into the nature of fear itself. And no matter how much work we do with any object, there will always be another along in just a moment. Working with the objects of fear does not decrease the tendency to be afraid. It only alters the object from which it is reflected. Better to work with fear itself. Indeed, rather than ask only, "Why am I afraid?" confront the *real* questions. What is fear? (All states of mind, even the heaviest afflictive emotions, can be investigated.) How does it feel in the body? What is its physical pattern? What is it doing in the belly? Is it more evident on one side of the body than the other? What is happening behind the left knee, the right knee? What is the jaw doing? Where does the tongue lie in the mouth? Does it press against the roof of the mouth, against the bottom teeth, does it curl against the palate, does it move to one side or another, does it stay steady?

"What is fear?" is a deep investigation that can take us beyond fear. "Why am I afraid?" is a superficial analysis which often keeps us trembling at every passing shadow. "What is fear?" is a big exploration of the small. "Why" is a small inquiry into huge entanglements, which helps but does not heal.

Having explored the body pattern that accompanies fear, we enter now its mental patterning—its tone of voice, its vocabulary, its intentions, its associated mental states. We know the difference between fear and joy because each has its own qualities. What are the qualities of this state of mind we call fear? Relating to the fear instead of from it, the very willingness to enter and investigate it is already an act of fearlessness. The healing is already on its way. To investigate the uninvestigated. To come to our edge and take one step further into that which lies just beyond the boundaries of our fear.

To work with fear directly rather than projecting the cause of discomfort onto another is to recognize the nature of fear as an uninvited selflessly mechanical process that naturally unfolds when triggered. Watching fear at first as content, as small mind rumination, eventually opens us to its big mind process: just *the* fear in *the* mind. It is not something one judges or even attempts to withdraw from. Instead, one approaches fear with a merciful awareness and gentle understanding, that though what we see in the mind may be unpleasant, by observing it, we discover *who we are not* and can continue unimpeded toward our true nature.

When we speak of "going beyond the mind," we are speaking of expanding awareness to levels of consciousness beyond our conditioned fears. To go beyond the mind means to go beyond the old. It does not mean to stop thought, but only not to be stopped by old thinking. It means to observe from inherent vastness the acquired smallnesses we occasionally mistake for our life. Beyond the conditioned mind lies that which is sought beyond anger and expectation, loving and hating, winning and losing, fame and shame, name and form, birth and death.

When we go beyond the seductive contents of our fear, we enter, fearlessly, the process of its unfolding and experience directly, beyond minds big or small, the enormity of the heart in which such concepts and fears float.

When we are relating to fear instead of from fear, the music changes. It's not that an old tune won't play from time to time, but that these latent tendencies no longer feel driven to dance. The Top 40 is still playing in the back room—there is still some fear, anger, distrust, doubt, longing—but one does not feel compelled to react in wild gyration. Tapping the toe now and again will do. Fear may still arise out of old momentum, but it is responded to with such mercy and awareness that one is not afraid. Though fear floats through the mind, the inner experience is a fascination and even joy in not being caught in the same old ways, of not even being frightened of fear, of living life anew, of being fully alive in the moment.

When fearfulness is absent from the mind, what remains is the natural state of beingness unobscured by grasping to fear. And that natural state is loving kindness.

Is it not perfectly ironic that it is the investigation of fear that makes us fearless? Just as it is the exploration of anger that teaches us to love, and the investigation of ignorance which brings wisdom. We learn to love by exploring what its absence feels like. We learn to be kind by examining how unkindness conditions the mind and body.

As the arms of the Beloved open to us, relating to ourselves from the heart, fear has so much space in which to simply be, so familiar are we with its nuances, that it no longer closes us. But, in fact, awakens us to the pain in the heart of all sentient beings, and calls us each to open to the healing we all share.

~

A MEDITATION
ON
AFFLICTIVE
EMOTIONS

*This is a meditation for investigation of the identification with
dense mental states, such as fear, doubt, anger or pride, which
can contract the mind and narrow access to the heart.*

Find a comfortable place to sit and take a few smooth, deep
breaths into the body.
Although the mind has many voices, let its words just float.
Watch the momentum unfolding.

Just let thoughts think themselves as the even flow of breath
begins to soften the body.

Let the belly soften to receive the moment. In soft belly we
have room for it all. In this softness allow awareness to roam
free in the body, exploring sensations.

Notice any areas of tension or denseness.

Notice areas of pressure or movement. Of heat or cold.

The tinglings, the vibratory quality.

Softly allow awareness to receive the body.

Does this state of mind have a correlation in the body? Is there
a body pattern for this emotion?

Feel the sensations that accompany this state of mind as they arise in the muscles, bone and flesh. Feel the physical imprint of this mental state.

Explore the sensations in the stomach and belly. Is there tension? Holding? Resistance?

Let awareness move gently into the chest. Is the breath constricted? Is there some desire for control which attempts to shape and hold the breath?

Let the attention be drawn to whatever sensations predominate. Explore the body pattern of this state of mind.

What has mind labeled these feelings?

Does it call them fear?

Does it call them anger?

Does it call them joy?

Acknowledge the state of mind. Note it. Each state of mind has its own particular qualities. What are the qualities of this moment?

Let awareness explore the moment to moment process of this feeling in the body.

Are these sensations changing?

Do they move from one area to another?

Is the body pattern of this state enunciated more in one area than another?

In the back or the neck?

In the gut?

What are the sensations in the tongue? Is it pushing against the teeth? Pressed against the roof of the mouth? What holding is exhibited there?

What is occurring at the top of the head?

Noticing, area by area, the mind's expression in the body.

Examine the constant unfolding of thought silhouetted against this wordless presence at the center of sensation.

What are the voices in the mind/body?

Simply listen. Nothing to answer back. Just receiving.

Note the intonation of these voices, their intensity. Allow the awareness to settle a bit more deeply into its listening.

Is it an angry voice?

A frightened voice?

A confused voice?

Listen to the tone.

Is there a noticeable intention in the voice? What is the intention of this state of mind/body, of this emotion?

Does it make you feel better or worse?

Does it wish you well? Does it take you closer to your true nature? Does it accept you as is?

What might be the effect of bringing forgiveness or love into this mind/body? Would it resist letting go of its suffering?

Is this a voice we wish to take counsel from? Does it lead us to wholeness or defeat?

Is there self-care in that voice? Or is there judgment, or pity, or doubt?

Just listening. Just receiving the moment as it is.

Do these feelings have a point of view, a direction they insist you travel? Where is the love? The mercy and kindness? Where is the healing in their offering?

Now allow the attention to enter into the deep movement within this state. Feel its energy, its changeability, its process unfolding in space.

Is it a single emotion or is it made up of many different feelings? Does it display a single mood or is it constantly changing expressions?

Perhaps many feelings are noticed. A moment of pride dissolving perhaps into a moment of anger.

A moment of aggression dissolving into a moment of self-pity.

A moment of judgment dissolving into a moment of hopelessness.

Each feeling melts, dissolving constantly from one state into the next. Begin to focus on the process, not simply the content.

Notice the quality of change within this seemingly solid state. Focus on the movement within.

Let the awareness focus into a moment to moment examination of the discrete elements which constitute the flow of this experience. See the multiple tiny thoughts and sensations which form the framework of this experience.

Notice the impersonal nature of these states we took so personally. Notice how they plead their case. Notice how they insist they are real and insist they will go on forever, even though they are constantly changing.

Notice the repetitive quality within. Notice how each voice, each sensation, each feeling, melts automatically, one into the next.

Watch how naturally each thought ends. Watch how spontaneously the next thought begins.

Observe the next voice, the next feeling arising. Watch how each state of mind/body is in process, arising and dissolving into the next.

Notice how the process is constantly unfolding.

Let it all float in awareness. Let it unfold moment to moment.

Watch how each state arises uninvited. Constantly coming and constantly going. Watch the incessant birth and death of thought.

Watch how life is constantly unfolding all by itself. Observe how thoughts think themselves. Notice how feelings feel themselves.

Give these constantly changing sensations and thoughts a little more space, a little more room to unfold in a soft body, an open heart.

Let the belly breathe all by itself. The chest clear. The throat open. The tongue soft and gentle in the mouth.

Just receiving the moment as it arises without the least clinging or condemning.

Nothing to change. No one to be.

Just the merciful space of exploration in which the moment to moment process unfolds.

All which seemed so solid before is seen constantly dissolving in space. Not creating the moment, just receiving it.

Watching it all as process unfolding, observing wholeheartedly what is.

Letting each moment of experience arise as it will in a spacious awareness. Floating. Constantly unfolding in vast space. Watching thought come and go in spacious mind.

Letting sensations arise and dissolve in soft body. Allowing.

Soft belly noticing even the slightest holding. Soft breath opening around even the least tension.

Receiving. Observing. Resting in being.

Letting come. Letting be. Letting go.

Space for it all.

This moment an opportunity for liberation and healing.

This unfolding, life itself, so precious, so fully lived.

VI

~

EVERYTHING
THAT HAS
A BEGINNING
HAS
AN END

CHAPTER 50

ENDGAME

SEPARATION, DEATH AND CONSCIOUS DIVORCE

E VERYTHING THAT has a beginning has an end. Indeed, the end is inherent in the beginning. Even at the moment of birth there is a contract with death. One in time will experience the death of the other.

Opening now to the impermanence of your relationship makes the moment so large. To be motivated by fear of the future does not serve anyone well. To be motivated by gratitude for the present gives us room to love now, here in this fragile millisecond we are allowed together.

Ondrea says there are three "kind-of-koans" in relationship. A koan is a wisdom riddle used in Zen training to confound the mind and present the immediate heart.

She says the first of these relationship riddles is, "Who is this person?!" This takes time and attention.

Then as bonding occurs the koan becomes, "How can I live with this person?!"

Trusting the process, the most mystical of all unions occurs—two humans becoming mercifully human together in love.

Then she says, when true hearts are shared, the koan becomes, "How can I live without this person?!"

The Thai Zen master Achaan Chah offered the teaching that "The glass is already broken." When a devotee asked how anyone could find happiness in a world of such unpredictable happenstance and impermanence, Achaan Chah held up a fine crystal goblet presented to him earlier. He said that he liked the goblet very much: the sun splayed rainbows onto the water as it passed through the glass, the fine crystal rang when tapped. But that when the sleeve of his robe brushed it from the table, or the wind blew it from the shelf and there it lay in its new incarnation, its light broken into a hundred shimmering shards, he was not disappointed or surprised. Because he knew that the glass was already broken. Even when first seeing the glass, he had acknowledged its impermanence and appreciated it "for all it was worth." In fact, he said, because of its incessant potential for change, he appreciated it all the more in the form it had momentarily taken, while it lasted. And recognized that "goblet" was just one moment in its process—one name in a thousand shapes and incarnations from dust to pearl.

In the same way, this relationship you are in is already broken. If no karmic wind blows it from the shelf before then, death will certainly affect it eventually. Every relationship only has a moment more to complete itself. It is here in the contemplation of endings that we learn yet more painfully about living with the consequences of love. Indeed, the more intensely bonded a couple may be, the more intense their absence across the breakfast table. Some, speaking of the incredibly painful time when their beloved died, have told us that they were in some ways relieved that the person they loved died first. They were willing to be alone on their own deathbed in order to be present for the death of their beloved. Willing to go on alone as part of their commitment to their loved one's process. This is the heart of the true lover, open to whatever arises in the alleviation of their beloved's suffering.

But death, of course, is not the only denouement of relationships. Of the many romantic or even harmonic love couplings you've developed, only one, if any, will be beside your deathbed.

From all these earlier relationships some type of separation has occurred. Most of your relationships disappeared like Narcissus into the denser realms of consciousness. Indeed, even death cannot break a bond like the disunion of hearts. The loss of a desired relationship through divorce, because it has an added element of abandonment, can be yet more painful than a loss through death. Divorce is more final than death. In divorce the relationship is ended. But in death, many continue their relationships on one level or another long after their beloved has passed beyond/within. Death breaks the human heart, but abandonment shreds it.

One day we experienced both these kinds of losses with two women in their mid-sixties grieving for their husbands. One was in the waiting room of a hospital, having just been told that her husband of forty years had died of the heart attack he suffered while shoveling snow from their driveway. Her enormous outpouring of loss opened the hearts and melted the bellies of all who were near. Her helpless cries, the tremolo for lost loves from the beginning of time.

Two hours later, Ondrea's blouse still dappled with the widow's tears, a gray-haired woman approached us in the parking lot. Having previously attended one of our workshops, she embraced us, shaking, saying that her husband of nearly forty years had run off with his secretary. Her choking lament and frantic helplessness hardened the bellies and disturbed the hearts of all within earshot. The abandoned woman's grief was greater for the rejection and coldheartedness which she felt was "aimed like an arrow at my heart."

The first woman, over the next year, built an altar in her home to her husband. Lighting candles regularly. Speaking to him often. Hearing him daily. Dreaming of him, playing with him, making love to him. The relationship as strong as ever. Experiencing an unbroken connectedness which even death could not disturb, she would have been the last to say she was without relationship. "He's always with me, and though sometimes I feel alone, I'm never really lonely." She celebrated her forty-first wedding anniversary dancing with him at dusk on the porch they had built together, continuing the mystery of their union. Open to the next moment, fully alive in big "don't know."

The second woman, over the next year, experienced an interminable grief, full of shattered expectations and burning distrust, as she removed from her home everything that reminded her of her husband. She said, "If I had been widowed I would grieve my husband's death, but being divorced I need grieve my own." In her own way, she "altered" the house to suit her healing. Her heart imploding, her breath thin as a sparrow's, she did not seek to love or dream. But as she began to trust at least herself enough to grieve, she embraced her wounded heart and began offering to herself the loving kindness never fully received and all too soon retracted. She said she realized that no one could save her life but herself, the grieving mind sinking into the healing heart, her pain turned toward service to others and the space between breaths.

She said the more she explored the anger that separated them and allowed forgiveness to fill that separation, the easier it was to feel gratitude for the good times and remember herself as the Beloved during the difficult ones.

Each woman living alone with the consequences of love as best she could. Each following her own unique path through her own particular pain to discover, just beneath the helpless separations of small mind, the inseparable heart. Each saying good night to the Beloved just before closing her eyes. One to her deceased husband, the other to herself.

Most of our relationships do not end in death, but are interrupted by the vagaries of the mind. Although the premise of this book is that relationship is a rich field of work on oneself, that does not mean that every relationship is a working relationship. Ideally, in each relationship each partner would maintain a mindfulness of the priorities of the heart. But that, unfortunately, is not always the case.

Working for a while with an individual who does not wish to work on themselves can be profound work on ourselves. A deep yoga of letting go of attachment to results or even expecting gratitude for acts of kindness or consideration. However, if the sense of separation continues unremittingly and there seems no meeting of the minds possible—and the heart has gone out of the equation—the two may, with a deep sigh of disappointment and a certain sense of self-respect, acknowledge their unwillingness to commit any more energy to the "continued unworkability" of the unraveling collaboration. But though the two may not find common ground in the mind, they may still share a common desire that their separation not condition in them further separations. A willingness to make this *the last divorce,* used as a healing of all they left behind.

Of course anyone, in an ongoing evolving relationship, may at times feel that it isn't working. Even in the most workable relationships, a desire to withdraw may arise on occasion, when our Narcissus refuses to let go or has become threatened by the clarity of its own reflection. Because of this tendency to defend that which causes us suffering—the self-image, our fears and longings—we suggest to most couples who have been attempting a working relationship that even if they do sense that parting is appropriate, they might consider exploring together for at least three months the causes and future remedies of the qualities in themselves that might lead to the ending of the relationship. Creating a unified separation. The essence of a conscious divorce or separation is forgiveness.

One of the dangers in a book such as this is that there may be, in our attachment to this process, a preferential leaning toward one-on-one collaborations that seems to suggest that a committed relationship is "better" than any of the multiple variations on the theme, including no relationship at all. This is not so. We were not born to be in relationship, we were born to discover our true heart "by whatever means necessary."

We are simply attempting to convey the inherent possibilities for those naturally drawn to this relationship practice. Nor is this book meant to keep couples together. It is only an invitation to be fully alive. To be awake for the process, not lost in "magical thinking" instead of committing to mystical union. Recognizing a gratitude slowly growing for this moment in which everything is in either a state of growth or devolution. Understanding that even what began as a conscious relationship can, without proper tending, degenerate into a wild egoistic dual or frozen-hearted stagnation, and eventually fearful withdrawal. As the man said, if we aren't busy getting born, we're busy dying.

Even a mystical union can be broken if the delicate balance between essentially separate psyches and essentially similar hearts is not maintained. It can happen if complacency weakens the focus. Or the partners get too far outside themselves, so "into each other" that they neglect their personal practice, and defer investigations of that which separates for superficial rituals of togetherness. Or such a union can simply change if the partners each become so thoroughly a "child of God" they become like brother or sister, siblings in the human family, so exquisitely sensitive and kind to each other, so open to each other without any attachment or desire.

With all the grace that Ondrea and I have experienced, our relationship learning has not always been so painless. We, too, have learned the art of relationship through the practice of falling down. And learning lightly to pick ourselves up once again. This is my third marriage. This is Ondrea's second. Eventually you get the teaching! In my first divorce, the relationship disintegrated because there was nothing holding it together. When our mutual attraction to various unwholesome activities fell away, no common ground remained. We literally drifted apart, she to Mexico, I into another relationship. Yet after a decade she wrote and we made contact once again. We continue to exchange letters on occasion, supporting each other's climb.

My second marriage came without intention or much consciousness, as did Ondrea's first. It was a commitment, not so much to a lover as to the exquisite children that came forth from that body/mind (perhaps more the former than the latter) connection. The divorce, five years later, was attributed to "irreconcilable differences." It was a powerful teaching that even a "bad" relationship can be good work on yourself when you are mindful and listen with the heart (which I now recognize I did all too infrequently). Considerable anger and unkind game playing had become the rule of the day. Quite different than the first marriage's natural parting, there was not so much a wish to "get on with our lives" as there was a deep disappointment and distrust in the potentials of relationship itself. It was a profound recognition that the years of deep separation were a reflection of the numerous unattended wounds and griefs that preceded our never-wholehearted meeting. And our desperate attempt to "make relationship" where one did not naturally exist. Where valence never occurred. Both acknowledged very different attitudes toward everything from the purpose of life to the time it takes to cook a three-minute egg. Our only concurrent joy was the children. I could not abide the anger that often filled the air, hers as well as mine. But in momentary flashes of sanity, we recognized, at least as friends, if not as lovers, that the relationship could not continue without considerable hard work, which neither felt the relationship was worthy of. Each felt it had become a "dumping pit" in which to toss our emotional detritus. Through some shreds of remaining wisdom, we acknowledged that the divorce was going to necessitate a kindness and consideration that had often been lacking in the marriage. And so we consciously focused on the care and acclimation of the children during our transition. In many ways our divorce was more conscious than our marriage. Recognizing the power of forgiveness, that the last step is as important as the first, we continued to communicate regularly for some time thereafter. As our triangulation had always been on the children, even more than on the relationship, much less each other, the divorce went very smoothly and mercifully. The kindness and concern for each other's well-being created a bond seldom experienced in the previous years.

A year and a half later, when my ex-wife was to be remarried, she and her husband-to-be, an old friend, asked if I would be best man at the ceremony. And a year after that when their twins were born, I was asked to be godfather for their infant girl.

Perhaps one of the reasons that I am on such healing terms with my two previous wives is that no matter how separately we suffered at any time, no matter how angry or judgmental, there was more of a sense of mental exhaustion than any wish to cause harm. And in each case, forgiveness and a processing of the past in time occurred naturally. Because there had never been the slightest threat or intimidation, there were no uncrossable chasms. Mental abuse served us all too well! Of course, when there is any element of physical abuse, it cancels all contracts. It is in itself an act of divorce. Although it may be forgiven, it is almost always a mistake to continue the relationship, imagining that previous commitments can be relied on.

It is very difficult to turn pain to healing if one has lost trust in the process. If abuse in the past, or previous dishonesties and infidelities have narrowed the passageway to the heart—densening the armoring over the grief point—it may be necessary to take a few steps back from the fire and cool down. If attempting to maintain a relationship in the midst of distrust has become more like fighting for your life in a blazing thicket than building a campfire in a sacred circle, a skillful distance might be created in which one can sit by the fire and reflect on its creative or destructive potentials.

It might be added here that in spiritual communities the word "retreat" means a time of quietness and contemplation from which one returns to the world greater than before. Some relationships require just such a retreat—not a withdrawal, but a secluded entering into our suffering and fear. This is not the retreat of backing off. This is an attempt to stabilize the mind and encourage the heart. At times when only divorce seems practical, such a period of quiet introspection can help us rediscover the ground beneath our feet and allow, in time, insight and forgiveness to heal the past. But before one can even attempt forgiveness they must recognize that one cannot force the process, but only open to it. Sometimes one needs to let go of even forgiveness in order to investigate the "unforgiven" in ourselves, before the next step can be taken on this new ground. When forgiveness arises naturally, encouraged by a willingness not to suffer, or cause suffering, the process of our healing continues unabated.

A conscious divorce or separation can reverse the conditioning that conditioned so much difficulty. Parting lovingly from an often unloving relationship realigns the possibilities of the next relationship. It allows us to let go and let be. It offers us the alternative of relating *to* that within ourselves and others which is unloving in a very merciful way. To practice forgiveness for self and other in a single breath. To take the next step, leaving no scuff marks from the last.

Just as it is fruitful to define what each expects from a relationship, to agree upon priorities in a relationship or marriage contract, so it is skillful when parting to find some ground for mutual agreement which approximates a divorce contract. Such agreements seem to aid in the healing process of letting go. Perhaps most important for our little mind not to get lost in the paranoia that accompanies abandonment, anger and self-image issues is a clear stipulation not to betray the other's secrets. Indeed, the first precept of such a commitment to conscious separation may be to keep silent all confidences. To hold sacred those moments when the heart revealed itself, so as not to condition mistrust or abuse the confidentiality of "pillow talk." It means to be a whole person even when that wholeness is challenged. To relinquish the power of fear and humiliation that each holds over the other. To be kind. To maintain some semblance of "common courtesy."

Because neurotic grasping can be at its small mind high point during the process of a separation, the next precept is to define completely and share honestly all that has accrued during the course of the relationship: materially, emotionally and spiritually. To make divorce a "coming into one's own" rather than a "tearing apart from one's *other*."

And, if there are children, a commitment to an openhearted sharing of time and energy. Never letting the children become hostages on the battlefield from behind which each ambushes the other. In any conscious divorce contract, the relationship triangle broken, a new triangulation arises at whose apex are the children.

And perhaps the third commitment might be to explore alone the grief that could not be heartfully shared, but acted itself out in bold gestures and subtle aggressions. Because small mind can be so treacherously clever, and Narcissus so needy, in the face of feeling unloved, the grief work done at this point is as powerful as any. It is the prelude to forgiveness, which is the true finishing of business.

It is not that Ondrea and I are doing "the work" perfectly, but just that we are doing it at all! From Ondrea's marriage twenty-eight years before and my two divorces, we had to learn something! Nothing teaches us about love like observing its absence. In the more than fifteen years we have been together, all that previously didn't work in relationship has come to us as a wonderfully beneficent teaching in how to maintain heart, even when mindfulness is weak. How to be loving even when Narcissus continues to complain.

We have come to recognize, with gratitude, bowing to all previous lovers, that all the sad expectations and disappointments which once turned us away from a deeper relating, now related to, have awakened us to other possibilities and brought us to this moment where nothing is impossible.

There are two questions often asked by those contemplating divorce. The first is, "How do I know when my work together with this person is finished?" Our answer is often that your work with that person may never be finished, but your time together may well be. If you say your work with this person is done, we would ask you, Is there any anger remaining? Is there the least protection of your image in that other's eyes? Are you still posturing while hiding from them? Are you each still tabulating unfinished business? If so, your work together is not exhausted, but your willingness may be. In which case, is forgiveness a possibility? Even in the consideration of ending your relationship, how do you plan to complete what feels undone? In truth, our work with another is never finished until we forgive another and ourselves. So the quandary isn't really, "How do I know when our work is done?" but how can we use this situation to propel our healing? And, of course, the answer is whispered from within: only mindfulness and heartfulness will restore the world. Only big mind has room for the moment "when prayer has become impossible and the heart has turned to stone."

The second question often asked is, "How bad does it have to get before separation or divorce is appropriate?" And our answer usually is that, first and foremost, if there is the threat of violence, a divorce may be a healing long overdue. And if the abuse is subtler, "trading tortures with your tongues," how much more suffering can you stand to give and receive? How long can you live without mercy? Is the mind so agitated with complaint and judgment that it cannot hear its heart? Is it time to step back and reflect if the relationship is really unworkable or just more in need of energy than you're willing to commit? Or have you "gone the distance" and still feel helpless and hopeless? And how will you heal deeply the aftermath of this relationship before jumping into the next?

Some take on a relationship to work on a particular issue that both are in the midst of attempting to heal, creating a "limited partnership contract." Their commitment may be more to a mutual process than to a long-term relationship. And if their process comes to completion, is functional for their healing, the relationship may dissolve when they have no further work together. Their hearts are not closed to each other, they are simply not in the modality of a committed, triangulated relationship. Even temporary relationships can be very powerful collaborations when mutually acknowledged as another step toward completion. Such partings are not usually accompanied by the previously mentioned confusions or questions. They are more like artists collaborating on a work of art. They have come together on a particular project and, having completed their work—perhaps to expand the boundaries of intimacy, work together on an illness or perfect a deeper sense of trust—continue on individually into their own lives. In such cases, the clarity of the first step—the original "limited partnership" agreement—conditions the clarity of the last.

Clearly, our learning process is at least awkward, if not painful, and at times rather confusing. But nothing teaches us what an open heart means like a heart that is closed. Priorities clarify slowly. But when commitment to another encourages in the heart a sense of workability of that which previously seemed unworkable, it softens the gut and opens the mind to the possibilities of the joy and healing which accompany our entrance into deeper levels of consciousness.

It is said that the longest journey begins with the first step, but it also is ended with the last. That last step is as important as the first. It is the first move of the next journey. How we end one relationship affects how we begin another. It is a teaching in continuum. Just as a divorce contract can be as crucial as a marriage agreement, a divorce ceremony is as important as a wedding. Each is a ritual of transition. A subtle mourning, a considerable expectation. Each has the power to heal or to enslave. But a divorce ceremony is not a wedding ceremony in reverse. It is another whole moment of birth. Another opportunity for lightenment. A triangulated divorce offers the anger and confusion into the great "don't know" vastness of the sacred, and feels the ground return beneath its feet. It is a balancing of heaven and earth. It is the next moment in the life you so long for.

In the last twenty years we have presided over several weddings, funerals and divorces. All had similar qualities in common: a sense of imminent change, an expression of the heart unusual in large groups and a feeling that one's life would never be the same again. In each, the participants were brought together in the shared heart, to say goodbye to the old and enter the new wholeheartedly. In one divorce ceremony we gathered in the rather sumptuous backyard of the parting couple. In the center of the garden, a small fire burned in a perfect stone circle. Around the fire stood their closest friends. A fine African carving, a very meaningful wedding present, was placed lengthwise across the flames, and as the four-foot-long wooden staff ignited at the center, burning in two, they played "their song." There was no enmity. Indeed, each was a bit tearful in the midst of this gentle recognition of profound incompatibility. As the center of the carving smoldered and burst into flame, the two spoke softly through the smoke, on either side of the fire, of the gratitude and appreciation they had for what had been experienced together. Acknowledging that the bad times were over, they sent their wishes across the firepit for each other's well-being. When the carving had burned through, we picked it up and broke it over a rock and handed a smoldering half to each of the no-longer-lovers. Each holding a two-foot section smoldering at one end, they made smoke rings, the Zen circle, in the air. And they bowed to each other, and took their half of the carved wooden staff and dropped it into the fire. Their relationship symbolically consumed in the flames that separated them. As the music began, congratulations were offered to each by all their friends. The love in the garden was palpable. Their relationship was past, but the world of love was still present.

After the ceremony, one mentioned that their wedding, which had been rather rushed, did not have as much of a sense of connectedness as this parting ceremony. Much unfinished business was concluded in the party, which went on long into the night. The music and dancing and a festive potluck banquet contributed by so many who had shared in the joys and confusions of the relationship from its inception, and wanted now to participate as wholeheartedly in its final unfolding.

It was not unlike the story a fellow told one day in a relationship workshop. "My wife and I, for many years, had a very unconscious relationship. We hardly knew if the other was in the room. What had begun with some measure of love had degenerated into an annoying gamesmanship. But by some awkward grace, we kind of 'caught it' just in the nick of time as it was about to completely unravel, and made a conscious decision that the end would be a hell of a lot more awakened than what had preceded it. We made a conscious commitment to a conscious divorce. We forgave each other. That was a few years ago. Now we're both in relationships that are just perfect for us. Once she was my wife, now she is my sister."

A divorce ceremony is a forgiveness ceremony. It is saying good-bye, recognizing that goodbye means God-be-with-you. It is a blessing ritual that disentangles minds and allows again a meeting of the hearts. Such a ritualized disengagement allows a healing in which the injuries and vague cruelties, the insensitivities and delusions of the past, are brought into a merciful awareness. It is, even when hearts are separate, a meeting of the minds that does not seek to punish, but only to be free of being the cause, or object, of injury or unkindness. A healing awareness which brings insight into the nature of the "unhealed" before it acts itself out in future relationships. It is an evolutionary step toward oneness.

No matter how many relationships on the evolutionary ladder, or how many uncomfortable partings, as a friend says, "Never give up on love!" The Beloved is just around the next unknown corner. In relationship, as in the rest of our life, we may be reborn before we are aware we even existed. The heart may present itself sooner than the mind expects. Love is in constant potential and sometimes the mind is the last to know. But the heart may sense from across the room, from across worlds, that the beloved is approaching and the journey of another lifetime is about to begin.

CHAPTER 51

~

DEATH
OF A
LOVED ONE

T A RECENT WEEKEND workshop a fellow approached whose face seemed familiar. He said that he and his wife had attended a relationship workshop some years before but that now it was time for him to attend a dying workshop alone. He asked if he might tell us a story. He told us of a close and working partnership with his wife, whom he loved greatly. For years, having enjoyed together trekking and climbing in the mountains, they decided for their tenth anniversary to visit Hawaii to climb an extraordinary waterfall they had a photograph of on their bedroom wall. It was a dream that had often warmed them on cold winter nights: a multileveled waterfall that descended in stages of silver cataracts and emerald pools, surrounded by jungle. So they journeyed to Hawaii to play in the falls' rainbow mists as celebration of their ten years together.

Climbing the table-rock levels slowly and deliberately, enjoying each moment of this dream, they stopped about two-thirds of the way up to catch their breath and take a mental photograph of the spectacular view. "We were ecstatic and soaked." Watching the torrent in gratitude and awe, he turned to share the moment with his wife. But she was not there. She had disappeared from the huge moss-covered rock. He looked into our eyes incredulously and said, "I turned around and she was gone!" She had slipped unheard from the water-splashed table rock, the roar of the cataract absorbing her last sounds. In a nanosecond, the beloved of ten years had slipped away silently. The "love of my life" had disappeared into the unknown.

Her particular touch, her odd humor, her ever-connected gaze, her compassion, her bright words, her blazing smile, her unique fragrance—gone. And in its wake, an absence in every breath, in every step, the earth hollow beneath stone feet.

"I turned around and she was gone!" What if, right now, you turned around and your loved one was gone? What has been left unsaid? What has not been given? What have you not allowed yourself to receive?

Having accompanied so many to the threshold of death, we have seen how often relationships are the most difficult attachments to relinquish on the deathbed. I recall being asked at a hospice if I would visit a comatose patient who had been sent there to die some weeks ago, but seemed to be "stuck and unable to let go." The staff explained they had done everything correctly, followed the "recipe," even told her it was okay to die. But when I entered the room I sensed something else was happening. Although she had been told it was okay to die, that's not how it seemed to her. For her, it was not okay to die. The fears of what might become of her six young children and her alcoholic husband after she died was creating an agonizing grasping at her severely withered body and its considerably diminished life force. Though she was in a full, nonresponsive coma, as is our custom I spoke to her about the condition she found herself in. I told her I recognized her dismay at the children not being able to survive such an enormous trauma. And of her distrust in her husband's capacity to keep the family going. But, I told her, I had seen many such situations, other families in which a mother left behind several children and how remarkably, evolving through a period of considerable sadness, each pitched in to help the other. As I told her stories of various families having worked through such situations and how resourceful children can be, and even how such traumas can at times bring out the best in people, tears began rolling down her cheeks from beneath her closed lids. As I told her I knew it was not okay with her to die and that that was okay too, but that her children and husband would somehow find their way through, a release of tension was noticeable throughout her body. She died two hours later. Even in coma her concern for her loved ones was unabated. Even in coma she knew that love was more powerful than fear. And that she could take refuge and trust the Beloved sufficiently to surrender her body and her family to the mercy of the universe.

Recently we received a letter from a dying woman about to depart her family. Ondrea wrote to the woman saying:

> Of course your heart is breaking. This is natural and not to be abhorred. Let it break. Allow it to expose itself completely. Say all that is to be said. Hear all that is to be heard.
>
> It is time now for the healing that goes beyond cure. Give yourself completely to each day. Make those audio and video tapes you have been thinking of for so long. Leave yourself behind. Let them know your heart, your voice, your image, for the years to come. Protect nothing. Enter wholly your life. Let it last them a lifetime.
>
> Send yourself loving kindness each day. Send the body forgiveness. Don't expect the emotions to be rational. That would be irrational. Watch any old judgments or mercilessness sent into your pain. Have mercy on you. Treat yourself like your only child. Treat your children to themselves. Remind them of their strength and beauty. And remind yourself of that as well.
>
> This is the process that you and I were born to do. Be soft with the disappointment. Understand that all you feel is natural. Be merciful. And when a bit of clarity allows, relate *to* these feelings with kindness instead of relating only *from* them with fear or any sense of failure. You have lived an enormous life. Trust the process.
>
> We have experienced so many losing their loved ones— children, parents, lovers, husbands, wives—and noticed again

and again how it deepened and refined their heart. It is a hard teaching, but one they will be able to soften to in time. Trust their process. The Beloved, your own great nature, awaits you and your loved ones alike just beyond the body.

Treasure yourself. I know this isn't easy, but your heart knows the way by heart. Rest in being.

Ondrea

Ondrea and I lived with the possibility of death for some years. Cancer, and ten years later lupus, on more than one occasion, threatened to remove Ondrea from my world. At times I watched the mind become numb with pain. The Buddha's first two noble truths of attachment and the suffering it entails, smoldering in the marrow. Waves of helplessness overwhelming all but love. The experiment of hearts on the brink of dissolution. Unable to keep my beloved alive, sitting in the empty living room, Ondrea resting in the bedroom, as the sun sets far outside and philosophy disintegrates in the shadows, a great heaviness overwhelms the body. A repeated panic ricocheting in the rational mind. Struggling to regain mindfulness. To surrender and allow mercy the moment. Offering up our pain to the heart of the Beloved, embracing the illness and the grief which surrounded it, something apparently left just enough room for grace to enter and inexplicable healings to occur. Or should I say "explicable" only in the mystery.

Now both cancer and lupus have receded from Ondrea's body. It is difficult to understand all that is entailed in healing—it seems to be composed of equal parts of wisdom and "don't know." But clearly it was love and mindfulness of *self* and *other* which so enhanced our empathetic connection and allowed each morning to attune to Ondrea's symptoms before she said a word. And our growing ability to meet the unpleasant with mercy and awareness, to keep our hearts open in hell.

Besides death and divorce, there are also the separations and little deaths that occur from the radical change in a loved one due to any number of causes from injury to illness, as well as stroke, old age, Alzheimer's, or even the emotionally shattering uncovering of childhood trauma. Much less the stultifying aftereffects of a violent incident or intense grief. Some say, "They are not the same person I married": the commitment wavering as the long-crafted model of that person disintegrates into their pain or confusion or fear. To the degree that we have been open to our pain and grief previously, we will be able to embrace this grieving of what is passing. We will be able to let go of the past to be present as needed. Sometimes in the darkness we need hold the light for another. Sometimes we need accompany a loved one through hell. It is not easy, certainly not what we bargained for. But the time for bargaining is over. Now only being will do. Now only playing our edge, entering the fire of our unfulfilled desires and our love.

I remember speaking to a woman in a workshop who was confronting just such a "loss of model" in her brain-damaged husband. Speaking of her unending love for him, she said she would "stick it out no matter what," though it was terribly difficult. Sharing stories of others working through the same predicament with mindfulness and forgiveness, I added, "Well, anyway, whoever said it was going to be easy?" To which a young woman's voice rose from the back of the room, "Oops, I'm sorry. That must have been me!" And oh, how the beloveds laughed!

We're all traveling the same river, bailing as hard as we can to "empty our boat." Confronted with impermanence, no one can tell us what the next appropriate step might be. The grace of "an impossible situation" is that it opens us to new possibilities. And service takes on a meaning very close to home. Each doing the best they can, any way they can. At times, perhaps, remembering the Beloved.

When death breaks the shared heart, the world bursts into flames. There seems nowhere to turn. And all we can do is sit down where we are and let the images and absences burn. Until our tears extinguish the flames and leave the world smoldering. When, eventually, the smoke begins to clear, in months or years, a few blades of new grass may be seen emerging from the spent embers. The broken heart slowly reuniting in a profound appreciation of all that had been. The shared heart mending into the oneness. Absolute absence dissolving into ultimate inseparability as the mind of grief sinks into the heart of healing. Melting into a single-heartedness, the relationship continues, in or out of the body.

And when, and if, a new relationship eventually approaches, we may be able, having so completed our "business" with the past, to offer ourselves wholeheartedly.

On this path of relationship there is always another step to take. A step closer to the heart. It is the step one takes remembering Suzuki Roshi's comment, "Everything is perfect but there is always room for improvement." It is the next perfect step, from small mind to big, from big mind to the enormous mystery of the heart.

The teaching couldn't be clearer: don't waste a moment, don't waste a lifetime!

ABOUT THE AUTHORS

Stephen and Ondrea Levine, known widely for their groundbreaking techniques in healing, share the path of self-discovery and the daily expedition toward grace. Having raised their three children and moved into the deep woods, they have for the past seven years been committed to a "relationship experiment of considerable song and intensity." Focusing nearly all their energies on the exploration of tandem healing—physical, emotional and spiritual. For those curious to take this process deeper, the Levines have made available cassette recordings of the guided meditations and techniques that form the superstructure of this work. For a catalogue, send a self-addressed, stamped envelope to:

> Warm Rock Tapes
> P.O. Box 108
> Chamisal, NM 87521

Presently, Stephen and Ondrea continue the process, learning day by day.